THE
Undisciplined
Horse

THE
Undisciplined
Horse

ULRIK SCHRAMM

Trafalgar Square Publishing
North Pomfret, Vermont

English translations of *The Undisciplined Horse* and *The Trouble with Horses*
© J. A. Allen an imprint of Robert Hale Ltd 1986, 1988 & 2003

Translated from the German works *Das Verrittene Pferd* and *Die Untugenden des Pferdes*
© BLV Verlagsgesellschaft GmbH, München 1983 & 1986
First published in Great Britain as two separate works 1986 &1988
This new edition comprising both works 2003

ISBN 1-57076-251-1

This new edition first published in the United States of America
in 2003 by Trafalgar Square Publishing,
North Pomfret, Vermont 05053

The right of Ulrik Schramm to be identified as author of this work has been asserted
by him in accordance with the Copyright, Designs and Patents Act 1988

Library of Congress Control Number: 2003102742

2 4 6 8 10 9 7 5 3 1

All black and white photographs reproduced from original
edition of *The Undisciplined Horse*
Colour photographs © Bob Langrish, except for those on pages 143,
and 164 © *Horse and Rider*

Edited by Martin Diggle
Design by Paul Saunders
Line illustrations by the author

Colour separation by Tenon & Polert Colour Scanning Limited, Hong Kong
Printed by Midas Printing International Limited, China

Contents

Translator's Note

The terms 'parade' and 'arrest' used in the text are technical terms for which there are no precise equivalents in English. A parade or partial parade is not a 'half-halt', but an interplay of all the aids – seat, legs and hands – to ask the horse to flex its hocks in preparation for any variation or change of gait. For any change of gait, one rides the horse forwards, even to the halt, regardless of whether the change of speed is acceleration or deceleration. An arrest, on the other hand, is a stoppage, restraint or check with leg, seat and hand, used when the horse is disobedient or inattentive.

Introduction

I T IS GENERALLY RECOGNIZED that there are many self-styled 'riders' and 'trainers' and very few truly competent ones. It is also true that there are very few really obedient horses and a lot of more or less disobedient ones, and that riding is not a pleasure if the horse either does not understand the rider's instructions or refuses to obey them promptly and cheerfully. This is true everywhere – in the stable yard, the manège, the show-jumping ring, the dressage arena or the hunting field – and no matter whether the rider is entirely dedicated to the skill of horsemanship or whether he rides purely for recreation. Perfect agreement cannot exist between horse and rider if one member of the partnership does not enjoy the sport and does not measure up to its demands, or when serious differences of mind are allowed to persist during training and afterwards.

I believe that many disagreements stem from the traditional teaching of riding, which has been concerned almost entirely with the establishment of an effective seat and with the mechanics of movement. Seat is obviously an essential element in mastery of the horse, but the rider's head is surely as important as his seat; thus, seat and aids are undeniably indispensable organs of physical influence, but the psychological factor is even more important.

Nevertheless equine psychology continues to be a much-neglected part of the education of riders. This is a pity because riding is not truly a sport if unity of mind does not exist between rider and horse. This perfect accord is unfortunately too rarely seen, while ugly displays of bad temper are not uncommon. It must be said of course that very few riders are truly brutish tyrants; most of those who battle against apparently stubborn horses are not aware that it is their incompetence, ignorance or thoughtlessness that provoke the animal's resistance. However, while riding is said to be a good teacher of self-discipline,

Perfect harmony between
horse and rider.

one wonders how much truth there is in this commonplace, since it is not
uncommon to see normally temperate persons losing their usual good manners and self-control whilst riding, to the point of cursing without restraint
and plaguing their horse with inappropriate applications of whip, spurs and
bit. Horses cannot talk and explain themselves and since some do not even
retaliate, such riders too often feel justified in their actions and make insufficient attempts to discover the root causes of their upset.

So far as real oafishness is concerned, overriding ambition and an inflated ego are the main sources of the brutality that sometimes spoils equestrian sports. These unlovely characteristics must surely destroy the pleasure of riding and, if an outlet for them has to be found, would it not be better for those displaying them to chase prizes in some other endeavour in which a living creature cannot be shamefully abused? That said, one can accept that some who have committed isolated acts of tyranny are not tyrants at heart, but simply over-keen and fired up with competitive fever. If such people would discipline themselves and learn to ride more skilfully and intelligently, they would probably achieve better results, and also restore their horse's zeal.

Further to this, it is understandable that a sportsman with a keen competitive spirit should be willing to drive his own body to the limit of its endurance, but in equestrian sports the horse ought to be treated as a team mate who must be able and willing to participate, and not as a piece of equipment that can be used to the point of destruction. I feel very strongly that any display of horsemanship must be a pleasure to watch; leaps and intricate movements should show the grace expressed in ballet dancing. The rider's face should reflect happiness rather than dogged determination and an anxiety to avoid losing points. In dressage, fluency should matter as much as precision in the execution of movements, even when there are prizes and trophies at stake. The horses, too, should look serene. Some do seem to enjoy the ambience of a competition and look light, pliable and calm; but there are some very unenthusiastic and constrained victims that have to be relentlessly spurred on. Competing on a horse full of zeal and confidence in its ability, showing freedom of movement and pliability is fun; but this is not a description that can be applied to competing on horses that require major coercion to perform. For this reason – personal enjoyment – even if not from more altruistic motives, riders of the latter type would be wise to question how they have arrived at their current position.

Of course, we cannot suppose that *all* cases of unwillingness or lack of co-operation on the horse's part are inevitably the rider's fault. We must remember that, as with humans, there are some incorrigible dullards and blockheads amongst equines and these can never be persuaded to offer useful degrees of co-operation. For anyone to claim that he can transform the disposition of a stubborn, apathetic horse is as fatuous as maintaining that he can motivate an elephantine hunter to strive to win a Derby, or a weedy Thoroughbred to excel in a puissance jumping event. This illustration, however, highlights another point: the difference between inherent and acquired unwillingness. The distinction here is between the occasional horse that is pathologically opposed to exerting itself either physically or mentally, and the horse that has become unwilling to do so because unreasoned and unreasonable demands have persistently been made of it. Over-exertion is ugly in all sports, but especially displeasing in the equestrian ones, and this brings us back to an earlier point. If human sportsmen are driven by some inner compulsion or by economic considerations to flog themselves to mental or physical destruction, that is their own affair – but they have no right to overtax a horse to the same end.

In the following chapters, in which I will survey the causes of equine insubordination, I will stress that intractable problems *must* arise during handling and training if we do not consider most carefully the physical and psychological aptitudes of a horse before deciding on its utilization. Although breeders have for some time endeavoured to produce suitable types, there are still many horses quite incapable of fulfilling the difficult requirements of modern competition. If we do not recognize the constraints that nature (or inappropriate breeding) have placed upon such horses, they will not only fail to live up to our unrealistic ambitions, they will also fail to achieve the performance level that would have been within their compass, had we proceeded with more restraint and good sense.

CHAPTER ONE

Understanding Equine Behaviour

Years ago, horses performed the duties now taken over by the mechanized vehicles, and people either rode or went by carriage to get from one place to another, and worked the land, as it were, in joint harness with the horse. The lives of people and horses were therefore closely linked, with a greater inter-dependence between man and horse than is the case today. As a result – and, indeed, through necessity – a basic 'horse knowledge' was handed down from one generation to the next, this being derived from a practical knowledge of the jobs the horse was required to do and the relative ease or difficulty with which the horse performed them. Unfortunately, with the horse's traditional tasks now having been replaced by machines, much of this 'horse knowledge', or 'horse sense', has been dissipated from large sections of the human population. It is somewhat ironic that nowadays, when the horse is used largely for sport rather than for essential work, too many people regard it is nothing more than a piece of apparatus, which they employ with a lack of consideration and understanding. Such people desperately need to acquire some knowledge of equine psychology to protect both their horses and themselves from the consequences of serious behavioural problems, which may be engendered in the horse through the rider's uninformed and inappropriate actions. Of course, not all such actions arise out of brutality or thoughtlessness: in many cases, the perpetrators are decent people who wish to treat their horses well. The difficulty is that, in many cases, actions motivated by kindness, but unsupported by knowledge or reason, have the opposite effect to what is intended.

Although, in general, the old-fashioned 'horse knowledge' did not equate to a comprehensive understanding of equine psychology, it is still the case that the best trainers had an understanding developed – albeit often instinctively –

to a high degree. This quality is manifest in an empathy for how the horse feels and 'thinks', and in a general rapport. It is typified by the nineteenth-century authority Steinbrecht, who wrote: 'Correct understanding of the mental qualities of the horse and their expression, and the ability, based on this knowledge, to influence them is essential, and becomes even more so as we become involved with more advanced training. Correct assessment of temperament and an insight into the horse's nature are just as essential for success as correct assessment of its physical qualities'.

Nevertheless, it seems that this most important facet of equine training has not, down the years, been explored or emphasized to a degree commensurate with its importance. Ever-increasing numbers of books are available on the subject of training both horses and riders. These books are based on various systems, approaches and philosophies, originating in early or in more recent times, but the majority have been and remain concerned primarily with the mechanics of riding. The scientific study of equine psychology, and the production of books that relate to this, are of relatively recent origin, despite the fact that, when a problem arises, it is the horse's psyche which is most likely to be at its root.

The aim of this present study is to provide the basis for a better understanding of equine behaviour by examining *why* our horses react in such and such a way. This psychological approach is not inherently difficult and, once the benefits are appreciated, any sensitive, observant rider will, with a little thought, be able to formulate his own ideas on the subject. Indeed, this process reflects one of the principal methods of animal psychology – self-observation or 'introspection' – whereby certain elements of equine behaviour are rendered perfectly comprehensible to man. This does not mean that we should judge the horse in human terms, but rather that we should consider the analogies and dissimilarities between the species, and use them as a basis for understanding the horse's behaviour. This will help us to understand that 'good' and 'bad' do not necessarily have the same meaning for the horse as for the human. A refusal to jump into water, for example, might seem incontrovertibly bad to the cross-country rider, but to the novice horse, with no previous experience of doing so, and no knowledge of the depth or what may lurk within it, remaining on dry ground may seem unequivocally the 'good' option. An ability to see things from the horse's point of view is, in fact, the starting point for realizing that most equine behavioural problems and resistances are the result of mistakes on *our* part. Fear, inability to comply and failure to understand what is required are all too often the reasons for the horse doing the wrong thing and for the associated behavioural problems, as are impatience and asking too much or too soon.

If we are to understand the horse more fully, it is first necessary to realize that the modern horse is the result of a very long period of evolution, which began more than sixty million years ago in the Eocene period, long before man came into existence. (The horse's first encounter with man was that of a wild animal with a hunter. Later, man followed the herds around nomad-style, killing what he needed for food and clothing. Then he learnt how to manage the herd, and thus began a process of selection.) We should always bear in mind this protracted evolutionary period when we examine the horse's instinctive behaviour; since it provides the basis for understanding how it developed. In fact, not only will it enable us to understand the horse's reactions, it will also help us to avoid nasty accidents which are sometimes a consequence of these reactions, for example, the injuries which can result from kicking, shying and bolting.

We must first remember that the horse is by nature a very active animal, designed to travel long distances to find water and grazing. Also, being a prey animal or 'creature of flight', it is particularly swift to respond to perceived threat and adept at manoeuvring at speed and running long distances. The swiftness of the horse's responses relates directly to the sensitivity of its reflexes, which are far swifter than those of a human – a fact which can be both a boon (when the horse finds a 'fifth leg' after stumbling) and a drawback (when the horse shies violently at something its rider has not registered). Even in a domestic environment, where these attributes are rarely necessary for survival, it is the pleasure which the horse takes in movement that remains its most noteworthy characteristic. Another characteristic which has been of great importance in the horse's development is its ability to adapt to its environment. The horse is found almost all over the world, and only the ice in the north and the tsetse fly in the south have stood in its way. The ability to adapt to extreme climatic conditions is connected with a high degree of skin activity. The horse's enormous capacity for sweating (which is greater than that of any other animal) is a sign of this. The other factor related to this skin activity is the horse's sensitivity. The closeness of the nerves to the surface of the skin explains the horse's ability to respond to the most minute stimuli, a characteristic for which it is well known. The horse's feet offer another example of its sensitivity. The horse is able to pick up the slightest vibrations in the ground through its feet – a faculty that may serve as an early warning system.

The horse's powers of thought and its ability to draw conclusions seem relatively limited in comparison with those of other domestic animals. Máday says that the horse can reason, but adds: 'whether it actually has ideas and forms judgements and conclusions has not been established because these activities have not yet been precisely explored and defined'. Yet it is clear that the horse does form simple ideas and judgements, and in some cases it even displays the rudiments of an ability to draw conclusions. For example, horses know how to simulate (e.g. lameness) and in cavalry stables there were frequent cases of horses which regularly rubbed off their headcollars, waited until the guard had passed, and then went looking for food or to visit a friend. Perhaps we might say that reasoning, in this sense, is not the ability to think abstractly but, as Blendinger says, it is more the horse's capacity for 'forming conceptions from sensations received in a state of attentiveness, and linking them up with other observations and conceptions'.

Whatever the precise status of its reasoning powers, the horse's reactions are quite distinctive and can be understood with reference to the lifestyle of its ancestors (creatures of flight). Moreover, this ancestry has given equine nature some noteworthy characteristics: the horse has an incredibly good memory, a highly developed sense of direction, a pronounced herd instinct, a dependence on habit, and an extremely discerning sense of smell. The herd instinct seems to transcend a simple survival mechanism: the horse is genuinely a gregarious animal, with a marked need for friendship and, as such, is very sensitive both to good treatment and praise and also to reproaches.

Whilst on the topic of basic instincts and characteristics we should mention the horse's sexual instincts, which can give rise to problems – especially if they are not properly acknowledged. As in all creatures, these instincts are very powerful, and any training regime that sets itself up in direct conflict with them is asking for trouble. In recent years, more people have taken to riding stallions, but this does not mean that the potential problems involved have been overcome. In riding schools and livery yards, stallion keeping is usually fraught with problems. Stallions tend to create unrest in a mixed yard, and it is rarely practical to turn them out, so there is as yet no way of ensuring a trouble-free existence with a stallion in the yard. Although some stallions have an excellent temperament and are no trouble at all, it is well to remember that stallions generally are mentally and physically tougher than other horses, and this will be apparent in their reactions to inappropriate treatment. Mares are not usually troublesome in the same way as stallions, but they do have periodic problems of their own. The first stage of oestrus or 'heat' is characterized by flirting, enticing and resisting. In the second phase the resistance has disappeared and the mare is ready to be covered. The mare's general behaviour may reflect these tendencies. In the first phase she may be ticklish, she may squeal, make threatening gestures, urinate and swish her tail ('don't touch!'). In the second phase, which often lasts little more than a day, the rider has the impression that he is sitting on a passive, immovable body, over which he has practically no influence, and which is stupefied and completely dead to the legs and hands. Not all mares behave in this way, but some do. Mares of this type are unusable to all intents and purposes during these periods. Obviously, punishment is inappropriate. The best thing is to leave them alone.

The horse's ability to express its feelings is well known. Although many riders and trainers pay insufficient attention to the signs, the play of the horse's features is far from invisible. The eyes, for example, are capable of a wide range of expressions. A calm horse has a different look in its eyes than a frightened one. Trust is also expressed in the eyes, as are attentiveness and willingness, or indifference. Everyone knows the blank look on the face of the exhausted horse which has been plodding around for hours on end with one riding school pupil after another on its back and the disturbed, even wild-eyed look that accompanies resistance in the horse which has been unreasonably asked to do things beyond its comprehension or capacity. (The physiological peculiarities of the horse's eye and its vision will be dealt with when we discuss shying and jumping.)

Not just the eyes, but the nostrils and mouth play their part in the horse's expressions. There is Flehmen's posture (associated with sexual arousal and response to certain odours), yawning, baring the teeth in threat, and the pendulous lower lip of the weary horse. Neighing and snorting also have a wider range of expression than is generally thought: these vocal expressions can be used to convey fear, excitement or surprise, and they can be used either in play or as a warning.

The play of a horse's ears and the carriage of the tail are other highly significant forms of expression. The ears can show attentiveness, unwillingness, willingness or menace. Moreover, the physiologists claim that the horse always

In yawning (*left*) the mouth is opened and the eyes half-shut, while in Flehmen's posture (*below*) the mouth remains shut and the eyes are open.

looks in the direction in which its ears point. In addition to its occasional role in pointing up back problems, the tail carriage is also expressive of the horse's moods, in particular high spirits, excitement, worry and tension. It is significant that, over the years, enormous efforts – some highly dubious – have been made to get horses to adopt a 'spirited tail carriage', for example, when presenting them to potential buyers. Finally, the horse may express itself through gestures of the limbs: pawing or stamping with the forefeet, to convey impatience and annoyance, or raising a hind foot in a 'keep your distance' warning.

We have established, then, that the horse is an extraordinarily sensitive animal which feels things very strongly, and it uses these forms of expression reflexively to communicate with its fellows, and also with man. It is important, therefore, that man should learn to understand this language, using his powers of comparative reasoning. An example of this is the horse's attitude towards noise. Horses have acute hearing and are very sensitive to noise, but this does not prevent them from making loud noises themselves, for example, kicking the sides of the box at feed time. Even though this may seem unwarranted to a flustered groom, we can understand that, in the horse's terms, it is done for maximum emphasis. When schooling a horse or working in the stables, we should be mindful of the horse's sensitive hearing and, not wishing to provoke an alarmed reaction, we should speak softly, and should not shout or scream. We will note that, in certain circumstances, a loud rebuke will be received as a more severe punishment than a blow. On the other hand, being spoken to quietly is a pleasant experience for the gregarious horse and speaking to it in a monotone has a calming effect (in this instance the actual words are irrelevant: 'it is the tone which makes the music'). Music, too, provided that it is without loud, sharp accents, calms the horse – although certain rhythms can have an exciting effect. (It must be added here that it is not true that horses adapt to and follow the beat of the music when performing trot, passage, etc.

Tail carriage (*from left to right*): normal, excited, active, tensed.

In fact it is the rider who unconsciously keeps with the beat or tries to go with it. In the circus, the band usually has great difficulty in keeping in time with the horses in the liberty acts.)

Although mere tone of voice can be useful in calming the horse, it is a fact that horses learn the intentions of certain words very quickly. A loud 'No!', or 'Good boy' spoken in a different tone are not the only expressions the horse can recognize. In fact, given repeated use it can understand a wide range of words, even when they are heard nearby as opposed to being addressed directly to the individual. Riders will often find that their horses break into canter by themselves when the other riders in the school are told to 'canter on', even before they are influenced by the herd instinct of seeing their fellows in canter.

Since the horse's hearing reacts with such extraordinary sensitivity to nuances of tones, our 'conversation' with the horse should be considered a psychological means of communicating with it. In fact, the number of tones of voice, and the categories of tones, which the horse can distinguish is probably much larger than we think. It seems to understand them particularly well when they are accompanied by visual or tactile signs. In this respect, Spohr remarks: 'The person who attempts to correct a horse which is playing up without using his voice will succeed only with difficulty'. We should, therefore, talk to our horses when we are working them and when we are handling them in the stable. By doing so, they will become more attentive, they will focus their attention on this contact, and their understanding and relationship with us will develop.

Returning to the sensitivity of the horse's skin, this can be greatly to the advantage of handler and rider, provided that knowledge of the quality is used wisely. The skin in the neck and shoulder zones is particularly sensitive and horses love having their withers scratched. Everyone has seen pictures of foals or older horses scratching each other. Scratching a horse's crest is a good way of making friends with it. A horse which will not allow you to catch hold of it by its head can often be persuaded to do so if you run your hand slowly along its crest, from withers to poll, scratching as you go. The area directly above the elbow is less sensitive. The sensitivity of the rib area and flank to the action of the whip or spur varies from one individual to another, and it has not yet been established whether, for example, the many horses which react violently to the whip, and yet have had no bad experience of it, fear it as an invisible enemy. They can, however, be accustomed to it by skilful training.

The sensitivity of the schooled horse to the slightest pressure of the leg is of fundamental importance in dressage training. The contact between horse and rider is established mainly through touch, hearing and smell. The horse has the rider on its back permanently under observation, and still manages to watch what is going on around it at the same time. Since a horse is far more sensitive than its rider, and can concentrate more intensively on him than he on it (provided it is not asked to do so for excessively long periods) it can sense the rider's emotions, and will react to the slightest indication of happiness and confidence or, indeed, of fear, anger or mistrust. In this respect I must emphasize that the horse's sensitivity can be a two-edged sword – the very quality that can enable the horse to respond to the lightest of aids may also manifest itself in swift and vigorous responses to pain, fear or rough and inconsiderate treatment.

Besides sensitivity, the other main characteristic of the horse, mentioned earlier, is its inherent need for activity. We know that wild horses covered long distances every day in search of grazing. They alternated between trotting and cantering, with the trot predominating. Hence the manner in which horses are kept nowadays has a profound psychological influence on them. The horse's natural craving for exercise – which reflects its whole lifestyle and not just the fact that it escapes danger by running – is expressed in the enjoyment it derives from it. This is seen most clearly in horses turned out in the paddock and there is further irony in the fact that the change in the horse's role from that of a working animal has not necessarily been to its advantage. In days gone by, work horses were out and about for many hours each day, so that, in addition to exercise, they had contact with the outside world and with the person who worked them, looked after them and fed them. However, many horses nowadays, especially sport horses, are often confined to their stables for twenty-three hours out of twenty-four. Stalls are the worst form of stabling in this respect, because the horse is tied up all day looking at a blank wall. In many stables, horses have no regular contact with the outside world. They have to be at man's beck and call, prepared to do and put up with what man wants, for an hour each day, whether they like it or not, and to do little else besides. Even the regular contact with one human being may have been lost since, in many cases, the horse nowadays is presented to the rider already saddled and bridled and, at the end of the ride, it is probably not the rider who untacks it.

Most people who keep horses do not realize how much the horse is capable of in terms of performance, and that lack of exercise leads to every conceivable form of mischief and bad behaviour. Lively, intelligent horses in particular tend to react in this way, because they need more exercise and more to occupy them than placid, lethargic animals. One hour of exercise per day is insufficient, and the pent-up energy seeks an outlet, either in the form of resistance or as some substitute for exercise, and all sorts of almost perverse habits develop. Punishment is not the answer to the problem, which must be solved by means of regular, meaningful work – and more work. It is significant that, despite other problems, the horses with the least tendency to develop these bad habits are the so-called 'school horses' found in riding establishments, and this is because they are often worked for several hours, carrying and putting up with all sorts of different pupils and their mostly negative influences.

This basic need for exercise notwithstanding, there is a whole range of behavioural problems that result from the horse resisting excessive demands. Such demands go far beyond the horse's basic need for stimulation, requiring responses which are beyond its current physical or mental capability. Either the trainer has attempted to go too fast, or the goals have been set too high or tackled inexpertly. It is only too easy to sap a horse's enthusiasm for its work, and this may not simply be a result of confusion. Excessive demands often lead to painful tendons and joints, and even to irreparable damage to the back and hindquarters. Depending upon the precise nature of the demands made and the constitution and spirit of the individual, a horse subjected to these pressures may either resist with all its strength or resign itself dejectedly to its fate. (In the latter case, of course, the fact that the horse's spirit is broken will still not enable it to do things of which it is incapable.) Arriving at either impasse in the name of sport is a scenario that should have any rider or trainer questioning both their intellect and their conscience. It should be a golden rule never to resort to coercion until *all* other means available have been exhausted and no solution has been found which is in keeping with the principle of a caring education. Regarding rough treatment in general, horses do not understand it as a defining act of dominance, or as punishment, but simply as hostile behaviour. It causes them to stop listening to the rider and to concentrate upon defending themselves – in other words, it increases, rather than diminishes, the horse's resistance. Always remember the principle that the horse is far more likely to comply if it has been kept in a good mood, i.e. 'sweet'.

This rule was established by De La Guérinière right back in 1733, when he wrote: 'One should guard against lumping all the horse's faults together as vices. Usually the horse has simply failed to understand what the rider wants, or else his disobedience is caused by a physical defect'. There would certainly be fewer broken down, ruined and badly trained horses today if this precept were respected. De La Guérinière also put the onus for successful training firmly on the rider by adding: 'Aids and punishments should be given discreetly (without unnecessary movement). Their effectiveness lies primarily in the rider's skill and speed of reaction. The punishment must be simultaneous with the fault, otherwise it will do more harm than good. Above all, a horse must never be punished in temper or anger, but always calmly. Finally I should like to say that the ability to use aids and punishments correctly is one of the finest qualities of the horseman'.

The dictionary definition of *Untugenden* (the German word for 'bad habits' or 'vices') is 'behaviour, in domestic animals, which deviates from the normal and habitual behaviour of that species of animal, and which restricts its use or makes it dangerous to associate with. Examples of vices in horses are restiveness, kicking, biting, shying, playing with the tongue, weaving…' The expression 'restiveness' crops up frequently in old books on riding. The dictionary definition is 'Habitual disobedience and resistance by the horse, e.g. misbehaviour in the stable, in harness or at the forge, or out on the roads or in traffic. Restiveness can interfere with, or prevent the use of, the horse in an organized work situation. It may result from inexperience, or it may be inborn or inherited. Physical or psychological disturbances may also be the cause'. It will be apparent from these definitions that behavioural problems can manifest themselves both in the stable and under saddle. It is also the case that horses discover an amazing number of ways to keep themselves busy or to avoid doing something they do not want to do. In the coming pages, we will examine 'bad habits', both the more common and the more obscure, in the interests of finding causes and solutions. The only habits not discussed in detail are masturbation (which usually requires veterinary intervention) and oddities such as eating dung, soil, wood and hair (which are usually signs of dietary deficiencies or metabolic disorders, again requiring veterinary advice).

To conclude this introduction to understanding equine behaviour, here are a few guidelines from some who have studied the matter in depth. Spohr has written: 'Handle your horse kindly and as frequently as possible. Be nice to him when you go up to him and when you leave him. If you must punish him, do so firmly, or even sharply if appropriate, but never act in anger or with uncontrolled violence. Punishment must always be followed by reconciliation. Do not allow anyone else to treat your horse unkindly, least of all his groom'. To this, E. F. Seidler adds: 'Every horse must be treated differently, in accordance with its own peculiarities', while, in simple terms, V. Krane underlines one of the most important principles of equine training: 'It is the many small victories we achieve which develop the habit of obedience'.

CHAPTER TWO

Stable Vices and Problems In-hand

Wind-sucking and crib-biting

Wind-sucking and crib-biting are two of the most dreaded vices. They result largely from boredom, although heredity can also play a part. There is a theory that a horse which is stabled next door to a crib-biter or wind-sucker will contract the habit itself, which suggests that horses also have an underlying urge to mimic. This urge, combined with curiosity ('What are you up to?'), can certainly lead to a horse adopting the practice.

What is wind-sucking? The horse opens its mouth and at the same time contracts the muscles on the underside of the neck. This results in the larynx being locked in position or drawn downwards. The gullet is opened and air can flow into it. This air is then either swallowed or allowed to flow out again, and the dreaded belching noise results. This habit can interfere with the digestive process, sometimes causing severe colic. The incisor teeth are also affected, because in order to contract the necessary muscles, the horse generally catches hold of something with its teeth – for example, the edge of the manger – hence the association with crib-biting. In some cases, however, the horse manages to contract the necessary muscles to suck in the air without catching hold of anything in its teeth. In other, rather perverse cases, the object caught hold of may be the top of the horse's own foreleg.

In Germany, crib-biting and wind-sucking are vices which must, by law, be declared when a horse is offered for sale. Although every horse owner must be wary of horses with these vices, many such horses suffer no serious adverse effects, that is to say they have no feeding problems and no history of colic as a result of these practices. It is, however, a fact that these vices can arise as a result of feeding the wrong things, such as sugar in particular. Any observant horseman will have noticed that, after a horse has been eating sugar, it starts licking its manger, the walls of the stable, etc. Although it still has a long way to go – from licking to nibbling, then biting, then clamping its jaw, and then finally sucking air – this is where these problems can start. One often hears that horses should not be fed titbits, let alone sugar, in the stable, and this is why.

Crib-biting horse and resulting damage to the teeth. Similar damage occurs to the teeth of horses which grind them on bars, etc. Painting the paddock fence with preparations of various kinds has little effect.

These habits can also develop as a result of an attempt by the horse to alleviate an empty feeling in its stomach, for example, when it has been fed too much concentrate and insufficient bulk food. All too often there is a tendency to give the horse too little exercise and at the same time to feed it up with too much concentrate and cut down on the roughage. When the unfortunate animal then attempts to make up for this by eating its own bed, it is put on sawdust or peat and does not see any bulk feed the whole day through. Feeding sensible proportions of bulk feed to hard feed, in a way that takes account of the horse's physiology and metabolism, will reduce the horse's propensity both to these vices and other problems. If a horse that is easily bored is stabled for much of the day, it is a good idea to split the overall daily ration into six to eight small feeds, in order to keep it occupied and prevent it from developing bad habits. Since picking at bulk food serves to prevent boredom, especially at night, the largest portion of bulk food should be fed in the evening.

While correct management, in terms of sufficient exercise and an appropriate feeding regime, may prevent the formation of these vices, stable design is also a factor. Any projections or bars in the stable provide the horse with an opportunity to adopt or pursue bad habits, in that it will tend to catch hold of them or chew them out of boredom or to amuse itself. A prime example is the edges of mangers, and these should be wide enough so that the horse is not able to catch hold of them, since some horses attack them with relish. Concrete and porcelain mangers tend to be thick enough in this respect as a result of their construction. However, some plastic mangers have replaceable edges because the manufacturers realize that this part is the most vulnerable. Such designs are patently not suitable for known crib-biters and wind-suckers and, indeed, such horses are best fed off the ground. Bulk feed can simply be piled on the floor and concentrates fed in a skep or bowl, which is removed after feeding. Although it requires more work in keeping the stable clean and tidy, feeding in this way is the most natural for the horse.

Other features of stable design that are an invitation for the horse to catch hold include dividing walls made of vertical wooden bars set wide apart, horizontal rails (which are ideal for chewing) and internally nailed planks (just right for pulling off – and the exposed nails are an additional danger). Rather than these, the stable walls should be of smooth construction and devoid of unnecessary attachments. If a see-through partition between stables is required, heavy-gauge wire mesh in a steel frame is a practical solution, with the holes too small for the horse to get its teeth through. The other feature that is immensely attractive to crib-biters and wind-suckers is the top edge of the stable half-door and this will inevitably need protection. A simple metal covering may reduce damage to a wooden door, but it will not prevent the horse from catching hold of it. Sections of piping have been employed with some

Any projection will provide an opportunity for crib-biters and wind-suckers to pursue their bad habits.

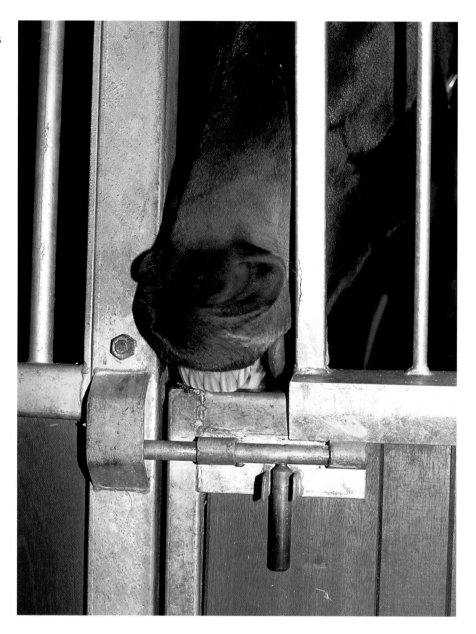

success, but these must be of sufficiently large diameter to prevent the horse from getting its mouth round them. Metal grilles, filling in much of the top section of the door, will prevent the horse from biting the door, but these must be of such construction that the horse cannot grab them, and they may increase the horse's sense of confinement.

Where boredom is a concern, substituting stable furnishings with 'toys' that the horse can play with safely may reduced the likelihood of these vices developing. The stable should be a place where the horse can rest, but not where its mind becomes stultified. The subject of toys will be dealt with further in the following section on Chewing.

Apart from the largely preventative measures discussed, what can be done if your horse already crib-bites or wind-sucks, or is starting to do so? It is noticeable that lively horses are particularly prone to these habits and, once they have contracted them – especially through too much standing around doing nothing – they will not give them up readily. As mentioned earlier, a horse can become so practised in the art of wind-sucking that it no longer needs to catch hold of anything in its teeth in order to do so. In this case it is no use just removing everything the horse can grasp. Although it is a prevention and not a cure, a wind-sucking strap can help up to a point with both wind-suckers and crib-biters. It must be worn all the time except when the horse is working. It must fit properly and be neither too loose nor too tight. It is attached to the headcollar by a strap at the poll to prevent it from slipping down the neck.

Many horses learn how to continue their bad habit despite being fitted with a wind-sucking strap.

This strap is, however, a half-measure which has its disadvantages. The horse will try to rub it off, and if it is not tight enough the horse soon learns how to wind-suck in spite of it, even if not to the same extent. Horses still in the early stages of the habit can sometimes be cured by means of a 'flute' bit (wind-sucking bit) attached to the headcollar. Like the wind-sucking strap, this must be worn all the time, both in the stable and in the field. A Tattersall ring bit achieves the same result by stopping the horse wanting to play with things with its mouth. However these measures must be used immediately, before the habit becomes ingrained.

Painting surfaces in both stable and paddock with tar or other unpalatable coatings is often attempted as a deterrent, but is only successful to a limited extent. Apart from the fact that the horses get covered in these coatings, they do not last, and are often less effective than one might imagine.

Electrified wire, however, has proved fairly successful for deterring crib-biters from catching hold of paddock fencing. The electrical pulse in the wire is so unpleasant for the horse that it at least respects the fencing in its paddock. The same method can be used in the stable if there are interior surfaces that need protecting and the wiring can be run safely. In fact you must use any means you can to outwit your horse, who will, in his turn, find the most devious ways to indulge his habit.

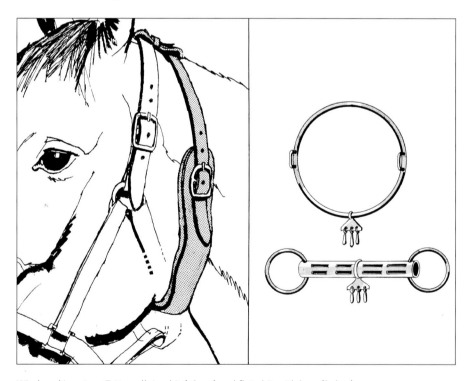

Wind-sucking strap, Tattersall ring bit (*above*) and flute bit with keys (*below*).

If all such methods fail, a further course of action is surgery, in which the sternal, oesophageal and submaxillary muscles involved in wind-sucking and crib-biting are cut on the underside of the neck near the throat. This is a drastic, expensive and messy operation, which leaves a visible break in the musculature which makes up the bottom line of the neck. This break varies in size depending on the skill of the surgeon. About 80 per cent of horses operated upon in this way are permanently cured of their habit. In my experience, once the decision has been made to take action against an established crib-biter, this is the best solution. The scar left by the operation grows together perfectly, leaving only a slight disturbance of the lower line of the neck. The less developed the underside of the neck, and the greater the surgeon's skill in making a, so to speak, cosmetically balanced cut in the musculature, the less significant will this disturbance of the neckline be. You need a strong stomach to be able to watch this operation.

Chewing

Horses may chew, or lick, the walls of their stables from boredom or for amusement or because they are suffering from a salt or mineral deficiency. (Eating soil or dung are also caused by dietary deficiency and require investigation by a vet or a qualified equine nutritionist.) In days gone by, horses grazing on natural pasture used to eat their choice of mineral-rich herbs and grasses, and so kept themselves 'topped up' with the minerals they needed. Nowadays, horses are cooped up in their boxes for far too long each day and are fed on specified foods year in, year out. They cannot look for what they need, but instead have to eat what is put in front of them. M. Schäfer says that for this reason, when feeding in winter, he adheres as closely as possible to the horse's natural choice of plants by feeding the best, sweet hay in the morning, and sweet hay plus hay from acid meadows in the evening. The horse's roughage requirement must be satisfied, even in cases where the crude fibre intake has to be rationed to prevent the horse from getting too fat. Often horses are bedded on peat or sawdust because they have attempted to compensate for the shortage of bulk food by eating straw bedding, even when it is dirty. Schäfer speaks of 'feeding factors', which are requirements that need to be satisfied. Normally a horse spends a total of twelve hours a day eating. If this requirement is not fulfilled there is a risk that the desire to eat will lead, for example, to the horse chewing anything it can get hold of, the more so because its ancestors obtained essential substances by chewing bark and branches.

The best way to satisfy the horse's fundamental requirement for salt is to hang a salt-lick in the stable. This is better than adding a few spoonfuls of salt to the feed, first because the horse can access the salt when it wants to and second, because licking the salt is a more constructive pastime than licking walls or chewing the stable fitments. (Alternatively, a mineral block may be substituted). It is also a good idea to put branches in the stable for the horse to chew, if for no other reason than to keep it occupied. Obviously the branches must not come from any trees or shrubs that are poisonous to horses, so their source should be checked carefully. Bark contains tannin, the exact amount depending upon the type of tree, and branches with buds on them contain bitter substances which horses will eat. Young horses in particular, being more active than older ones, enjoy having a branch with which to occupy themselves, although it should not be too thin or too brittle. As mentioned in the previous section, toys with no nutritional value can also serve to alleviate boredom. A variety of commercially produced horse toys are now available, but even something as basic as an empty cardboard box – without staples in it, of course – can be put in the stable. A horse with a lively mind will find all sorts of things to do with it!

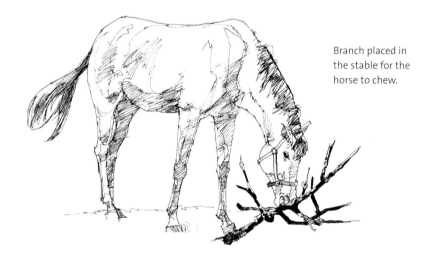

Branch placed in the stable for the horse to chew.

Mutual mane chewing is associated with back and wither scratching. It is distinct from the frenzied biting or chewing by a horse of its own coat, which usually indicates some skin disorder. Two horses scratching each other's backs from crest to tail with their teeth make a charming sight, but the result in terms of damage to the mane is catastrophic. Before long, unsightly holes appear in the beautifully tended mane, and it is weeks or months before the chewed tufts of hair have grown back again. In short, the mane looks thoroughly moth-eaten. To put it just as bluntly, there is nothing that can be done about it. It cannot be termed a bad habit since nibbling the mane is part of normal social grooming, in which horses (provided they are friends) will nibble each other in the places they cannot reach for themselves. This is an occupation to which horses are completely devoted, and it is out of the question to try to stop it. The only thing you can do is split up the two horses concerned into different paddocks, because, as has been said: when it comes to getting your back scratched, not just anyone will do!

Grinding teeth on the stable bars

In addition to signifying crib-biting, deformed incisor teeth are also the sign of the advanced stage of another bad habit: grinding the teeth on the bars of the stable. In order to understand this habit we must first make a brief study of the horse's eating habits. Horses living in the wild used to eat over the course of the whole day. The size of the horse's stomach does not permit it to take in a large quantity of food all at once, as cattle do. Except when it is desperately hungry, the horse bites off a few blades of grass at a time, chews them thoroughly and swallows them. Consequently, to get enough food, it has to eat grass for at least five hours a day. In contrast, horses nowadays are given concentrated food at specified times. Since it is known that a horse cannot make do with one meal per day, as a dog can, it is normally given hard food three times a day.

Feeding times should be strictly adhered to. This is necessary because the horse has a strong sense of time. For example, school horses know exactly when the lesson time is 'up'. There are numerous stories about carters and grooms and their horses which demonstrate the horse's awareness of time. Interestingly, the horse's inner clock is always slightly 'fast', making the horse react before the time arrives for something to happen. Thus unrest automatically sets in at the stables as the normal feeding time approaches. If the food is, in fact, late, this unrest will be compounded. Horses quickly get into bad habits as a means of working off their feelings, and these habits are further exacerbated by the fundamental desire for food.

Obsession with food is less pronounced in herds of horses grazing on large areas of grassland. These horses keep their distances, and only graze close together if they are especially close friends. In stables the situation is very different. The increased preoccupation with food is (according to Blendinger) a manifestly neurotic exaggeration of a natural mode of primitive behaviour. Obvious signs are laid-back ears, bared teeth, kicking the sides of the stable and grinding the teeth on the partition bars. Here again it is the energetic, intelligent horses which express themselves most forcefully.

Grinding the teeth along the bars of the partition grille or on the edge of the manger has particularly unpleasant consequences if these fixtures are made of metal. Concrete mangers, or other pre-cast concrete structures, are no better. Before long, blemishes and signs of abnormal wear appear on the incisor teeth and the horse's ability to eat (graze) may be impaired. As with crib-biting, the first course of action is to remove all opportunities for practising the habit. This may be easier said than done, but as a horse-keeper one should go to the trouble of ensuring that there is as little as possible for the horse to catch hold of with its teeth. It may also be a good idea either to feed such horses before the others (if this does not just shift the problem elsewhere), or to tie them up temporarily in such a way that they cannot get hold of anything. Finally, although this problem may be inherent in some impatient horses, it is worth remembering that, in many cases, it is induced or provoked by poor human timekeeping.

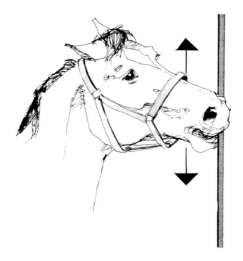

Grinding the teeth on vertical bars and horizontal objects is particularly harmful when these are made of metal, because they act like a rasp. Concrete is no better.

Banging and kicking the sides of the stable

The causes of this habit are usually the same as the previous one. Again, the horses concerned are not of a dull, indolent nature; they are lively, active and sensitive. They kick the sides of the stable out of excitement and impatience, and also to draw attention to themselves. Moreover, man is partly to blame for this habit: the bad practice of distributing titbits encourages horses to beg, and to try to get attention by banging or kicking. Not only is this an annoying habit, but knocking the limbs against the walls can have unpleasant consequences, such as capped hocks. If not treated immediately these can become hard and press on the joint, with even more unpleasant results. The knees too can be damaged. Remedial measures consist on the one hand in padding the sides of the box (swinging bail partitions in stalls should have plaited straw wrapped round them), and on the other in strict adherence to the rule that the horses must not be encouraged to beg. If the kicking results from a preoccupation with food, tying the horse up at feeding times should be considered. It must also be mentioned that– especially where it is not a regular habit – kicking the wall may be a sign that something is wrong, for example the horse has some form of irritation or injury. In such cases the veterinary surgeon must be consulted.

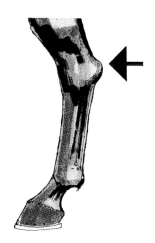

Capped hock.

Pawing

Pawing the ground in the stable is nearly always a sign of impatience and a craving for exercise; a tired horse rarely paws, except when it intends to lie down. With this as with the other habits, it makes absolutely no sense to shout at the horse and punish it with a whip in an attempt to stop it. This sort of treatment will only lead to restlessness, head-shyness and resistance, in fact quite the opposite of the desired result. Here again the principle applies that disobedient horses are only made obedient through work. As well as taking pleasure in exercise, the horse has a physical craving for it. When it paws the ground, this means that it wants something – at least, it wants something other than to stand in its stable. Pawing is a way of expressing eagerness and impatience; it is the horse's way of saying 'I want'. If the horse has discovered that it obtains something from man when it paws, it will quickly get into the habit of begging, and then you will never stop it from doing so. Horses also paw when they are hungry or thirsty, without the handler having done anything to cause it. Here again they are trying to say that they want to go out – to get a drink or something to eat. (In some cases, pawing that cannot be related readily to the foregoing explanations may be a sign of distress in an ailing horse, but this is likely to be accompanied by other signs of ill-health and is distinct from lively impatience.)

Insofar as pawing indicates a craving for exercise, the weekly 'day off' (rest day) should be mentioned. Where this signifies a day of confinement, it is an example of misplaced 'kindness'. The rest day should be a period of relaxation, not time spent doing nothing. For a horse, a day of enforced idleness is not a rest day but sheer torment and, as we have already seen and shall see again, it causes numerous behavioural problems and disorders, and serves only to keep the vets in business. The worst kind of day off follows a long ride or a competition. The event takes place on a Sunday morning, for example, so the horse spends half of Sunday plus all of Monday cooped up in its box, perhaps with aching muscles, and is deprived of the exercise it desperately needs to loosen up its muscles and disperse the lactic acid which has built up. It would make far more sense to turn the horse out or at least take it out for a walk in-hand. A rest from being ridden and from stress, accompanied by a measure of freedom, are what the horse requires. If circumstances preclude turning out or leading out, then at least the horse should be let loose in the indoor school for a while.

Throwing feed about

Some horses toss their food right and left over the sides of the manger onto the floor before they actually start eating. This is a senseless trick, since they then proceed to retrieve it all out of the straw. Foals often pick up this habit from their dams. The first course of action is to put only part of the feed in the manger at a time: a full manger only serves to encourage this sort of behaviour. If there is only enough food to cover the bottom of the manger this will cramp the horse's style! A second possibility is to change the manger. You can now buy mangers with an inner lip which prevents the food being pushed out. You can also fit bars across the manger. This will stop the horse swinging its head from side to side and so knocking the food out. A manger with a large lump of suitable material in the bottom will also make it difficult for the horse to push the food out, because it will have to put its nose down by the sides of the lump to reach it. If the manger is big enough, a salt lick, whole or in pieces, can be put in the bottom.

Another solution worth considering is to feed the horse at ground level. This can be done using a shallow container of suitable construction, such that the horse cannot injure his feet or forelegs by treading or kneeling in it. (In the interests of both container and horse, the former should, in any case, be removed after feeding.) Alternatively, if the floor surface is suitable and clean, the horse can be fed directly off the floor. There is no reason why the horse should not eat off the ground as nature intended. The only prerequisite, as has already been said, is an area of clean floor from which it can eat its feed without picking up pieces of dirt, sand and wood. Some horses are masters of the art of dismantling and destroying their mangers in record time. Unless they can be put in a stable with an integral concrete manger, these horses are best fed on the ground.

Weaving and box-walking

Weaving is a tiresome habit in which the stationary horse rocks its forehand continuously from side to side, usually with its forelegs slightly apart. The weight is transferred from one foreleg to the other, which causes undue wear and tear on the joints and tendons of the forelegs, the more so since this swinging may go on for hours on end. Although it can be exacerbated by excitement, weaving is without doubt a way of compensating for confinement and lack of exercise. Other animals kept in captivity (e.g. elephants, camels and bears) are also prone to weaving. It is noticeable that horses which receive sufficient exercise, either in the form of work or through being turned out, rarely take up weaving.

Weaving can spread from one horse to another, so, bearing in mind that horses like to imitate, weavers should be placed where other horses cannot see them. In this context of seeing, or not seeing, other horses, we should note an apparent paradox in equine behaviour. In well-designed yards, the stable doors open outwards over the yard. The top part of each door can be, and in most circumstances is, left open. The horses can watch what is going on in the yard, can see each other, get plenty of fresh air, and do not feel hemmed in – or at least we think that they do not. In fact we are wrong, since horses stabled in this way often weave. It is true that they can feel part of what is going on, but

In weaving, the tendons, ligaments and joints of the forelegs are continuously under stress.

they cannot go out of their boxes, however comfortable these may be, and they may then begin to weave as a way of compensating for this. Matters are made worse if there is something exciting going on outside the stable, either to one side or, worse still, directly opposite. In some such cases, depending on the size and temperament of the horse, and the precise construction of the stable, it may be advisable to keep the top part of the door shut and to open the bottom part.

Rocking from side to side with excitement when the feed is due can also lead to full-blown weaving. As previously stated, horses know exactly when it is feeding time – even if the person responsible for feeding apparently does not!

Once a horse has started to weave, it is extremely difficult, if not impossible, to stop it. Anti-weaving bars may be fitted across the upper half of the stable door, but many horses will simply take a step backwards and weave behind them. As with all bad habits, you have to experiment with the unlikeliest of cures in order to find one which works. People have tried painting black and white vertical stripes on the walls of the stable so the horse has the impression, when it weaves, that the stripes are oscillating. Weights attached to the fetlocks have been tried, but here the risk of injury has to be taken into account. However, attaching weights to the horse's body which make counter-movements when the horse weaves has sometimes been found helpful. Another method is to attach to the headcollar a rope which runs through a ring fixed firmly to the wall and is then attached to a significant weight. This can be a stone weighing about 11 kg. This device is adjusted so that, when the horse is still, the weight rests on the floor. However, whenever the horse weaves, it has to pull the weight. It is quite possible that weaving then becomes simply too much bother!

A habit not far removed from weaving is eternally walking round in circles in the box. As a basic principle, a tired horse will rarely show any desire to box-walk. Horses adopt this practice through boredom or stress. A stable companion, in the form of a goat, for example, should be considered. There are many cases of friendships between animals, with both animals benefiting from the relationship.

Treading on the opposite foot, and crossing the feet

With the first habit the horse treads on, or rubs, the coronet of one hind foot with the opposite foot. This often results in injury to the coronet. Like the habit of weaving, this arises from boredom and is difficult to cure. The only possible course of action is to fit overreach boots, so that at least the horse cannot injure itself.

With the second habit, the horse stands habitually with one forefoot crossed over the other. Here again, overreach boots offer the best protection against injury.

In winter, particular attention should be paid to the removal of all studs for the period that the horse is in the stable. In some areas it has become general practice to leave them in, but the effort to remove them should be made, since they are potentially an additional source of injury (e.g. abscesses).

It is also advisable to consult the veterinary surgeon if there is any suspicion that the horse is resting one foot on the other to take the strain off its tendons. If this is the case the horse is probably suffering from inflammation of the suspensory ligament.

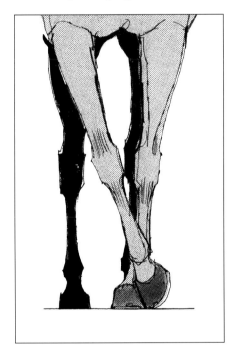

Crossing the feet.

Treading on the coronet of the opposite foot.

Rubber overreach boots: pull-on and quick-release.

Rubbing the tail

This problem is more common in summer than in winter: the horse has an itch so it rubs the top of its tail on walls, railings or trees. First the hairs become dishevelled, then a bald patch appears, and, in advanced cases, sores develop. The itch is either on the dock, or in the anus or genital region. In the first case, dirt is the cause. The hairs at the top of the tail should therefore be brushed meticulously every day with a dandy brush. Sweating horses in particular provide a favourable habitat for the mange mite, and if mange is the cause of the horse rubbing its tail, the veterinary surgeon must be informed because this is a notifiable disease. In both the above cases a 2 per cent solution of salicylic acid (salicylic acid collodion) or a 10 per cent solution of benzyl benzoate (in alcohol) have been shown to be effective. When working with these solutions, care should be taken that they do not come in contact with the anal or genital area. It goes without saying that the anus and underside of the dock should be washed daily with a sponge.

The itching may also be caused by worms. The veterinary surgeon will advise on this. Horses should, in any case, be wormed several times a year. In some horses, allergies to grass proteins or weeds can also cause itching. Here again, the veterinary surgeon can advise.

Mares in season may also tend to rub their tails. Fitting a tail guard or bandaging the tail (with due care) will protect the tail in such cases.

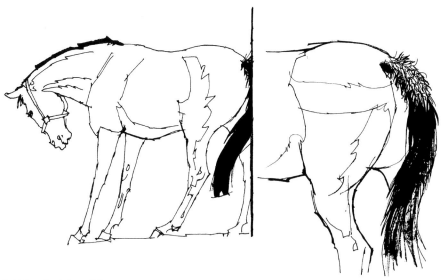

Rubbing the tail, and the consequences.

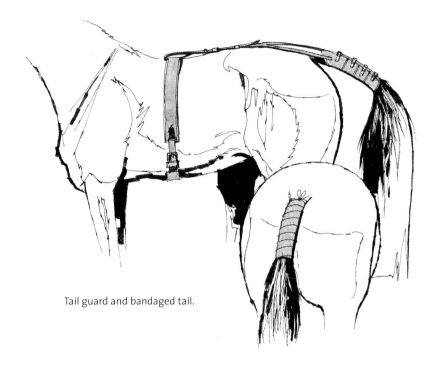

Tail guard and bandaged tail.

Rug-tearing

Rug-tearing is an expensive habit. Rugs are not cheap, and some horses will reduce any rug to shreds. Unless the cause of this practice is skin irritation, it simply means that the horse does not wish to wear a rug on its back. Horses are rugged much too often and, on occasions, when rugging is not appropriate. The horse's protective covering – that is, the coat – is designed in such a way that the stabled horse can withstand temperatures as low as −6°C. The important thing is that there are no draughts and that the atmosphere is not damp or steamy. Sweating horses should never be put away until they have been thoroughly dried out, either by leading them round or by rubbing them down. If a horse has a very thick winter coat, and inevitably sweats up when worked, an appropriate type of clip should be carried out. Horses cooled down properly after work will not come to any harm from dry, cool or cold air provided they are properly fed and have a good bed. So, especially if the horse is signifying destructive displeasure at being rugged-up, why rug at all?

Sick horses, however, do sometimes need to be rugged. So what should be done if the horse is still in sufficiently good spirits to try to get rid of its rug? Often, attempts to dislodge a rug are provoked because it has not been fitted properly and/or it alarms the horse. For example, the rug slips under the horse's belly during the night, and the horse tries to rid itself of its uncomfortable burden. It can also happen that the rug gets torn as the horse stands up, because the horse has trodden on it or become entangled in it. It may then hang down round the horse's legs, causing panic. The horse may also panic if the rug slips off over its head or is left dangling around its neck. Such reactions cannot be considered the horse's fault and the basic point is that rugs should fit (and be fitted) in such a way that they cannot slip. In addition to a crupper they should have a sewn-on surcingle which fastens round the belly. Diagonal straps at the back, holding the rear ends of the rug together under the horse's belly, are also a good idea. A second surcingle about 20 cm behind the first is recommended. This helps hold the rug in position and makes it more secure. Obviously, they must also have a breast strap at the front. Fastened properly, these methods of attachment ensure, once and for all, that the rug does not become a nuisance by slipping.

If a horse really needs a rug yet is an incorrigible rug-tearer, a proven preventative device whilst fitted is the muzzle or mouth guard. However, it does not look very nice, and it verges on cruelty because it prevents the horse from eating and drinking. It must, therefore, be removed at certain times and there is no guarantee that the horse will not take advantage of these moments to indulge its habit. Also – especially if it has a lively temperament – the horse will try everything to get the muzzle off or to demolish it. A chain muzzle is a better form of prevention because it allows the horse to eat and drink to some

Different rug fastenings.

extent, but prevents it from getting hold of the rug in its teeth. Another possibility is a clothing bib, which is like the back half of a muzzle. This also allows the horse to eat – but not to bite its rug. This device is particularly recommended.

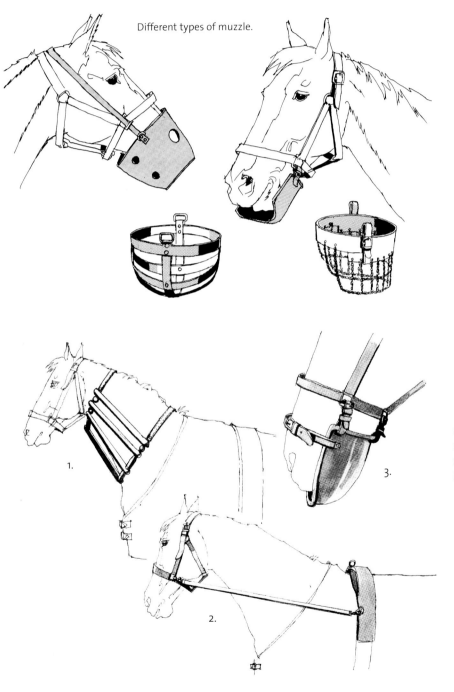

Different types of muzzle.

Devices used for preventing rug tearing: 1. neck cradle; 2. anti-rug-tearing bar; 3. clothing bib.

Two further pieces of equipment should be mentioned, although they are not recommended. The first is a wooden collar made of slats, which is known as a neck cradle. In this, the horse is able to eat and to move its head to some extent, but it cannot turn its head and neck, and so cannot reach its rug. This device is unpleasantly restrictive. Even worse is an anti-rug-tearing bar, which is attached at one end to the headcollar and at the other end to the roller. This is even more restrictive than the cradle. It allows hardly any movement at all and is definitely cruel. Even tying the horse up for long periods is more humane than these two methods.

Apart from horses that tear their own rugs out of irritation, there are over-playful individuals that may tear the turnout rugs of companions in the field. This is obviously undesirable and – if the torn rug is someone else's property – highly embarrassing. Furthermore, a torn rug, unnoticed for a while, has the potential to cause an accident. If a horse is known to indulge in this behaviour, he is best turned out in an adjacent field, in sight, but not in reach, of his companions.

Playful horses can damage the rugs of their field companions.

Biting

Biting has various causes. In days gone by, some horses were even taught to bite and kick in battle. However, modern selective breeding procedures serve to eliminate negative characteristics, so that nowadays horses are rarely born vicious. Those that become so are usually the products of seriously rough, incorrect handling.

Biting may result from teasing, desire for food, or incorrect grooming. It may also be a symptom of lack of exercise. Often it has developed through incorrect education of the horse as a foal. Young foals entice people into playing with them, especially if there are no other foals in the field, and before long, unless the humans quietly admonish any unwarranted behaviour, the games become rather rough. The foal does not realize how strong it is in comparison to man; it looks upon him first as a playmate and then as a sparring partner and, if not corrected, it soon loses its respect for man. Too often, it is not until this point that the human partner reacts and this may be by making rapid threatening movements, and by hitting the horse. The horse's confidence is thus shaken and it may then retaliate (albeit sometimes as a defence) by biting.

Ticklish horses, also, soon resort to biting if subjected to rough treatment whilst being groomed, therefore soft brushes and gentle grooming strokes

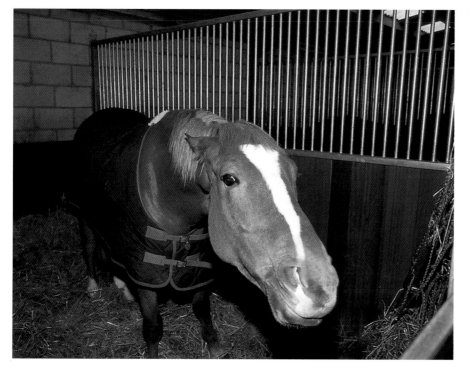

Warning signs from a horse that may be preparing to bite.

35

should be used on the horse's sensitive areas. Similarly, some horses, and mares in particular, will bite when the saddle is being put on or the girth is being done up. In irritation and annoyance, they sink their teeth into the manger or a post, or into the person who is causing the discomfort. Particularly sensitive and strong-willed horses are especially prone to this habit. In such cases the handler should consider how he could make the unpleasant procedure more acceptable to the horse. Hitting the horse is pointless, as is shouting at it. The horse will simply associate the abuse with what it sees as an unpleasant process, and it will not prevent it from feeling the girth being tightened. Talking softly and fondly, and patting the horse's neck is a better course of action, and diversions should also be attempted. This is one case in which it may be expedient to offer a titbit. The girth should be done up very gradually, perhaps only one hole at a time. Sometimes it also helps to lead the horse forward a few steps, then tighten the girth a bit more. The rider should then be helped on, so that the saddle is not pulled out of position and the horse does not feel restricted by a tight girth. Especially if a hitherto amenable horse starts trying to bite when being saddled, it is well to check that the saddle has not become damaged, or is no longer a good fit.

So far as social influences are concerned, it is notable that an energetic 'lead mare' turned out with horses at grass will usually ensure that the hierarchical order is quickly established and maintained, with a minimum of biting! When man intrudes in this society, matters often take a different course. Jealousy, aggression and ill-will can turn horses into biters. However, there are many cases of biters turning into pleasant, useful animals once their confidence has been restored. It is wrong to isolate biters. Often, swapping stables or transferring the horse to another block or yard will bring about a change, because behaviour in the stable also depends on the horse's attitude to its neighbours. Horses have strong likes and dislikes: if they are unsettled, neuroses often develop. Since a horse's attitude towards different people varies, a person whom the horse accepts should be chosen for the job of reforming a biter. Certainly, care should be taken to ensure that biters are not teased in the stable, whether by other horses or humans. It is a good idea, when trying to cure them, to let them go a bit hungry, so that, when fed, their interest is focused on the food and not on their human handler. Again, a confident handler who will talk soothingly to the horse is beneficial.

Máday says that, according to the experience of a certain circus director, it is possible to break a horse of the habit of biting by teaching it to retrieve objects. An alternative view is that it is best to get rid of a chronic biter at the earliest opportunity.

Kicking, and difficulties with shoeing

Another form of malicious behaviour is kicking. However, like biters, kickers are not born that way. Even though young foals make reflex movements with their hind legs, these are instinctive, not malicious, acts. Horses become kickers through incorrect handling. The reaction to wrong handling can reach the point where the horse lays back its ears and lashes out at the very approach of a person. Some horses are masters of the art of suddenly lashing out without any visible warning signs. However, a clear distinction must be made between kicking out of malice and kicking because the horse is overfresh, anxious to be fed, in oestrus, pregnant or ticklish. There is a saying 'Beware of the front legs of a stallion and the hind legs of a mare'. Another saying, which refers to kicking at feeding time, is 'If you want to discover a person's true character, disturb him when he is asleep; if you want to discover a horse's true nature, all you need do is disturb it at feed-time'.

In this section, we shall deal with the habits of unmounted horses that lash out at people or other horses. Kicking out under saddle will be discussed separately (see Chapter 8, Lawless Horses). In some cases, as we shall see, kicks and related acts may not be aimed deliberately at the handler, but this makes no difference to the damage caused if they happen to connect.

In days gone by, kickers were hobbled in the stable, or had ropes attached to their hind feet at one end and to their headcollars at the other, and run through a ring attached to the lower part of the roller. The result was that the horse punished itself when it kicked. However the best solution is to try to win back the horse's confidence with endless patience and calmness. Here again the horse's liking for a particular handler plays an important part, and the horse should be attended in its stable by this person only. Kickers are more difficult to deal with in stalls than in loose boxes, since one should never approach a kicker from behind, and this point should be borne in mind when accommodating such an animal. Generally, when approaching a kicker, it is best to talk to it first, then walk briskly up to its shoulder without hesitating. Once the horse has succeeded in frightening its handler, it will always have the upper hand.

In most cases of kicking, mistakes have been made when the horse was a foal. Foals should be accustomed at an early age to having their feet picked up, being handled all over, and being groomed. In addition to the educational value, it is important that a foal learns to pick its feet up in order that they can be carefully trimmed to prevent the development of any postural faults, which could have serious consequences. A little trouble at the outset pays dividends in later years. Allowing its feet to be picked up is something a horse learns relatively easily, but all too often youngsters are allowed to get away with stroppy behaviour, and handling the feet may even be omitted altogether. Alternatively, the handling may be carried out roughly, which causes distrust and dislike of the process. However, while harsh, frightening procedures should be avoided, the training must nevertheless be serious and purposeful, and the foal must not look upon it as a game. Now and then it will be necessary to hang on tight, because once a foal has learned that the handler is not so strong as itself, it will keep trying to pull its foot away.

One factor that often causes problems in teaching a youngster to pick up its feet is that people often go about it the wrong way. A horse will lift both fore and hind legs more easily if they are pulled forward slightly. Bending the foreleg at the knee can also be tried. The leg is held by the fetlock, around which both hands are cupped. (In Continental Europe a helper is employed to hold the horse's foot while the farrier shoes it.) With a hind leg, it is important that the fetlock rests on the handler's thigh so that it cannot be pulled away. If a horse is very resistant to holding up a hind leg, and it has a reasonably long tail, one answer is to wrap the horse's tail around its fetlock. Then, if it kicks out, it punishes itself by wrenching its tail. Especially in the early stages of teaching a horse to hold its feet up, it is a good idea for a helper to distract the horse's attention by playing with its top lip or stroking its forehead.

Particular calmness and firmness are necessary when it comes to trimming the feet, especially since this lays the groundwork for actual shoeing. If a foal proves fractious, a tried and tested method of improving its behaviour and easing the farrier's task too is as follows. A suitable stable is chosen, and plenty of straw is put down so that the foal cannot slip. A helper leads the foal up to the wall and stays with it throughout the operation, talking to it soothingly,

Lifting up a forefoot. To make it easier to hold the foot up, it is advisable to rest the horse's knee on your thigh.

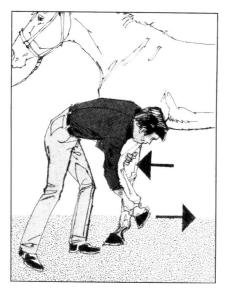
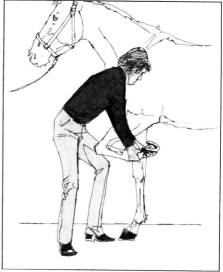

Lifting up a hind foot. The foot can be rested on your thigh.

Winding the end of the horse's tail around the hind foot while it is in the air tends to have a quietening effect. It also has the advantage that the horse more or less holds its own foot up.

patting it and praising it. A second helper pushes the foal's croup up against the wall, lifting up the tail as he does so. The farrier can then see to the foal's feet by himself.

Of course, one does not always have the advantage of training horses from a young age, and it may be that a mature horse is acquired which refuses to pick its feet up, kicks out whilst being shod, or is otherwise difficult to shoe. One example of this general difficulty is the horse which will not stand still, but hops around on three legs. The farrier's work is hard enough, without him having to cope with such antics and it is noteworthy that, in days gone by, when the horses went to the farrier, and not the farrier to the horses, many forges had a 'shoeing frame', which immobilized the horse completely. A modern ploy, which may at least reduce the fidgeting of a fractious horse, is to go for an energetic ride to tire the horse before it is due to be shod. Again, it cannot be stressed too much that most bad behaviour would never arise in the first place if horses were worked sufficiently, and, above all, regularly.

Another method of countering fidgeting and generally fractious behaviour is to apply a twitch. When using a twitch it must be remembered that its purpose is to distract the horse and not to inflict pain. In other words, it should not be twisted so tightly that the end of the nose turns blue or the skin comes off. Instead, the twitch should be used to play with the end of the horse's nose, and should only be turned more tightly when necessary. It should be loosened as soon as the horse does what is required of it. Patting the horse lightly on the neck and speaking soothingly to it at the same time help it to calm down and not think about what is happening to it. If this method fails, then a sedative in the feed, or an injection from the vet may be the only answer.

Speaking of vets, behavioural problems such as kicking may arise when the vet calls. Some vets know how to deal with difficult horses, and others do not. Horses are very easily put off. One clumsily given injection is enough. Next time, the horse will fly into a panic at the very sight of the vet at the stable door. The solution to this problem is great tact, patience – or even another vet.

If confirmed kickers need their feet restraining or lifting while various procedures are carried out, there are various methods that may be considered, all of which rely on the use of a rope. These are detailed in the accompanying drawings.

As mentioned earlier, some forms of kicking may not be done with the deliberate intention of striking a handler, or they may, at least, not start out in this way. One example of this is that pawing, which may begin as a form of begging, can degenerate into a more aggressive striking out with the front feet. Of course, many people give their horses treats, but horses differ in their natures, and we must know where to draw the line if – preferably before – the 'begging' starts to get out of hand. If your horse does start striking out at people with its forefeet, the whip is the only answer. However, its use (from the front, on the cannon bone) must be immediate. If you have to run and fetch the whip the punishment is too late, and is ineffectual, because the horse cannot associate the two events.

The reasons for banging or kicking the sides of the box or the stall parti-

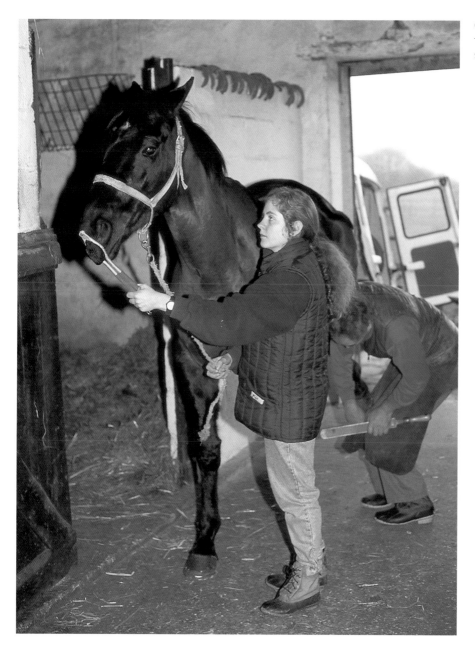

Correct use of a modern twitch to calm a horse whilst shoeing.

tions have already been discussed, together with the possibilities of injury to the horse. Clearly, such activities can also have unpleasant consequences for any person who gets in the way. Particularly in the primitive stabling provided at many competitions, care must be taken that kickers cannot do any damage – whether to the stable, themselves or the handler. This need for caution is heightened by the fact that competition horses may be wearing studs in their hind shoes.

The twitch should never be kept permanently tight: it should be loosened when the horse has done what is required. The unfortunately common practice of tying the twitch in position (*right*) is totally unacceptable.

(*Left*): Raising and securing the foreleg of a kicker. In an emergency the stick (which must be round) can be pulled out quickly.

(*Right*): The correct way to secure a tail as part of the restraining arrangement.

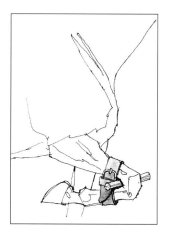

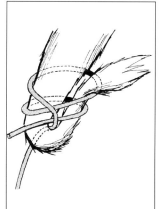

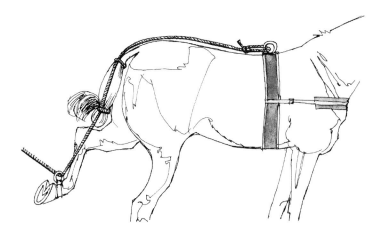

A good method, though it can present problems (e.g. how to get the strap round the pastern).

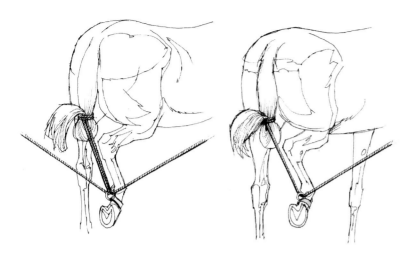

Two more ways of holding up the hind foot of a kicker: (*left*): method for use with two helpers; (*right*): method for use with one helper.

There is one other habit sometimes seen in stabled horses which, in a way, is associated with kicking and can have unpleasant consequences. Nervous horses sometimes react to various situations by trying to crush their groom – or anyone else in the stable – against the wall. This seemingly threatening and potentially injurious practice is, however, usually a sign of terror rather than malice. A horse trying to avoid being kicked by another horse can be seen to protect itself by leaning its flank against the flank of the other horse. Thus, when a horse crushes a person against a wall (perhaps because it is afraid of punishment), this is a defensive reaction and not a malicious one. Although the action remains highly undesirable, the reason behind it must be understood, and the horse should not be punished for it. In the horse's mind, this would confirm the need for the action. Instead, it makes more sense to calm the horse and convince it that there is nothing to be afraid of.

Finally, a few words about kicking from over-exuberance. Many accidents have been caused by horses being led and released incorrectly when they are turned out in the field. However happy horses may be at the prospect of this freedom, they should still be obedient, and they can be trained to go quietly and obediently to the field. It is a big mistake to release the horse at the gate and let it go charging off. This is where kicking can have disastrous effects. On entering the field the horse should be turned so that it is facing the handler, and it should not be released until it is standing quietly. In this way it can never reach the handler with its feet, even if it then charges off bucking and kicking. Believe it or not, it is quite possible to educate a horse to behave calmly and quietly when it is given its freedom. However, taking two or more horses to the field at the same time should be avoided wherever possible. Too many things can go wrong on the way to the field and when entering it.

Kicking among horses turned out at grass can only be prevented, not cured. The first essential, when introducing any horse that might conceivably be a kicker to a group, is to remove the hind shoes. However, known kickers should be turned out separately from other horses. Even so, it is advisable to round off the corners of the field with diagonal rails to prevent any horse from being trapped in a corner in the event of any argument within the herd.

Rounding off the corners of the paddock with diagonal rails prevents horses from being trapped in the corner and kicked.

Getting cast

A horse is said to be cast when, having lain down, it gets stuck against a stable wall and is unable to rise unaided. Getting cast is not a vice. However, some horses manage to get cast time and time again even in large stables, and this can still be termed a bad habit, albeit one which is caused by clumsiness. Horses can also get cast in stalls. Obviously the first thing to do when this happens is to release the horse from the tie rope or chain; if this cannot be done, the headcollar must be cut off. In stalls partitioned with swinging bails the rest is simple: the bail is detached, the adjacent horse moved out, and the cast horse is able to get up by itself. In stalls with solid partitions, or loose boxes, help must be summoned and attempts made to move the horse into a better position by pulling it round by its tail or by ropes attached to its feet. This should be done calmly so as not to panic the horse. Care must be exercised when pulling the horse by the tail – a broken tail is a nasty injury! It is a mistake to hit the horse to try to make it get up when it is simply not in a position to do so. As a last resort, ropes and slings can be used.

Before helping a cast horse, it is essential to know just how a horse gets up. It does so in the opposite sequence from a cow. It rolls onto its tummy and brings its hind legs as far forward as possible under its body. It then extends its forelegs one at a time to the front and uses them to lift the body. This enables the hind legs to push off from the ground with a jolt, which goes right through the body. This sequence must be understood because this knowledge will enable the handler to put the horse's legs in a position that will make it easier for the horse to rise. Before attempting any drastic intervention, it is also worth making a calm, if rapid, assessment of the situation. If the horse does not appear to be badly stuck, and is making a concerted effort to get up, without panicking, give it time to gather its strength: sometimes this is all that is needed.

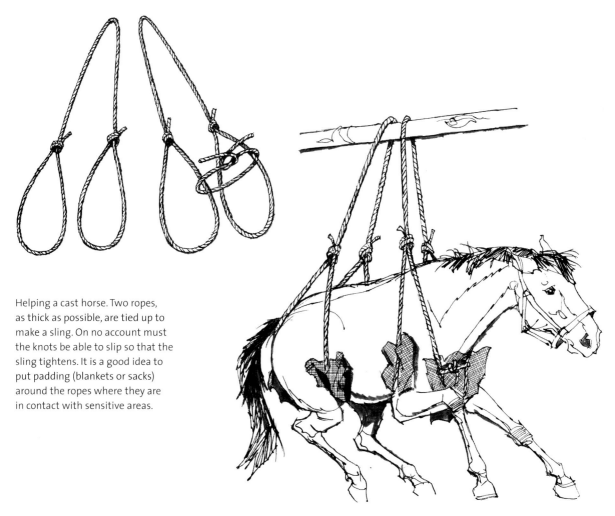

Helping a cast horse. Two ropes, as thick as possible, are tied up to make a sling. On no account must the knots be able to slip so that the sling tightens. It is a good idea to put padding (blankets or sacks) around the ropes where they are in contact with sensitive areas.

When attaching slings to help a badly cast horse, care must be taken to prevent it becoming excited. If it does panic it is advisable to pin its head to the ground by getting an assistant to kneel on its neck and press down with his hands on the jawbone or behind the ears. This may sound a drastic measure but, in fact, it is a useful way to prevent the horse from wasting its energy as well as to prevent it from getting injured.

Once they begin to feel the ground under their feet, many horses will take over the righting process for themselves but some, either through shock or extreme weakness, will have to be pulled all the way up into a standing position – and even then it may be some time before they actually take their weight on their feet. In such cases, the veterinary surgeon should be consulted. Further to this, it should be emphasized that the advice given refers to basically healthy horses that cannot get up simply because they have become stuck. Horses that cannot get up through illness should, of course, always be referred to the vet.

Horses with a tendency to get cast, or clumsy types which find general difficulty in getting up, should be provided with a deep litter straw bed, or a bed with a layer of peat underneath. Such a bed enables the horse to get a good grip with its feet, so that they do not slip out from under the horse as it rises. Asphalt or concrete floors beneath the bed should be grooved to provide further purchase. The straw should also be banked up against the walls to prevent the horse from lying right up against the wall. In addition to straw banks, sloping stable walls are a good idea because they allow the feet to slide upwards, and not downwards as with vertical walls. Horizontal laths on the wall (unless the horse crib-bites) will also provide a grip for the horse's feet. Three laths, with the top one 1–1.3 m from the ground, are sufficient. Such measures may prevent the horse from experiencing regular problems when trying to stand up, which can make it reluctant to lie down at all (see next section).

Bedding banked up against the stable walls to help prevent the horse from getting cast. Laths or ridges on the walls give the horse something to push against with its feet.

Refusing to lie down

Horses can, up to a point, relax, rest and sleep standing up (this is made possible by the construction of the skeleton and the way the tendons work). However, it has been proved that lying down is essential to the horse's well-being. Complete decontraction of the muscles cannot be achieved through long periods of standing, although there are stories told of horses which have never lain down in their lives.

There are several reasons why horses will not lie down. If the reason can be determined, and the cause removed, this will be to the horse's advantage – although this is not always possible. One basic cause, easily remedied but better avoided, is that dirty, damp bedding may be sufficient reason for a sensitive horse to remain on its feet. In many cases, the cause is physical and may be harder to alleviate. Old horses may simply have become too stiff. Or a horse may, for example, be afraid of the pain and difficulty experienced in getting up, because of degenerative changes in the hock. Horses which have experienced breathing difficulties as a result of a pulmonary infection whilst lying down, may also be reluctant to repeat the experience. Whether or not any of these reasons were contributory factors, horses with a history of being cast may also become frightened of lying down.

Psychological reluctance to lie down is often associated with insecurity – when, for example, a horse is moved to a yard. Nervous horses may also be afraid to lie down if there are mice running round in the straw, or even birds nesting in the stable roof.

Pulling back on the tie rope and slipping the headcollar

Pulling back on the tie rope and rubbing the headcollar off are not so prevalent nowadays, because few horses are kept in stalls. In many instances in the past, stepping back in the stall was the first step towards slipping the headcollar. The underlying reason for developing this habit may have been boredom, inquisitiveness or disgust at being perpetually tied up. Initially, the horse would step back as far as its tie rope would allow, a habit which might have unpleasant consequences in stables with a narrow gangway behind the stalls, or with another line of stalls on the other side of the gangway. Apart from the fact that they would foul the gangway, these horses would get in the way, upset the others, and cause kicking. Although responses such as hitting the horse's quarters with a broom were not unusual, such actions are not worthy of a good horsemaster and did not deal with the underlying causes. Neither, in fact, did tying the horse up short. This only led to the horse doing its best to get rid of the headcollar completely. A rope or chain might be put across the back of the stalls, but this had the disadvantage that horses might get into the habit of rubbing their hindquarters and tails on it. Similarly, a bar used for the same purpose carried the added risk that the horse might actually sit on it! Given the underlying causes of unrest, turning the horse so that it was facing the gangway for short periods was often the best way of minimizing the problem. Of course, where horses are still kept in stalls, these difficulties remain to be dealt with, but horses also need to be tied up on occasion for reasons other than being secured in stalls.

If, for any reason, a horse, exhibits a tendency to pull back on its tie rope, one way of dealing with the problem is to use a self-tightening headcollar, which causes the horse to punish itself by putting pressure on the lower jaw when the horse steps back. It is also possible to obtain from the saddler a special kind of headcollar with an additional separate headpiece-cum-throatlatch, which fits the head better. The self-tightening headcollars are also useful for horses which break their headcollars on purpose, since this habit starts with the horse stepping backwards. It is more advisable, and better for the horse's training, to let the horse punish itself than to resort to a great, heavy headcollar which can lead to an accident (although, as we shall see, there may be occasions when such a headcollar has its place). With horses which simply slip their headcollars, doing up the throatlatch so tight that the horse can hardly breathe is definitely not the answer. It is better to get the saddler to make up a special headcollar along the lines of those illustrated, or of a similar type.

Headcollars 1 and 2 serve to prevent the horse from pulling back when tied up: the horse punishes itself when it does so. Types 3 and 4 make it impossible for the horse to get the headcollar off.

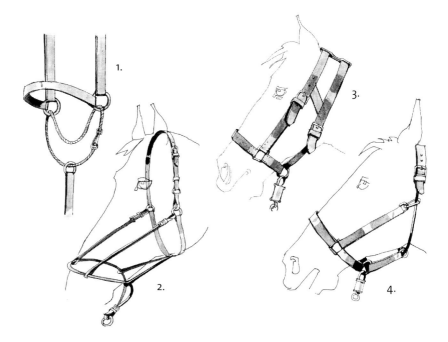

From the horse's point of view, getting rid of the headcollar is an understandable reaction to being constantly tied up, but the consequences can be disastrous. Depending on the circumstances in which they succeed in freeing themselves, they may endanger themselves or other horses and cause various degrees of upset, turmoil and destruction. It should be noted, however, that horses should be accustomed gradually to being tied up and (the old arrangement of horses being constantly tied up in stalls notwithstanding) they should not be tied up for unnecessarily long periods for no good reason. Although young horses should learn to stand tied to both sides in the gangway, if there is any resistance it is not advisable to tie the horse on both sides straight away. Even though the horse may not stand so still, it has to start off by learning to stand tied on one side. It will come to accept the other side too with patience and calming words.

If a horse pits all of its strength against being tied up, and panics to the point of risking injury to itself, then mistakes have certainly been made in its education. Depending upon the individual case and circumstances, different remedies may be attempted. The fact is that gentle, tactful handling and powerful resistance may both be equally effective in obtaining a horse's obedience – although temperament and underlying causes will be very influential in deciding which course to pursue. Paalman writes that, with horses which

refuse to stand tied, a piece of string which the horse can break easily should be inserted between the headcollar and the chain or rope. The horse will gradually give up the practice when it realizes that it can break its rope easily. This is perhaps one possibility. On the other hand, in different circumstances, this may be the time to resort to a really strong headcollar and, if necessary, a smack on the quarters to achieve the desired effect. As is often the case when dealing with horses, deciding on the right method is often a matter of equestrian knowledge and discernment.

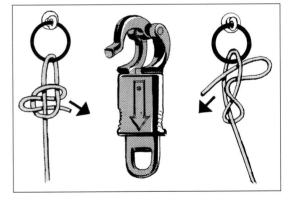

Two kinds of quick-release knot for use with a horse which is tied up. In the centre is a 'panic-clip', which can be undone by pulling.

Being difficult when led

Going back to a point made earlier, I should first say that horses which have been trained to lead as foals and have normal temperaments will not usually present any problems later. However, it is a fact that these conditions do not always pertain.

Horses which will not leave their stables, or refuse to be led, are tiresome, and can make people look very silly. The handler tries to lead the horse out of the box, but it refuses to budge an inch, and stands obstinately like a wooden horse, with its legs straddled. Or else they have led the horse somewhere, and for no apparent reason, when there is nothing to frighten it, it clamps its feet down and refuses to move. Often, in such circumstances, two fatal mistakes are made; *never*

1. turn and look the horse in the face unless you just want to calm it or coax it;

2. pull the horse, since the more you pull the more resistance the horse will offer, and you cannot hope to move half a ton or more of resisting horse. The bridle or headcollar will break, but the horse will not move forwards a millimetre.

The best course of action is to enlist an assistant to provide the necessary back-up. A short sharp tap, or whack if necessary, with the whip will show the horse that it must leave the box or that it must continue on its way. Talking quietly to the horse and praising it, and offering it some tasty morsel, will help get rid of any further resistance.

It is no good trying to pull a horse out of a stable if it does not want to come!

What should you do if you are alone? Making the horse go backwards a few steps can help, as can pushing it sideways with the shoulder, since getting it to move one step can provide the impetus to get it going again. In the first case, the backward steps must be induced with the minimum of compulsion – do not wrench the horse violently backwards since this will ruin its joints and spoil its good nature. If the horse is to be turned sideways, always do this by turning the horse away from you to the *right*, i.e. around its hindquarters. Never turn it left when leading it from the left. Another method which will probably get the horse going is to drive it round on its forehand with a stick, as when doing preparatory schooling work in-hand. Again, the stick should be used correctly as an aid, and not simply to beat the horse.

The opposite of refusing to move when being led is the horse that rushes forwards too impetuously – but this is still disobedience. If your horse behaves in this manner and does not respond to either a gentle or energetic tug on the headcollar rope, then the lead rope can either be looped round the horse's nose or passed through its mouth. The latter method is more effective, but should only be used when absolutely necessary. Never lead your horse with just your hand on its headcollar: there is always something which can happen to upset even the quietest horse, and if you have ever been left swinging from a headcollar because you could not get your fingers out, then you will know what can happen. This advice should be taken even more seriously when leading two horses.

The correct way to turn a horse is always to the right; if this method is used it cannot escape control. If the horse is turned to the left, the handler is liable to be taken off his guard and knocked over.

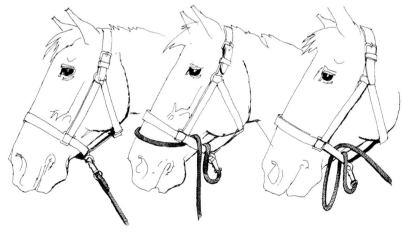

In order to lead a horse in a difficult situation, it is a good idea to put the lead rope over the nose or through the mouth. Afterwards all you have to do is slacken the rope off.

51

Rearing while being led is also a bad form of disobedience and this deficiency in its education should be remedied immediately. The method of leading with the headcollar rope through the horse's mouth, as described above, can be tried, but this may not be sufficient to counter determined attempts to rear. As an alternative, you can get lead ropes which have a length of chain set into them just behind the panic clip (quick-release clip), the purpose of the chain being to go through the horse's mouth. The horse cannot chew through the chain, which is also more effective than rope in exercising control. However, corrections with the chain must be made with discretion, otherwise injury to the mouth may result. If the rearing continues, an anti-rearing bit can be employed. This is a tried and tested aid, but is obvious from looking at its design that it can be brutal in its action and has the potential to cause serious injuries to the roof of the mouth. Again, therefore, it is a device that must be used with considerable discretion.

In order to teach overall obedience when leading a horse, it may be expedient to carry a schooling whip or stick in the left hand. This can be used on the horse's flank to encourage forward movement. Alternatively, if the horse keeps barging forwards and leaping about, it may be necessary to tap the horse on the nose with the handle of the whip. This must be done with discretion, otherwise it can induce head-shyness, but it may well be more effective and less damaging than jabbing the horse in the mouth. Unless the horse is really incorrigible, a couple of sharp taps at an early stage may nip the behaviour in the bud. As is so often the case, effective correction, applied early, may resolve a problem to the long-term benefit of both horse and handler. The aim is for the horse to learn to walk along next to you on a very light contact, neither rushing nor holding back. This has parallels with the horse at walk under saddle and you should use the lead rope in a similar way to the rein. For example, you can use your right hand to 'hook the horse back' (a 'taking' aid), but do not forget to 'give' with the hand again once your signal has taken effect. Talk to the horse and use the commands 'Walk on' and 'Whoa' smartly and clearly in conjunction with your physical signals. Take your time and always try the gentle way first.

For horses which are difficult to catch at grass, a practical method is to attach a short rope, about 20 to 30 cm long, to the headcollar. It does not hamper the horse while grazing, and puts you in a better position to catch hold of the horse than with no rope at all. Many horses do not like being 'grabbed' by the head, so sudden movements of this kind should be avoided. However, you can catch hold of a rope more readily than you can a headcollar. A knot in the end of the rope will give you more grip. When handling horses that are difficult to catch, it is *extremely* important to heed the earlier warning about not attempting to lead a horse with your hand through the headcollar.

Problems in saddling and bridling

It is incredible how absurdly some people go about saddling and bridling their horses. When just about every mistake in the book has been made, and the horse has developed the corresponding bad habits, the process of tacking up then becomes really tiresome. For example, everyone is familiar with the sight of a tiny person trying to put a bridle on an enormous horse. If a tall person can experience difficulties, someone small will be in a real predicament. The horse's head gets higher and higher, the person stands on tiptoe, yet still he cannot reach. The battle may end in anger and rough treatment. To avoid such a scenario, take your time and work your way slowly and thoroughly along the horse's crest, scratching it from withers to poll, like foals do to each other in the field. Try to find the spots where scratching makes the horse lower its head of its own accord to allow itself to be scratched, stroked and 'kneaded'. Once the horse will lower its head voluntarily, there should be no problem in fitting the bridle, provided that this is done with care and patience.

Head-shyness is usually an acquired characteristic. It is caused by bad handling or bad experiences, such as the use of force to put the bridle on, blows to the head, a badly fitted or overtightened twitch, bad experiences with the veterinary surgeon, etc. It will take a long time to get rid of this habit – if indeed it can be cured. Traces of it will remain, and you must be careful not to act in a way that resurrects the problem. The golden rule is no rapid movements, and a lot of tact and persuasion. A horse which has become nervous in this way must have, or acquire, confidence in you. Whether the horse is afraid or not depends on the person who handles it, and how that person behaves. When redressing head-shyness, it is a good idea to talk to the horse constantly and to be generous with titbits so that eventually the horse takes the bit willingly and allows the bridle to be pulled over its head and ears without pulling away. The important thing is to make the procedure as agreeable as possible for the horse, since it clearly finds it worrying.

It is a general rule that the horse must be kept happy not only when it is being worked, but also when the tack is being put on. This will also help the horse to begin work in a relaxed frame of mind. Let us go through the normal tacking up procedure step by step. First, there is the decision about the order in which saddle and bridle are to be fitted. This depends partly upon location and partly upon the horse. Ideally, there is a headcollar and lead rope available, there is a safe location at which to secure the horse, and the horse is happy to be tied up. In this case, although many people would still choose to fit the bridle first, there may be circumstances in which fitting the saddle first has its advantages. These would include saddling a 'cold-backed' horse, or one sensitive to being girthed up – topics we will consider shortly. If, on the other hand, you are tacking up in a loose box and either no headcollar is available, or the horse will not be tied up, you will be more or less obliged to fit the bridle first, since you can then put your arm through the reins and keep control of the horse. Failing to do so invites a situation in which the saddled horse keeps running away from you round the box. This will develop into a bad habit, which the horse will not readily forget. It goes without saying that any situation in which a horse might break free wearing only a saddle (such as a show or a hunt meet) is one to be very much avoided – in such circumstances, fitting the bridle first should be a rule.

For the purposes of illustration, let us assume that we are fitting the bridle first. We begin with the horse wearing a headcollar, even in the stable, because, first it is easier to get hold of it, and second it is safer, especially if the horse panics. The first step in putting on the bridle is to slide the reins over the neck, with the headcollar still on. The handler then positions himself on the left of the horse, level with its neck, undoes the headcollar, and takes it off. (If the horse is not in an enclosed environment, it may be necessary to fasten the headcollar temporarily around the horse's neck. However, horses should only be secured in this fashion briefly, and should never be left unattended.) The handler holds the bit on the open palm of his left hand and pushes it gently but firmly into the horse's mouth, pressing lightly with his forefinger and thumb if necessary. At the same time, with his right hand, he pushes the headpiece of the bridle over the right ear, holding the noseband up with it, by the nosepiece. The left ear is then pulled through, and the noseband and throatlatch done up.

What should be done if the horse refuses to be bridled, and puts its head up higher and higher? We have already seen how to avoid this problem developing, or how to address it in the long term. In the short term, always have a titbit with you, and give it to the horse before you start to put the bridle on. The horse will want another. Few horses are so contrary that they throw their head up straight away, but if it does so, give it another titbit. Hold the horse with your right hand on its forehead, stroking it. This hand is then ready to pull the bridle over the right ear, then the left. There is no sense in trying to pull a horse's head down against its will. Once it has been grabbed a few times, had the bit shoved roughly into its mouth, the noseband wrenched tight, and both ears forced painfully through the bridle, any horse will turn sour!

Usually the main problem is trying to push the bit into the mouth when the horse is evading upwards with its head. If this is the case, instead of holding the bridle by the headpiece, hold it in your right hand by the two cheekpieces about 10 cm above the

Horse playing up whilst being bridled.

bit. Stroke the right hand up and down the nose to try to get the horse to comply. The left hand remains open, with the bit on it, ready to push into the horse's mouth in the usual way. If the horse resists the right hand, firm counter-pressure, given if necessary, is usually sufficient. Do not forget to make much of the horse when you finally succeed in your aim. Incidentally, some horses have extremely sensitive whiskers on their muzzles, but even if this is the case, they should not be cut, because this would mean depriving the horse of important organs of touch.

Always leave yourself plenty of time to put the bridle on. In winter, when the bit may be icy cold, no horse will particularly enjoy having such an instrument put in its mouth. When doing up the noseband take care not to get any of the horse's feeler hairs caught in the buckle. Especially if the horse and tack are not your own, it is always wise to check the position of the bit in the horse's mouth. The corners of the lips should not be pulled upwards, but neither should the bit hang down so that it touches the tushes. (When fitting a bit initially, a measuring stick pushed carefully through the mouth from side to side will give the width of the mouth, to which 1 cm should be added on either side.) Particular care should be taken when fitting curb bits. The port should not be too high and the cheeks should not be too close to the sides of the face. The curb chain should be turned (clockwise) until it is flat, and should lie in the chin groove. A rubber curb guard may help if the horse is particularly sensitive in that area. There should be the same number of spare links on the right as on the left. Bad experiences with pinching bits (e.g. worn eggbutt joints, or even narrow loose-ring snaffles) may be a reason for horses to play up when it comes to putting the bit in. Remember, also, that with a drop noseband there should be room for three fingers between the noseband

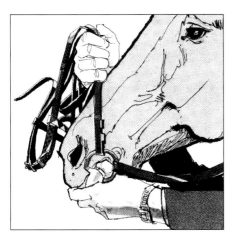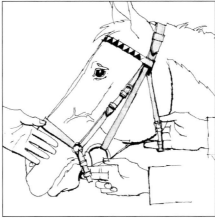

(*Left*): The correct way to hold the bridle and bit to put them on. (*Right*): Correct fitting of a snaffle bridle with a drop noseband.

and the bridge of the nose; that the nosepiece should not be too long; that the buckle of the chin strap should not lie against the lips, and that the browband should be neither too short nor fitted too high so that it pinches the base of the horse's ears. There should be room for the width of a hand underneath the throatlatch.

Moving on to the subject of putting on the saddle, if the horse will not stand quietly to be saddled, it can be tied up with the headcollar fitted over the bridle. When putting the headcollar over the bridle, care should be taken that it does not cause any part of the bridle to press against, or rub, the horse's head. Never secure a horse by its bridle, either directly by the reins, or by clipping a lead rope to the bit. It may be convenient to do so but, apart from the fact that the horse can wreck the bridle without so much as a second thought, it can sustain nasty injuries to its mouth.

Since horses are generally used to being led and handled from the near side, it is usual to put the saddle on from that side, but the side of approach is less important than the manner in which the saddle is applied. It should be placed slowly and carefully a few centimetres in front of its correct position, and then pushed back into position in the direction of the lie of the hair. Throwing the saddle on roughly and in haste is to be avoided at all costs – horses are nervous animals by nature. It goes without saying that the saddle area and the numnah should be clean. Careful checks should be made on both sides of the horse to ensure that the numnah (or anything else fitted beneath the saddle) is correctly positioned and not rucked up or pressing on the withers.

At this stage, praise your horse for standing quietly, or if it will not stand, praise and reassure it to try to educate it to do so. (If a fidgety horse is tied on both sides it cannot move away so easily when the saddle is being put on. If it is tied to the wall, let it move sideways until it is standing next to the wall.)

A common mistake is tightening up the girth straight away. First let the horse come to terms with the fact that it has a saddle on, and only tighten the girth enough to keep the saddle in position. You can busy yourself by putting your spurs on, or tidying up the mane and tail, and only when you have done this, gradually tighten the girth. If you have a horse which blows itself up like a balloon when being saddled, you will need to tighten the girth incrementally, otherwise you may find, when mounted – or attempting to mount – that the horse has outwitted you and the saddle is slipping. Sensitive animals – often mares – will resent having the girth tightened and these too require girthing up gradually. With such horses, it is often wise to keep an eye out for any attempt at nipping; a threatening look round should be countered by pushing the horse's head away, but this should be done with minimal force and should be accompanied by reassuring tones. With 'cold-backed' horses it is actually dangerous to tighten the girth immediately. Although some 'cold backs' may be linked to temperament, many are associated with physical factors. Whatever the root cause, horses with this condition will react strongly if the saddle is put on incorrectly (or the wrong saddle is used), and if the girth is tightened too quickly. A 'cold-backed' horse either bucks or refuses to go forwards and stands stubbornly rooted to the spot with its back humped. In extreme cases, the horse may even go down. When dealing with such a horse, girth it lightly, lead it round a few times outside the stable, and do not tighten the girth any further until you can see that it has relaxed. If need be, get someone to give you a leg-up, and always sit down lightly in the saddle – never crash down. At the start of the work session, first walk round for a while with the girth still fairly loose and only tighten it further once the horse has shown clear signs of warming up and settling to its work.

Difficulty with loading

Some horses will walk straight into the horsebox of their own accord, but they are in the minority. There are some ugly scenes to be witnessed at competitions when it comes to loading up. At the opposite end of the scale is the cowboy horse which, ready saddled and bridled, jumps of its own accord at least 80 cm on to the back of an open-topped lorry. Some horseboxes are constructed in such a way that they invite the horse to load, and recently, boxes have come on to the market which are equipped with a hydraulically operated system which can lower the whole body down to ground level. Some boxes are not so inviting, and this should be taken into consideration both when buying and when loading. You should try to make boxing a pleasant experience for the horse. Bad experiences while travelling will also influence it. All sorts of ghastly accidents have occurred, such as the floor collapsing and the horse's feet being dragged along the road, the horse going down in the box, being trampled on by other horses, getting caught up, breaking loose, jumping out, etc.

It goes without saying that the ramp must be solid and not shake when the horse steps on it. It must not be too steep, and it should be covered with straw. It should not be dark inside the box, which should be as roomy as possible to encourage the horse to enter. It should also smell clean, and the roof should not be too low, since this makes the horse feel restricted.

Sufficient time must be allowed for loading the horse, and there should be no chasing and shouting. Practise loading at home before the day of the journey. Make the horse familiar with the box; feed it frequently inside the box if necessary. Wait until the horse is hungry, so that it is pleased to go into the horsebox for a feed. If you have a box which takes more than one horse, you can perhaps find another horse which can be taken into the box first to encourage your own horse to enter.

If none of these methods work, what then? Only one thing is certain: you can no more pull a horse into a horsebox by its headcollar than you can drag it out of the stable against its will, as has already been explained. Neither can you push it into the horsebox. In order to avoid potential problems from the outset, and also to leave the horse in no doubt as to the fact that it must go into the box, it is advisable to use the best method from the start. Of course you can first try blindfolding the horse, or leading it round and round in circles until it loses its bearings. Of course you can try thrashing it to make it go in, or backing it up the ramp, or riding it in if the box is open at the top, but all these ways can go wrong, and you will finish up with a horse which is even more resistant. It has learnt that it can get away with it – and it will make good use of such knowledge! So why not do it properly from the start?

Take two lunge lines (two strong ropes will do), and attach them one to each side of the horsebox. The other ends are each held by an assistant. The two assistants each run the lunge line they are holding around the horse's quarters, and in so doing cross over to the opposite side of the box. The horse is 'enclosed' by the two lunge lines around its quarters. (At a pinch, one long rope, with an assistant at each end, may suffice.) Another assistant, preferably the one whom the horse knows best, holds the headcollar rope, and a handful of hay, a carrot or a similar delicacy. A fourth assistant stands behind with a whip at the ready. The horse is then pulled into the box by the two assistants with the lunge lines, while the one with the whip drives it from behind. (The whip should be used with discretion, tapping the horse if necessary to

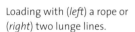
Loading with (*left*) a rope or (*right*) two lunge lines.

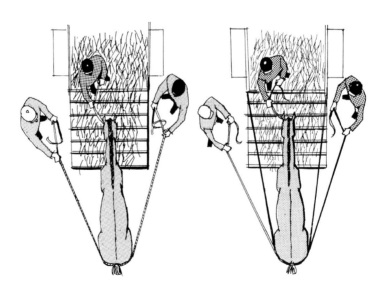

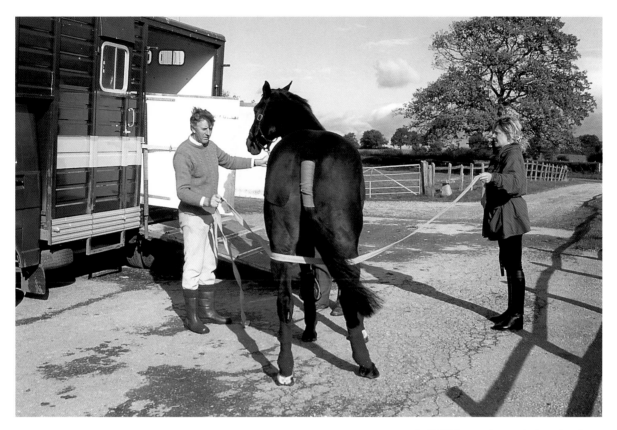

Loading with the help of lunge lines.

encourage forward movement – if it is used to beat the horse into the box, this is likely to reinforce his fear of the process.) It is important that the horse cannot jump off the side of the ramp. If possible, the box or trailer should be positioned so that one side, at least, is blocked off by a wall.

Often the horse gets as far as the bottom of the ramp but refuses to step onto it. One person should lift up first one forefoot and then the other, with the assistants pulling hard on the lunge lines at the same time. Once you have overcome this hurdle, the horse will keep going. There should be no shouting, but rather encouragement and plenty of praise! It is very important to shut the tailgate as soon as the horse is in. Not until this has been done should the horse be tied up. During the journey you should check regularly that everything is all right. Once the horse has learned that entering the box presents no problem, two men with their hands joined behind its quarters will suffice to push it in (with a third holding the headcollar rope, of course). Once the horse is used to being loaded with two lunge lines, the same system but with only one rope or lunge line can be tried.

When loading up after dark, remember that those horses which have a particular tendency to shy at things on the ground ('ground-shy') react very violently if they see the beam of a torch on the ground in front of them. You should check your horse's reaction before shining the torch on the ramp or inside the box to show it what is there. Lamps which illuminate a large area are better, but even so you should avoid shining any light on the horse from the front, since it may be dazzled and unable to see where it is treading. Furthermore there should be no reflective metal objects shining or glinting in the vicinity. All in all it is better to park the horsebox somewhere lighter and not light up the inside at all, because horses find this disturbing. Diffused lighting is quite sufficient, and is more pleasant for the horse than a bright light, which can trigger off violent reflex actions. With bright lights there are often moving shadows on the wall and ground, and these, too, can be a source of irritation.

Problems during unloading can also be avoided by being careful. Unload nervous horses first (have this in mind when deciding on the sequence of loading). Obviously, if it is possible to turn the horse round in the box, this should be done and it can then be unloaded forwards. When it is necessary to back a horse down, the horse should be supported on either side by an assistant to prevent it from stepping over the side of the ramp. Speak soothingly to the horse and back it down slowly. Do not turn it round on the ramp, because the next time it will anticipate this and turn of its own accord – rather too fast for comfort! In so doing it can easily step over the edge of the ramp and injure itself.

An assistant placing the front feet on the ramp often helps to get the horse started.

(*Left*) It is often sufficient for two helpers to join hands behind the horse's hindquarters. (*Right*) Off-loading.

Problems on the lunge

Before moving on to the subject of bad habits in the ridden horse, a few words about lungeing. It is beyond the scope of this study to deal with the techniques of lungeing in detail. Whether you lunge in a cavesson with side-reins, a chambon or overhead check reins, with a saddle, lungeing roller, long reins, or simply a lunge rein attached to a headcollar (though this last has significant limitations) is not a matter for discussion here. (These points are, however, significant, since lungeing, like riding, can be done either competently or incompetently. A horse can be put on its forehand instead of on its haunches, and it can have its mouth ruined and its neck and poll made stiff instead of supple.) My concern, for the purposes of this book, is that there are certain situations of which horses take advantage in order to misbehave, and it is these we shall consider.

As with so many problems in equitation, it is usually the horse's early education – or lack of it – that lies at the heart of problems on the lunge. It goes without saying that a young horse, which is always liable to present problems, should never be lunged without at least one assistant. It is difficult to sort out an unruly horse on the lunge without an assistant, and rough treatment is to be avoided at all costs. A properly marked out circle will be useful, and if a lungeing ring is not available a boundary can be improvised with straw bales. Whatever is used to mark out the circle, the horse should not be able to injure its legs on it.

For the first few days the assistant leads the horse by a short lead rein on the inside. The horse should learn during this period to keep to the line of the circle and to obey the commands. The principles of lungeing and how to give these commands should already be known by anyone undertaking to lunge a

(*below and opposite page*) It is better if misbehaviour on the lunge is not allowed to develop.

young horse. The important thing is that the horse learns that it cannot simply do as it pleases. One major advantage of having an assistant is that it is much easier to prevent the horse from developing the bad habit of turning in at the halt and walking towards the lunger. This practice is widespread, and is incorrect. The horse must remain halted on the track until the lunger walks up to it. It is therefore necessary to ensure from the outset that calmness and obedience prevail and that no insubordination is tolerated. This early education will be reflected later in the work under saddle. It also makes reschooling on the lunge easier if a sound foundation has been made for future reference.

CHAPTER THREE

The Pliant Horse

I CANNOT START TO ENUMERATE the various ways in which horses manage to thwart their riders without first defining the pliant horse. This is an obedient and submissive horse that is easily bent, yields readily to influence and is obliging in all that it does.

In years gone by, it was generally admitted that all horses, including hunters, had to be trained to a degree and be sufficiently pliant to meet the requirements of, what we nowadays term, an elementary dressage test. Nevertheless, the good saddle horse had to be adaptable, and horses which had been schooled to a highly polished level in dressage were still expected to be calm, self-reliant conveyances in the hunting field. However, the early part of the twentieth century marked the end of the traditional role of the horse in human affairs; horses were no longer necessary as transport, and so riding became just a sport divided into different disciplines, each of which seemingly required a special stamp of horse and a special kind of training. For example, the three-day event is more fundamentally a test of a horse's courage, stamina, experience and agility than of a rider's refined horsemanship; yet the rider must remember that a dressage test has to be performed. The marks for this, quite rightly, have relatively little influence on the outcome of the competition, but there are many horses that do not show even the modicum of pliancy required.

On the other hand, dressage has now become an exclusive sport, and of course in sport there is no other practical way of measuring performance than in penalizing inaccuracy and faults. Artistic quality is too difficult to evaluate objectively. Unfortunately, this system of judging has led some riders to resort to rough training methods and short-cuts which provoke resistance on the part of their horses. This explains why ludicrous parodies of the piaffe and passage are such frequent occurrences at Grand Prix level; what is more deplorable is the infringement at that level of the most important preconditions of pliancy – impulsion, purity of the gaits, ease of movement and smoothness of the transitions.

It should be noted that, in the nineteenth century, connoisseurs were already starting to lament the decline of the art of horsemanship. Now that dressage has become a competitive sport, it has to be admitted that artistic quality has declined even more. However, it is not my purpose to criticize performances at Grand Prix level; I am writing about the re-education of spoilt horses. This always implies a return to basic education. It must be understood of course that dressage is just a school of obedience and the basic principles apply to all the disciplines. It is not only the so-called dressage horses that have to learn to move willingly at the gait and speed and in the direction chosen by the rider, and to submit with grace to the latter's ascendancy. Any horse becomes tense when its natural agility and desire to go forward have been spoilt by faulty training procedures; and when the horse is tense all its joints become so inelastic that the rider also stiffens to preserve his own stability, and thereby loses the ability to control and guide his horse with precision and tact.

Signs of perfect submission

I will quote Hans von Heydebrecht in the following paragraphs, because his description of a pliant horse cannot be bettered. He has drawn a model that we should all want to emulate, but to be able to do so we must also want to learn to ride proficiently. A firm but easy seat has to be acquired, for failing this we will never be able to feel and correct instantly any incipient deviation from the standard he has set.

'The horse must be agile and sure-footed and its gaits must be pure. It must be driven by its desire to go forwards. It must displace its mass easily, without hurry or awkwardness precisely on the track prescribed by its rider. Its neck must form a graceful, ascending curve in front of the rider's hand. Its poll must be elevated, with the nose slightly in front of the vertical. Its ears must be the highest point of its body and they must show a relaxed activity that indicates attentiveness to the rider and submissiveness. The horse must look in the direction of the movement. Its lips must be closed, but moistened by salivation to show that it is contentedly "chewing the bit". The tension which it puts on the reins must be light, even and constant; then the small oscillations of the curb rein will reveal the lightness of the contact and prove that the horse is balancing itself by the proper use of its hindlegs. When the rider eases the contact, the horse's timing and carriage must remain unaltered; but if the rider

Movement of the High School: ballotade in-hand.

advances both his hands frankly or lets the reins slide through his fingers, the horse must advance its nose and must not attempt either to lean on the hand or to get above the bit. On the other hand, an imperceptible closing of the rider's fingers must cause the horse to shorten its steps or, alternatively, to move forward to a square halt and remain calmly at a standstill. Conversely, the slightest pressure of the rider's lower legs must produce a determined lengthening of the strides. All the movements must seem totally unconstrained and produced by the rhythmical activity of the muscles of the trunk and spinal column, and the smooth oscillations of the elastic back. The ease with which the rider maintains his poise must reveal the smoothness of the movement. Every stride must involve the elastic activity of all the joints of the hindlimbs; according to the degree of collection, the hindlimbs will act more or less as powerful extensible levers to drive the mass forward in long, flowing strides, or as elastic props balancing most of the weight of the body and lightening the forehand. Yet in the extended gaits the hindlimbs must not fail in their balancing role, and in the collected gaits the increased flexion of the hocks must be followed by a powerful thrust. The activity of the muscles of the hindquarters must enable the forefeet to be picked up easily and to alight

The extended trot, showing great impulsion and straightness.

lightly, the forelimbs to make expansive ground covering gestures, the shoulders to oscillate through a wide arc even in the collected movements, so that the forearms can be lifted to the horizontal and the hooves detached from the ground so easily that they barely seem to touch it before being picked up again. If the rider is observed in profile, he must seem to be sitting in the centre of the horse's back, with as much of the animal's body before him as behind. From the ears to the gently swinging tail, the topline of the horse must undulate smoothly; the neck must never be more inflected that the rest of the body. The withers must be higher than the highest point of the croup. If the horse is watched from the front, its hindfeet must be hidden from view – except of course in the two-track movements. The nose must drop from the pliant poll so that the ears are held on a plane parallel to the ground. If ridden "in position", the inside eye, inside shoulder and inside hip joint of the horse must be nearly on one straight line. The shoulders of the rider will then be parallel to the ground and his head will show between the ears of the horse. Body of horse and rider must appear to be fused together, virtually constituting a single mass that moves like an animated work of art with grace, power and precision.'

Exercise and cross-country riding

The above is of course von Heydebrecht's picture of a horse moving with all the energy needed for display in a dressage test. But is this how the horse should move during relaxing exercise? Well, we must understand that there is a difference between work and exercise. I insist that for exercise riding we should always use a light seat. Admirers of Western riding may not agree and I concede that cowboys cannot be expected to work all day long in a light or half-seat. Their knees and ankles would be severely overtaxed. But if one is not a cowboy or a Camargue shepherd, one does not have to remain astride a horse for hours on end, except in long distance competitions. In this latter case, it would be absurd to ride with extremely short stirrup leathers. However, twentieth-century cavalry when on the march used a light 'remount' seat and thus proved that it is practical to ride lightly for many hours without stress.

When the rider sits 'lightly' it is the suppleness of his hips, knees and ankles that enables him to preserve his balance easily and to link his movements to those of the horse. Though his buttocks must not rest in the deepest part of the saddle, they must remain as close to it as possible. His knees must always be closed to provide adequate friction or grip, but this grip must not be forceful, since a strong grip, besides being damaging to the health of the rider's joints and muscles, tends to unbalance the horse and inhibits the stabilizing

Both seats are faulty and entail ineffective and annoying lower legs: (*left*) the crutch seat; (*right*) the armchair seat.

and shock-dampening functions of the hip, knee and ankle joints. The effortless adhesion of the inner surface of the thighs to the saddle must still enable the rider to keep his calves in contact with the horse's sides and his heels well depressed; he must be able to use his legs to drive and to guide. His hands must be held at about the level of the horse's mane and must never press downwards and, when jumping obstacles and climbing uphill or downhill, they must advance in the direction of the horse's mouth.

A correct light seat. For cross-country riding, the light seat is less tiring for rider and horse.

The light seat requires a shortening of the stirrup leathers, but the position of the lower leg is very important. In both examples illustrated the leg position is faulty.

69

The light seat allows the horse to move easily and naturally at all gaits with regular, energetic strides or bounds, and to use the joints of its hind legs for dampening the jolts of the movements as much as for propulsion. Over undulating terrain and over obstacles, the rider 'sitting light' is in a better position to give the horse the essential freedom of its neck and is less likely to compromise its balance by being left behind or, direst of all faults, by sitting with slack loins. Since the rider needs his stirrups for balance, he is less likely to use his spurs inadvertently.

If the length of the stirrup leathers is not adapted to cross-country riding, the rider will not be able to go with the horse. Because his leathers are too long the rider (*left*) is left behind. The rider (*right*) is thrown up above the horse's neck and stiffens the forelimbs of the horse because the stirrups are too short.

The 'light' seat used for jumping or cross-country must be just as stylish as the 'full' seat. This is not only a matter of elegance. A faulty light seat compromises the balance and efficiency of horse and rider and damages the joints of the horse's forelegs. We should never imitate the unconventional attitudes too often seen in show-jumping and sometimes adopted even by champions; bungling amateurs who try to ape them show total ignorance of the basic principles of equilibrium. Style is absence of unnecessary effort, and this is the secret of efficiency.

CHAPTER FOUR

Conformation, Gaits and Temperament

T O START WITH, we will have to admit that a resistant horse is not necessarily an intractable horse. It may perform perfectly for a different rider
than its owner, who will then have to conclude that he himself is the
one that should go back to school. Yet a moderately good rider on a pliant
horse can look more stylish than a highly proficient rider on an insubordinate
horse. Even the uninformed spectator, although understanding very little
about the technicalities of dressage, can appreciate the difficulty of sitting with
ease on a tense horse, especially in the extended gaits. The elegance of the rider
depends on the horse's willingness to be driven.

Some resistances are linked to defective conformation, but temperamental
difficulties cause much more trouble than unfavourable physical aptitudes.
While bold, strong horses are relatively easy to manage, shy and skittish ones
can never be entirely reliable. We must, of course, understand that no horse

Restricted by a severe tension of
the reins, the horse is moving
with an extremely rigid back
and trampling forelimbs which
make it impossible for the rider
to sit to the movement. The
rider is gripping and her seat
hammers the back of the horse.

can be an all-round athlete and we can expect resistance if, for example, we try to force a sprinter to move slowly or a lumbering hunter to exert itself in a race.

Conformation

It must be said that some brilliant performers have not always been endowed with ideal conformation. Nevertheless, if a horse is well made, one would expect it to move well. Straight, unconstrained movement, scope consistent with mass and muscular strength, energetic engagement of the hind legs, transmission of their propulsive power to the forelimbs by means of active, elastic back muscles, ample oscillations of the shoulders and expansive, graceful gestures of the forelimbs can only be the consequence of the concurrent activity of all the associated muscles and of all the joints of a well-proportioned horse. In other words, if the gaits are good, the structure must be good.

Every defect of conformation must to some degree impair the ease and efficiency of movement. In the following brief survey of faulty points, the difficulties which they entail will be indicated. They may not render a horse unrideable, but they can be the root cause of some of the problems which arise during training. Certain evident imperfections can be either accentuated by other weaknesses or, on the contrary, mitigated by points of strength. Nevertheless, they must be taken into account when deciding on a programme of training. Further to this, although selective breeding has minimized the incidence of faults and weaknesses, and led to a distinctive 'type' of sport horse, we must not judge horses as if a perfect prototype existed; each individual part should not be measured as if it could be entirely perfect or absolutely wrong. It is better to base one's judgement on an overall impression.

One of the most important considerations is the height of the centre of gravity. If the horse's legs are too long in relation to its trunk, its centre of gravity will be too high and its balance more precarious. This is an obvious disadvantage for collection and also for galloping across country, especially if those long legs have to support a particularly massive body. Generally speaking, a rather long-legged horse is better suited for show-jumping than for the other disciplines, but of course its hind joints and its shoulder girdle will have to be examined carefully.

In contrast with the 'square' or leggy horse, the oblong horse is generally better balanced; it certainly enjoys the advantage of a lower centre of gravity, and this gives it better equilibrium and agility when galloping across country. If it misses a step, it can save itself from a fall more easily than the square horse. However the length of the trunk must not be the result of the (not at

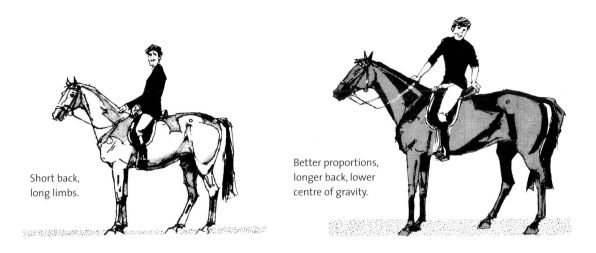

Short back, long limbs.

Better proportions, longer back, lower centre of gravity.

all uncommon) occurrence of a nineteenth rib-bearing vertebra, nor of an upright shoulder or a short croup. The latter defect will limit the range of movement of the horse's hind limbs and considerably impair performance, producing a scrimpy canter that quickly deteriorates into an inefficient four-time running action.

We can now turn our attention to other details of conformation.

Head

The size of the head must be relative to the bulk of the rest of the body. An excessively heavy head will have a seriously adverse effect on a horse's equilibrium. However, regardless of size, the head must be well set, neither too high (occiput higher than atlas), nor too low (occiput lower than atlas). The first defect restricts the pliability of the poll and the horse will tend to move with an exaggeratedly elevated neck and a poked nose; the second defect produces an excessively flexible poll with a nose that quickly gets behind the vertical and a neck so willowy that control can become virtually impossible.

Jaw

The shape of the mandible is very important. The mandibular space between the two branches of the lower jawbone which bear the lower cheek teeth must be wide enough to allow the flexion of the poll without painfully compressing the parotid glands. The light pressure of the vertical part (which furnishes attachment to powerful muscles) on the parotid glands gently massages them when the horse 'chews' the bit and thus produces the saliva that keeps the mouth moist. When the poll is correctly flexed, the bars are in a position that

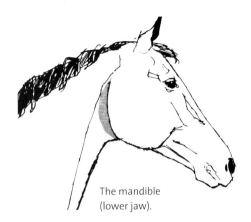

The mandible (lower jaw).

allows control by the rider's hands. The upper borders of the bars should be clean-cut; they are then more sensitive. The sensitivity of the bars and the pliancy of the poll are the factors that enable a good rider to control a horse with light, feeling hands. On the other hand, thick, fleshy bars give a less sensitive mouth. I warn my readers here against the senseless practice of preventing the chewing of the bit by tightening the noseband. The effect of this barbaric treatment is not merely impaired breathing; it can make a horse tortured in this way bolt out of panic.

Neck

The shape of the neck reveals not only the quality of the horse but also the quality of the training. It is often said that a properly trained horse can never be ugly; even horses that are not particularly favoured by nature can be made to look handsome as a result of skilful training. The muscles of the topline will develop, concealing marked hollows and protruberances. On the other hand, the ventral muscles of the neck must atrophy progressively as the horse learns to balance itself better without frequent reminders by the rider and to respond more promptly to the light indications of the hands. It will then be only too easy to induce a false lightness, with the horse permanently behind the bit, unless we have cultivated absolute obedience to our legs and acquired sensitive hands, so that we can get the horse to extend its neck and advance its nose ahead of the vertical. For all purposes the best sort of neck is rather long, though not frail; it should be set at a right angle to the shoulder; its topline should be slightly arched, its underside straight, and its width must decrease gradually from the withers towards the poll. A neck of this shape can never be the cause of resistance.

The swan-neck, on the other hand, is very tricky. Laymen are often charmed by its slenderness, but swan-necked horses are so prone to evade control that they often become rearers or jibbers. However, the ewe-neck is even more objectionable. It is usually associated with a badly set on head that is difficult to flex at the poll. Ewe-necked horses are practically unrideable. They run stiffly with a rigidly tense back and a poked nose, making it impossible for the rider to sit and to drive effectively. These faults are difficult enough to contend with when the rider is an expert horseman, but the average rider cannot be expected to control a ewe-necked horse; the horse quickly discovers too many ways of evading the influence of legs, seat and hands.

A short, even rather heavy neck, provided it is well set on, is a smaller disadvantage than either of the above. But only if the rider is capable of developing impulsion and does not, on the contrary, provoke the horse to arch and shorten its neck even more by setting his hands or by working on the bit with his arms. The worst fault of all consists in striving to lower the neck by means of alternate pulls on the reins. We Germans call this *windlassing*. *Windlassing* is a heinous offence. Riders who commit this sin simply fail to understand that in doing so they teach the horse to evade rather than to submit. It is a very bad habit and, like all bad habits, an extremely difficult one to correct. It loosens the base of the horse's neck and this teaches the horse to move crookedly, with its hindquarters to one side. When a horse bends its neck at the withers, control of the hind legs is impossible and no degree of collection can ever be achieved. The restraining effect of the rider's hands stops at the withers. It is absolutely essential that the base of the horse's neck be made perfectly stable.

Various neck shapes: (*top left*) a good neck; (*top right*) a rather long neck; (*bottom left*) a ewe-neck; (*bottom right*) a neck set on low.

For dressage, a neck set high is an advantage. It facilitates the elevation required in the more difficult tests. For jumping and galloping across country, a neck set on rather low is not a great disadvantage, but it does help the horse to lean on the rider's hands.

It remains to be said that, regardless of its shape, the most important thing is that the neck should be the prolongation of a long, oblique shoulder.

Withers

The withers should be long and gently sloping into the back. Long withers impart expansive foreleg action. They give the rider the pleasant feel of having a lot of horse in front of his body.

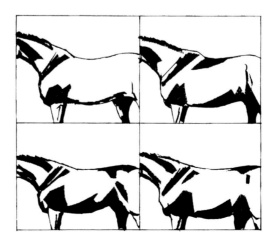

Various shapes of withers: (*top left*) short, sharp; (*top right*) long, gently sloping; (*bottom left*) short, low; (*bottom right*) long, low.

Elbows

The elbows should be well detached from the rib cage to allow the freedom of movement of the forelegs.

Forelimbs

Well placed forelimbs and sloping pasterns are another condition of ease of control. The movements of the forelegs must be straight; ugly dishing and plaiting can cause stumbling and injury.

Back

A short back is strong but stiff and does not allow the rider to sit upright without being jolted and jolting the horse – which induces the horse to stiffen its back even more. A short back does not necessarily entail a short stride, since stride length depends on the shape of the shoulders, the croup and hind legs, but it enables the horse to resist the lateral inflection of the trunk required in two-track movements. On the other hand, an excessively long back will impair the effective weight-supporting function of the hind limbs and the ability of the horse to move collectedly. The horse's strides will be rather short and hurried; show-jumpers however are not unduly handicapped by somewhat too long a back provided they canter well.

In the early stages of training, the rider must avoid over-stressing the muscles of the horse's back and must be quick to detect even slight irregularity of movement which is often caused by soreness. Hollow-backed horses are difficult to saddle, fatigue quickly and their back tends to sag under weight.

Various back shapes: (*top left*) straight; (*top right*) hollow; (*bottom left*) short; (*bottom right*) Roach.

Roach-backed horses on the contrary are immensely strong but so rigid as to be totally unsuitable for any equestrian sport. It must be noted however that even weak, hollow backs stiffen with the onset of fatigue. If weakness of the back is associated with a particularly sensitive skin, it is of the utmost importance to ride in a light position because the habit of stiffening the back is enduring and once acquired is extremely difficult to correct; it will then make the horse very resistant when advanced work is attempted. In some cases, it can be advisable to ask a person of slighter build to ride the horse, and he must be able to ride lightly without gripping forcibly because he must still drive the horse forwards with his seat when his weight is supported on the stirrups. Suitable exercises for loosening a tense back will be described in the next chapter.

A good seat depends on the elasticity of the horse's back but also on the shape of its rib cage. A tall rider on a slab-sided horse cannot keep his knees in contact with the saddle and his lower legs in contact with the horse's sides. Besides this very serious inconvenience, there is another important one; narrow-chested horses have less capacious lungs and tire quickly. They are also difficult to girth up and the saddle will tend to slide forwards and hamper the shoulder movement. On the other hand, a short-legged rider will not be able to keep his lower legs in quiet contact with the sides of a horse with a massive barrel of a chest. Even a long-legged rider may have difficulty in keeping his balance without gripping if the horse's ribs are excessively arched. I must remind you that strong gripping stiffens the hips and causes tapping with the legs. Tapping legs have no impulsive effect, but rather the reverse.

An unduly small belly may indicate poor health or an insufficiently bulky diet. Herring-gutted horses may be suffering from chronic indigestion caused by an excessively nervous disposition.

Hindquarters

The hindquarters must supply the driving power and their weakness cannot be compensated for by any other good points of conformation. The croup therefore must be well-covered by muscular tissue, giving it an outline resembling that of a melon rather than of a ridged roof. However, examined from the rear, the horse's hindquarters must be broader at the level of the stifle than at the level of the hip joint. A straight, horizontal croup or, conversely, a steeply sloping one provide insufficient leverage and are a source of difficulties. On the other hand, excessive prominence of the croup – a common defect of mares – being a consequence of relatively excessive length of hind legs, has the effect of throwing too much weight on the forelegs, causing lack of equilibrium, perhaps overreaching, and a tendency to lean on the rider's hands. The saddle easily slides on to the shoulders, impeding their freedom of action.

Self-carriage and collection are completely unobtainable with this kind of conformation.

Insufficient angulation of the joints of the hind legs detracts from the purity of the gaits. While a straight hind leg may not be a disadvantage for a show-jumper, it is most undesirable in a horse one would want to train for dressage. It produces a scrimpy walk that cannot be extended and prevents collection at all the gaits. At the trot, the hocks are snatched up and turned outwards and the soles of the hooves can be seen when one watches the horse from the rear.

The hocks must be broad and have distinctly defined planes. Untrained horses that rotate their hocks outward when the hind legs retract can be assumed to have weak hindquarters, but horses of excellent conformation will develop this fault when unskilled riders with heavy hands attempt to collect them. The hind legs must be carried forwards on a straight line and a little too much distance between the feet is preferable to a narrow base of support. Cow-hocks and bandy legs make a horse unsuitable for dressage. They are less objectionable in hunters, but of course they will wear out sooner than well-shaped ones. Minor defects of conformation can be neutralized by a good farrier, but not gross ones. These do not only impair performance; tendons, ligaments and joints will be gradually damaged by the excessive rotation of the limb segments consequent upon the weak conformation.

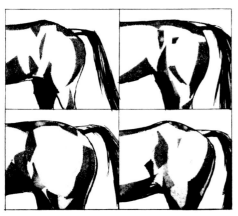

The croup: (*top left*) meagre, slanting; (*top right*) straight; (*bottom left*) nicely rounded; (*bottom right*) prominent.

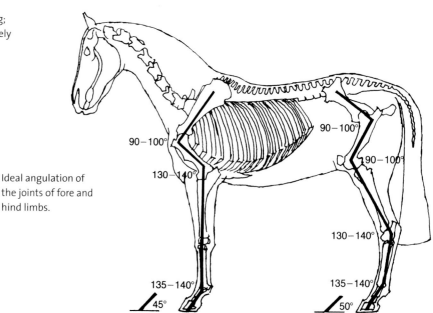

Ideal angulation of the joints of fore and hind limbs.

Tail

The horse's tail carriage is very significant. When a horse is running free or is being exercised on the lunge, the movements of the tail reveal the activity of the back muscles. If the tail is carried rigidly upright, if it is held to one side, if it lashes furiously, either horizontally or vertically, the erratic movements are sometimes a symptom of colic; usually however they are the obvious signs of a tense back and often of chronic irritability.

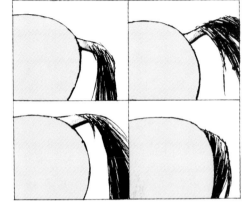

The dock must be the elegant prolongation of a back and croup of good conformation. It must not appear to have been appended as an afterthought. The tail should oscillate at each stride and bound, its movements revealing the smooth activity of the muscles of back and croup. A crooked dock is sometimes a symptom of organic abnormality; in this case, surgery is a purely cosmetic operation that cannot correct the basic trouble. However some horses hold their dock to one side when they are made to work in collection, and straighten it when the gait is lengthened. If this is the case, the rider must be partly at fault. A clamped down dock is always a sign of tension, caused perhaps by anxiety or pain. A dock carried rigidly erect indicates excitement or even morbid excitability.

The tail: (*top left*) set on low; (*top right*) appended as an afterthought; (*bottom left*) set on high; (*bottom right*) clamped down.

The gaits

Pronounced faults of conformation are not just blemishes. They are frequent causes of unsoundness; moreover they will inevitably mar the three basic gaits, walk, trot and canter.

The walk

The walk is the most difficult gait to improve and it is therefore important to watch very carefully a walking horse at liberty or being ridden on a completely loose rein.

On a loose rein, the horse's hind feet should overtread the traces left by the forefeet by one or two hoof lengths, depending on conformation. A naturally scrimpy walk is nearly always an indication that the canter will lack sufficient scope and that the horse should be unconditionally rejected as a good prospect for dressage; if any improvement is possible, it will never be sufficient.

Yet even when the natural walk of a horse is passably good, we must not forget that the walk is the most difficult gait to ride well, and the one most easily spoilt by bad riding. Dressage riders especially must always remember that there are four kinds of walk: the free walk on a loose rein, the medium walk, the collected walk and the extended walk. They must learn to ride each one. And they must also remember that nothing is more detrimental to the quality of the walk than a negligent body carriage and interfering hands. If we like to hack out with a friend to chat with, and if we must smoke and gesticulate, we must give the horse complete freedom of movement of head and neck. It is perfectly permissible to allow ourselves to be carried by the horse provided that we keep our lower legs in effortless contact with the horse's sides, accompany the horse's movements with supple hips, and let the horse have the reins; but once we start riding on a contact we must pay all our attention to rhythm, length of stride and straightness.

When judging the walk, the length of stride must be examined attentively. Excessive overtreading (by three or more hoof lengths) may well be a product of conformation; this means that the walk and also the canter will be difficult to collect and that the horse will most probably overreach when driven into an active trot. Faulty timing, that is a walk which tends towards pacing, is sometimes a sign of excessive nervous tension; it is more often the consequence of the rider's premature attempt to collect the gait, or again of a wrong conception of the driving (or pushing) seat. The walk must be ridden as attentively and skilfully as the other gaits. I will have more to say about this gait in the next chapter.

The trot

As regards the influence of conformation on the trot, we should remember that a less than perfect forehand, even a less than ideally long and sloping shoulder, can be compensated for, in any case to some extent, by very good hindquarters; on the other hand, the most beautiful neck and shoulder are useless assets if the hind legs are stiff and straight jointed. Attempts to extend the gait will then result only in hurried running, especially so if the hocks are turned out. Hence, when watching a horse trotting we must always examine it from the rear as well as from the front.

The canter

As for the canter, it must show plenty of scope and three well-marked beats followed by the silent time of suspension. The natural canter of the horse must appear effortless and elastic. It is impossible to sit to a hurried, jerky and

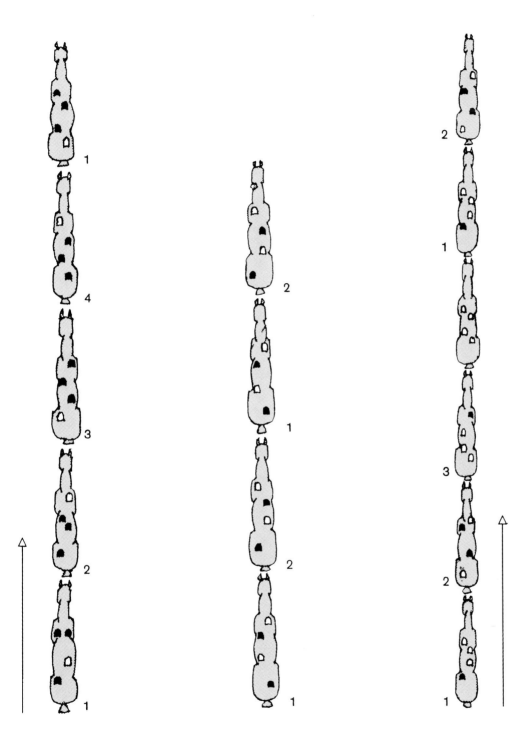

Sequence of footfalls at the three basic gaits: (*left*) the walk;
(*centre*) the trot; (*right*) the canter.

skimpy action and the gait is as fatiguing for the horse as it is for the rider. Since it is also almost impossible to induce a horse which has a naturally short, hurried gait to canter correctly, we should dismiss the possibility of training the animal for dressage. It nearly always is a leggy, straight-hocked individual, with straight pasterns and a short, stiff back.

Temperament

As I have already said, temperament matters as much, if not more, than conformation. Horses, like humans, are said to possess either a sanguine, a choleric, phlegmatic or melancholic temperament. Of course, in reality there are no clear-cut differences of temperament, but rather a blending and merging of traits.

Sanguine characters are lively, energetic, trusting and generous. We must not take advantage of their zeal by working them beyond the point of fatigue. Their upright, mobile ears are an outward mark of their attentiveness; their wide-open eyes express confidence and desire to please. Being contented horses, they usually have a good appetite and are good doers.

The choleric horse is also energetic and enduring, but is more easily provoked. There are wilful horses that can only be ridden effectively by sharp riders, able to nip incipient resistance in the bud instead of acting too late and having then to resort to a harsher correction. The choleric horse is not easy to handle and to train, but can be a good performer with considerable endurance. These horses too have expressive ears which may often display anger, and then the white of the eye may show. They are often impetuous and excitable.

Phlegmatic horses, on the other hand, are calm and of an equable disposition. They are good doers and are dependable, but not very keen to work and some of them can be bovinely stubborn. Their ears are upright but not very mobile. Their movements though not vigorous are not necessarily skimpy; they may indeed be quite impressive.

Melancholic horses are the least forthcoming of all. They appear calm, but they are stubborn and so wilful as to become downright rebellious, even when severely chastised. Their inert ears display their lack of interest; one of them may droop. Their eyes are usually small and distrustful, their movements indolent. They are frequently poor doers.

However, as I have said, there are no clearly marked differences between the different types. Changes of mood do occur, though they may be transient. In any case, one needs to have had a long acquaintance with many horses to be able to predict how they are likely to behave in various circumstances and how they should be trained. Besides which, there are other influences, apart from hormones, that can alter a horse's behaviour, such as, for example, inordinately acute sensitivity to noise. An extreme degree of long-sightedness can make a horse wary of stepping over something lying on the ground or cause it to balk at a newly made gap in a fence. The essential thing is to recognize the tendency of the horse as soon as possible and to reduce the frequency of occurrence of resistances by adopting the method most appropriate to the individual case.

Character and compatibility

While on the subject of temperament, it is pertinent to say that the rider's character matters as much as that of the horse. An inappropriate matching cannot promote harmony; ideally, size, weight and talent should be proportionate.

Now it often happens that one buys an animal rejected by a previous owner because of its intractability. The problem may not be apparent at the time of the purchase but will manifest itself sooner or later – fairly early if the new rider is experienced, rather later if he is less sure of himself – in any case too late to cancel the exchange. Even if a more skilled amateur rider, or a professional, takes over the training, the same difficulties which the original owner had been unable to cope with will have to be contended with. There are so many disgruntled riders who would find renewed enjoyment in the sport if they could be persuaded to part with an unsuitable partner and find another horse more compatible with their level of proficiency. Is it their conceit that prevents them from acknowledging that they are incapable of riding a particular animal and should part with it as soon as possible?

What are the character traits of rider and horse that make a pairing undesirable? Hot-tempered persons who cannot keep a curb on their emotions ought to realize that they will always make bad sportsmen, let alone horsemen; however, a combination of an ill-mannered lout and a fearful, highly-strung horse would be particularly disastrous. This sort of horse must belong to a rider who is patient, composed, self-controlled and inspires calm, who never allows his annoyance to surface when the same difficulties keep cropping up. Sensitive, emotional horses require very disciplined riders, justifiably confident in their competence to impose a degree of resistance commensurate with the degree of disobedience of the horse, for too much leniency can be as pernicious as harshness. A dull, ungenerous horse will never learn to work if its rider is apathetic or weak. Since it is well known that some riders always induce a horse to jog, it is logical to assume that various kinds of resistance may manifest themselves more strongly or, on the other hand, may diminish or may not be offered at all according to the temperament of the rider. Proper and timely reactions are not inborn, though they are more easily acquired by some persons than by others; they are educated reflexes, instilled by frequent repetition of carefully co-ordinated movements. There are, nevertheless, many not naturally talented riders who would manage better if they made an effort to grasp the relationship of cause and effect and if they were prepared to spend some time and effort towards acquiring a more efficient seat; they would then be able to feel incipient resistance and correct it properly and promptly before open disobedience demands punishment.

It must also be said that a horse's awkwardness is all too often the consequence of the rider's lack of concentration, of logical consistency or of insufficient determination and firmness. An understanding of the way the horse's mind functions is essential to all horsemen. Horses must trust their riders, but they must also respect them; pampering horses by allowing them to have their own way when this conflicts with the rider's requirements is as sure a recipe for unruliness as is brutality. It is in the stable that we can begin to spoil a horse by letting it find out that it can get away with disobedience. We cannot therefore be too firm in our management of such details of behaviour as willingness to lift up a foot on command, submission to grooming, saddling and standing still to allow the rider to mount. It is by a horse's conduct in the stable that we can first judge whether it is docile and well-mannered; this is where the seeds of resistance are most likely to be sown for the first time.

Nevertheless the horse has to learn to offer co-operation. The brawniest and heaviest man is powerless against an uneducated, strongly determined horse. But most horses nowadays are fairly docile animals and nearly all degrees of disobedience are the consequence of human mismanagement, even when atavistic traits of insubordination are present. However, as mentioned earlier, before resorting too quickly to punishment, we must always remember that we cannot expect unquestioning compliance to our orders if a horse does not understand what it is meant to do, or if it is physically incapable of achieving the performance expected. If the rider is irrational and inconsistent, incomprehension rather than obstinacy is usually the reason for disobedience or rebellion. (At competitions I am often astonished to see the ease with which a rider controls one horse, and the difficulty he has in getting another to perform exactly the same movement. Incidentally, a rider must avoid battling with a disobedient horse in the warm-up enclosure provided at competitions. He is likely to get himself and his horse into grave trouble. In the long run, behaviour of this kind does more lasting damage than is generally appreciated, because tendons, joints and ligaments of horses are easily strained during such wrestling matches, and the rider risks both frayed nerves and broken bones.)

A good partnership. The united resolve of horse and rider indicates a harmony of wills.

Mare, stallion or gelding? The choice is important. There are riders who will not contemplate a mare for the antiquated reason that a man's nobility is affronted if he rides anything but a stallion. This of course is nonsense. A much more valid consideration is the fact that mares can be seriously upset by the recurrent periods of oestrus. They are also prone to being ticklish, irritable and hollow-backed. These things are relatively unimportant in the case of purely recreational riding but matter very much in competitive riding. It is also a fact that mares are more prone to biting and kicking than are male horses. Yet a fair proportion are hardy, patient and endowed with plenty of stamina. The effects of the periods of oestrus vary. Some mares remain so unperturbed by the event that one does not notice it. Others become so irritable that they cannot be ridden while the mating season lasts.

Geldings are generally more dependable. They have, of course, their own character traits, but their quirks are not linked to recurrent sexual urges. Stallions, affected like mares by the activity of the sexual hormones, can be a considerable nuisance in a yard if mares are stabled close to them, and also when assembled at competitions, in the hunting field or in a troop. They can cause trouble in the manège if other horses are being worked there at the same time. These disadvantages assume less importance when they are kept in a small, private establishment. They are, however, usually more intelligent than geldings, more generous and hardier, but they have to be very well ridden.

Size

Matching the respective size of rider and horse matters also, especially for dressage. Nevertheless all equestrian sports must be pleasing to watch and should offer a spectacle of harmony, elegance and ease. The picture of a horse and rider combination is totally marred by gross disproportion. A diminutive person atop a massive animal is as unattractive a sight as a burly or lanky body on a dainty hack. Effectiveness however matters more than elegance, and so the question of size must be considered in respect of the seat, by which I mean of course a seated position which enables the rider to make the most effective use of his body and legs.

The rider should be able to keep contact with the saddle with the whole inner surface of his thighs and with his knees, which must be above the widest part of the horse's rib cage. If the knees are at the level of the broadest part of the barrel – either because the rider's legs are too long or because the horse is too narrow – it is impossible to preserve their constant contact with the saddle while at the same time having the lower legs at the girth, where their impulsive effect is most potent. A small, overhorsed rider will experience similar difficulties. But, as mentioned in our earlier discussion of the horse's back, the shape of the horse's rib cage matters at least as much as the size of the horse. Slab-sided horses and those with ribs arched like barrel hoops are always difficult to drive and control.

It is dressage riders especially who need to consider a suitable relationship between the respective sizes of the two partners, but gross disproportion is a disadvantage for show-jumping and hunting also. Allowing oneself to be transported on horseback is not the same thing as riding, and too great a disparity impairs effectiveness. I do not mean that on horseback one should never behave as a peaceful and quiet passenger; please do not misunderstand me, for I never meant to give the impression that we must constantly nag our mount. However, when performance matters, when precision, timing and balance are all-important, then the rider must be able to influence the horse with effective aids.

When the horse was an indispensable instrument of transport, riders had to cope as best they could with the most comfortable horse they could afford. Nowadays, for most people, riding is a sport, but is it a fair sport when small ponies are made to gallop, carrying the weight of a rider whose feet almost touch the ground? Every sport has its own rules, and equestrian sports should be governed by traditional principles. It is not right to throw all traditional customs away. I am not too worried about attire, but I am concerned for the animals which we use for our amusement. Their soundness and fitness for our game ought to be considered if we believe that there can be no sport without fairness. Each one of the various disciplines in equestrian sport makes special demands, for which horses must have the right aptitudes. Horses are not insensitive machines and it is not sporting to ask them to perform in events for which they lack the necessary aptitude.

It has been said that every rider ought to ride a custom-made horse. Besides the important matter of effectiveness and seemliness, we must also consider the effect of weight. An inordinately heavy rider will overtax the joints of a horse that is relatively too frail and will fatigue it quickly; on the other hand, a puny rider will never prevent a relatively oversized horse from taking charge of matters and perhaps injuring itself in the process. It is a fact that neither the underhorsed, nor the overhorsed, rider can be called a horseman or a horsewoman.

Overhorsed rider.

Underhorsed rider.

The most usual faults observed in a medium dressage test:

I. Crooked entrance and salute.

2. Hovering medium trot.

3. Collected trot with trailing hind legs; the horse is behind the bit and its neck is shortened. Ineffective seat and legs of the rider. This is not a properly collected trot.

4. Disconnected rein-back; the rider is pulling the horse backwards.

5. Medium canter with neck shortened by heavy hands.

6. Volte left; the horse's neck is bent, the hindquarters are turned out.

7. Left shoulder-in: twisted poll; the rider's hands are too high, his left leg is stiffened and ineffective.

8. The horse has stiffened its neck and hind legs when invited to chew the bit.

9. Disunited canter (inside hind has impacted before outside hind).

10. Abrupt transition to walk from canter; the horse has stiffened and is braking with its forelegs.

11. Hind legs trailing, the medium trot is not achieved. The rider's seat and legs are incorrect and ineffective.

12. Canter right with hindquarters turned in. The right leg and right hand of the

rider are preventing the engagement of the inside hind.

13. Turn on the haunches. The outside hind remains grounded. Rider and horse are badly positioned.

14. Incorrect exended trot. The horse is on the forehand and bearing on the hands. It is badly overbent and its back is rigid. The rider is gripping and jolting the horse's back.

15. An incorrectly collected canter, showing resistance to the bit and a rigid back. But observe the stiffened shoulders of the rider, his rigidly braced back and his knee grip.

Colour

As for colour, I have very little to say about it. The old notions about colour are as fanciful as the idea that the weather always changes with the phases of the moon. Constitution, stamina, attentiveness, docility and temperament are completely unrelated to the colour of a horse's coat.

As regards the colour of the eye, the reason why some horses show the white is that the iris is rather small and shows when the horse is irritated, because the movements of the ears and eyes are linked. Horses that have normal irises will not show the white of the eye even when they lay back their ears to display anger. But the expression of a horse's eye is very significant to the experienced horseman.

Black hooves are not stronger than white ones; whether one, two, three or four legs are white means nothing; chestnut horses are not especially wily because the colour of their coat is 'foxy'. A horse's character and behaviour depends purely on its genes, its upbringing and its training.

One can, of course, have a preference for one colour, but when selecting a horse for a particular purpose, all the other factors which have been discussed must be considered. Should one be faced with a problem of behaviour, one must know the right way of dealing with it and be competent to carry out the appropriate correction.

A good horse 'has no colour'.

CHAPTER FIVE

Causes of Resistance

BEFORE UNDERTAKING THE TASK of solving the various problems which horses can set, we must first learn to recognize the causes of resistance, for it is always on the root of a problem that its solution is contingent. In short, methods of correction must be adapted to the cause of resistance. It would be wrong to assume that every fault can be eradicated quickly or that there is only one unfailing recipe for redressing it.

Prevention and cure

Every unruly horse must be treated as if it were an exceptional case, but the remedy must depend also on the intelligence and ability of the rider. The essential thing is the early prevention of bad habits. The perfect horse simply does not exist, but some are more difficult to train than others. All riders must be prepared to admit that they can never cease to learn, for every horse will provide them with a new experience which leads to discovery. A horse may sometimes be accused of exceptional stubbornness, when in fact all that it needs is the right combination of aids in the right measure. It is probably incorrect to talk of a problem horse. All horses are going to pose a problem of one kind or another, and a rider with a good seat is always attentive and ready to feel and put right the slightest fault or irregularity before it becomes a habit. Curing a horse of a long-established bad habit is well-nigh impossible; preventing the formation of a bad habit depends on the rider and there are not many riders whose seats allow them to feel the first symptom of disorder.

The ignorance and lack of experience of the rider is often the cause of a horse's persistent or frequent irregularities. Yet even quite competent riders can be guilty of inattentiveness, and of unheeding serious irregularities or even refusing to acknowledge them. They often have to work on their horses without being supervised and they tend to drive too tenaciously and to lose the feel of the movement. From time to time, they ought to seek the help of an expert riding master. Things can look very different when viewed from the ground. The comments of dressage judges are sometimes useful, yet – even assuming that the person who sits in the judge's box is really competent – judges do not have to explain the cause of the irregularities for which marks have been deducted. The sole duty of a judge is to place the horses in order of merit by deducting points for the faults which he can see. The present system of judging does not permit him to give advice and, in any case, he has not got the time to do so. An enlightening conversation at the end of the day would be appreciated by the crestfallen competitor, but this is also usually impracticable. What the rider wants is not a certificate to the effect that his horse hovers at the trot, moves crookedly, takes an irregular, uneven contact – he wants a prescription that will cure the faults. Therefore it is to a good trainer that he must go. There are few good trainers, but some can be approached at competitions. Still, the best of trainers cannot offer a remedy that will work in one session because correction always takes time. Therefore the rider who chooses to train his horse himself must have clear guidelines and good knowledge of principles.

Horses are individuals

Since every horse is an individual that has been exposed to diverse conditions, every horse needs special treatment and there is no singular recipe for the cure of each fault. We must not forget either that the rider is an essential ingredient of the remedy. For example, the horse may have undesirable tendencies and these can be compounded by the faults of the rider; or, as mentioned in the previous chapter, temperaments can be incompatible or physiques ill-matched.

Furthermore, provided general principles are respected, one must be broad-minded and prepared to resort sometimes to methods which are condemned by some for being unorthodox. I know that I will expose myself to indignant reproach from some quarters for even mentioning so-called unorthodox procedures. I still maintain that, regardless of theory and tradition, the proof of the value of any method is that it succeeds in its aim, which is to teach the recalcitrant horse that it must move correctly and that it must be obedient.

The aids

However, before we can think of correcting the various cases of equine insubordination, we must acquire the mastery of the aids. It is of course impossible to describe the essential accord of the aids in a diagram; nevertheless it may be that some readers will find the adjoining representation informative. We must realize that every aid is useless when given in isolation from another. There must always be a fine interplay of legs, seat and hands (and of voice, whip and spurs to reinforce them if necessary). One set of aids may have to be given greater emphasis than another depending on the magnitude or the kind of resistance with which the horse opposes our impulses. The rational and discriminating use of limbs and body which is known as 'aids' must finally become a series of discreet indications which the horse understands and obeys instantly. And, to be able to intervene judiciously and instantaneously at the very first sign of stiffening or disobedience, the rider must be perfectly balanced and constantly attentive. If he can also realize the limit of his talent and of his horse's aptitudes, he will cease to torment himself or his horse and will discover that riding can be an entirely enjoyable activity.

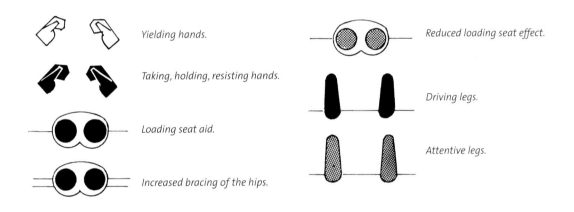

Yielding hands.

Taking, holding, resisting hands.

Loading seat aid.

Increased bracing of the hips.

Reduced loading seat effect.

Driving legs.

Attentive legs.

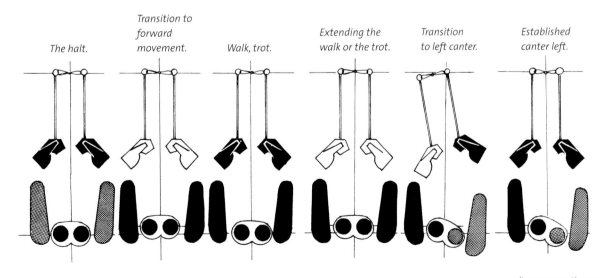

The halt.

Transition to forward movement.

Walk, trot.

Extending the walk or the trot.

Transition to left canter.

Established canter left.

diagram continues

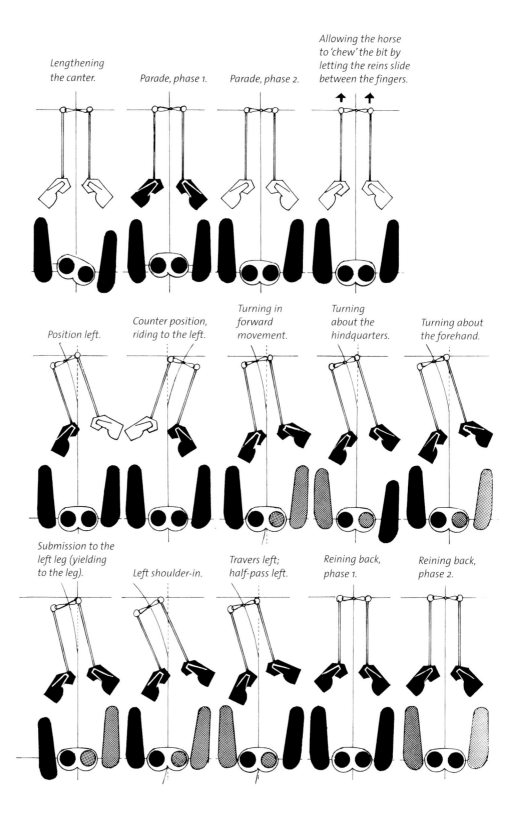

Lengthening the canter.

Parade, phase 1.

Parade, phase 2.

Allowing the horse to 'chew' the bit by letting the reins slide between the fingers.

Position left.

Counter position, riding to the left.

Turning in forward movement.

Turning about the hindquarters.

Turning about the forehand.

Submission to the left leg (yielding to the leg).

Left shoulder-in.

Travers left; half-pass left.

Reining back, phase 1.

Reining back, phase 2.

CHAPTER SIX

Redressing Spoilt Horses

MUTUAL UNDERSTANDING STARTS to be established in the stable. It is my firm belief that every rider should want to saddle his horse himself and, better still, that he should want to groom his horse. Even if one has a good groom, a superficial final polishing oneself can do no harm and gives one the opportunity to care for one's horse and establish a good rapport with the animal.

Grooming and tacking up

Grooming and tacking up provide the first opportunity of detecting certain signs of intractability in the horse. It is therefore important, and always interesting, to handle a newly acquired horse in the stable. This will allow us to find out how sensitive it is and which are the most sensitive parts of its body, to discover the extent of its docility and the ways in which it manifests any lack of submissiveness. Besides this, talking to our horse is the best way of gaining its trust. Horses that are in regular, amicable contact with humans become more dependent upon them, as dogs do, hence they become more reliable, easier to handle and more serviceable than those horses that have been degraded to the status of machines to let us play our games. Earning your horse's devotion is a small price to pay for a generous reward. For one thing, the horse will always be more attentive to the sound of your voice than to that of others. Moreover, even if you never find yourself in a situation so precarious that you have to rely entirely on your horse to get you out of trouble, you will still find that a trusting horse will understand more easily and obey more willingly the demands which you will make on it in the course of daily work. A quiet voice and a manner devoid of roughness and impatience should be employed as much in our dealings with horses as with small children. If we always behave reasonably, our horses should become so trusting that they will obey – even if doing so may cause them some inconvenience. And so we should make the effort to groom our horse, even if the person who is paid to do so has already done a perfectly satisfactory job.

Horses can tolerate a lot of handling and we should therefore claim the right to look after the one that we ride. We can clean the horse about the head and ears, brush out the mane and tail, rinse the eyes and nostrils, wash the anus and sheath or vulva and pick out the hooves. Some horses are inordinately sensitive and may at first object to all this attention; but we must remember that ticklishness is acute sensitivity to light touch and that it cannot be controlled by the victim, whether man or beast. We must understand this fact, for the ticklish horse will certainly never welcome a tactless handler. We ought to be equally considerate when fitting the saddle and bridle. Resolving difficulties associated with this process has been dealt with earlier (Problems in saddling and bridling page 53), yet it remains of the utmost importance to carry out these procedures in a manner that does not hurt, annoy or alarm the horse.

Mounting

Teaching the horse to stand still during mounting is the next very important lesson in obedience. We must not allow the horse to move, be it only one step forwards, sideways or backwards. If we cannot impose our ascendancy at this stage, there is little hope that we will be able to cope with insubordination in further lessons. There is a maxim in show horse judging: 'A horse goes as it stands'. As well as referring to how a horse moves, this can also be applied to the horse's behaviour under saddle. An obedient horse will have learnt to stand, so its behaviour while being mounted is representative of its behaviour in general.

This first lesson must be taught on the first occasion of mounting; today and not tomorrow. We must mount and then dismount until the horse has fully understood that it will never be given permission to move before we are completely prepared. The same lesson will have to be repeated every time we start to ride. Moreover, we should never give the signal to go as soon as we have put our feet in the stirrups and have sat down; we can give the horse a friendly pat and a word of praise to show our appreciation of its good behaviour, and take some time in arranging our clothes and adjusting the reins before we give the leg aid. We will thus spare ourselves the ridiculous predicament of riders of ill-mannered horses that move on while their passenger, with only one foot in the stirrup, has to haul on the reins as he tries to drag himself aboard.

Of course, teaching this lesson will be much easier if we make the process as comfortable as possible for the horse. In days gone by, people used to mount their horses habitually with a 'leg-up'. This was not only for reasons of convenience, but simply because horses stand more calmly without someone pulling them down and twisting them round on one side, swinging one leg through the air, digging a toe into their tummy, and finally crashing over 70 or 80 kg down on their loins. Thus accepting a leg-up on to a horse which has already learnt to stand should not make you feel you are being lazy, or cheating, particularly if it actually helps to maintain the horse's compliance. Similarly, if your horse is very tall, you can also let out the left stirrup leather a few holes to make it easier to mount, or you can use a mounting block. With mares, or any other animals which dislike being girthed up tight, it is essential to have an assistant on the right of the saddle to ensure that it does not slide to the left and then under the horse's belly. Obviously it is a good idea for the assistant to place the right stirrup in the correct position under the sole of your boot, because fishing around with the foot for the stirrup can sometimes irritate the horse and encourage it to fidget.

These points made so far, however, refer to redressing fairly minor acts of impatience and indiscipline – or to ensuring that we do not encourage the development of such behaviour. What happens if we acquire a horse in which serious disobedience has become deep-rooted – a horse which spins round, tries to bite, or bolt, or rears when we attempt to mount it? The answer is, essentially, the same – we must teach it to stand still. In such cases, however, the remedy may well take longer, and it may be both dangerous and impractical to attempt to rectify the problem unaided.

Therefore, unless you have absolutely no choice in the matter, do not attempt to tackle the problem on your own. It takes a lot of patience and calmness to make a horse with such problems obedient again. An assistant should stand at the horse's head, in front of it, with a supply of titbits. In extreme cases, the assistant stands on the right of the horse, holds the horse's right cheekpiece (not the reins) with his right hand and, with his left hand, hangs on to the right stirrup leather (at the top, by the buckle) to prevent the saddle from slipping, or being pulled, sideways. It is also his job to place the stirrup (turned the right way round) on the rider's foot. He may also turn the horse's head slightly to the right, which is what the rider should do anyway when he mounts. In extreme cases, it may be useful to have more than one assistant, one of whom may give a leg-up. It is important that the rider sits down softly, and does not suddenly weigh down hard on the horse's back, and that the horse is spoken to constantly and rewarded with bread, sugar or pieces of apple. Once you have mounted, with assistance, ride forwards immediately. However, do not be content with succeeding in mounting once, practise doing so repeatedly, gradually increasing the time you ask the horse to stand before moving off, because there is hardly anything worse than, for example, being stuck in the country with a horse which will not let you get on it.

If you do have to tackle this problem without assistance, try to position the horse up against a wall. Although this is feasible in the school, it is rarely possible to do so when you are out in the country. So what should you do then? You may be able to get another rider to position his horse alongside yours, on the right. If so, shorten your right rein, bend the horse's head gently to the right, and make sure you get on without digging the horse in the tummy with your toe: some horses object to this! Stand very close to the horse when you mount so that your centre of gravity coincides approximately with that of the horse from the outset, and slide into the saddle – do not crash down into it! Do not forget to praise the horse. And then practise mounting and dismounting: walk the horse forwards a few steps and then start again from the beginning.

As with many examples of bad behaviour, serious resistances to being mounted are often rooted in early handling. So what should we do if we have a horse which has never had anyone on its back – and in addition is sensitive, nervous and not at all keen on letting anything of the sort take place? The answer is, we should 'play around' with the horse, for example, when we have

Assistance with mounting when teaching the horse to stand. It is not essential to have quite so many helpers, but you do need two or three.

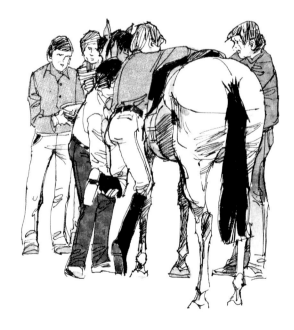

just given it a feed we should lean against its left side with one arm over its back, patting it in different places, talking to it and putting weight on its back. We should put a saddle cloth or numnah on its back and pat it with our hand. Later, we can put a saddle on top of it. (The horse must first be allowed to see and, especially, to sniff these items.) At first the saddle is only laid on the horse's back, and the horse is praised, patted and given food. The saddle is then taken off and put back on again, and at some point the girth is passed round the horse's belly, and then done up. The horse is taken for a walk – with the saddle on – and the saddle is patted and the stirrups pulled down, and then run up again. When the horse accepts all this calmly, we can start lungeing with the saddle in place and the stirrups run up out of the way and secured.

I am not very keen on the idea of introducing the horse to further weight by putting a sandbag on its back. It is not so much the weight that alarms the horse, but rather the basic fact that there is something on its back. The primitive fear inherited from its ancestors comes to the fore: the horse thinks it could be a beast of prey about to bite it at that vulnerable point, the withers, with fatal results. A better course of action is to allay the horse's fear so that it begins to understand that the whole thing is just a game, in which the person who gives the horse nice things to eat and chats to it, suddenly sits on it, without anything nasty happening. To achieve this, get someone to lift you up against the horse, lie across the saddle, and then lift your leg over the saddle. Keep your upper body horizontal at first, then gradually sit up. A bowl of food held under the horse's nose can be very helpful at this point. If problems arise during backing, it is advisable to work in the stable, and not in the corridor. Never tie the horse up for this purpose. Be satisfied with small beginnings, and never ask for too much at once. Never forget the basic principle that the horse must be kept happy. You will never get on the horse's back against its will, unless you do so rodeo-style, and that is not exactly what we are aiming at! If, after you have mounted the horse for the first time, you do encounter resistances, your assistants should ensure that this does not happen again. Once a horse has discovered that it does not have to tolerate a man on its back, it will soon learn how to stop people getting on it. The helpers must keep hold of the horse at all costs. A lead rein, not attached to the bit ring, can be helpful. Once a horse has managed to escape, it will do so again. In difficult circumstances, it is best if the rider dismounts immediately, the horse is calmed down, and the whole procedure begun again, rather than a fight developing between horse and rider. I would reiterate that, to start with, you should always be more careful than may be necessary, so as to avoid any such incidents or to nip any problems in the bud.

Once the young horse has accepted being mounted, it will have to learn to stand still under saddle. Nevertheless, this process should be undertaken gradually. Young horses should not be made to stand still for long periods, first because they lack the patience and concentration span of older, trained horses, and second because of the unaccustomed weight on their backs. The stationary position is quite tiring for back muscles unaccustomed to bearing a considerable weight; they will have to be strengthened by exercise before we can demand complete stillness for more than a very short time. Unsympathetic constraint at the halt will thus cause a young horse to fidget. It is only after some months of gymnastic work that the discipline of standing square at the halt can be imposed occasionally during the lesson.

Loosening muscles

Calm is an unconditional element of submissiveness. No horse is completely governable before it has relaxed unnecessary muscular tension. This relaxation of harmful excessive tension, which horsemen call 'looseness', is constantly mentioned in conversations between riders and in written works on the subject of equitation. Nevertheless, there are not enough horses that can be said to be properly relaxed and to move forwards freely.

The twelve signs by which we can recognize this looseness are:

1. The ample oscillations of the limbs.

2. The undulating movements of the spine.

3. The pliancy of the poll.

4. The placid obedience to the indications of either rein.

5. The 'chewing' of the bit.

6. The ease with which the poll can be inflexed in both directions, the mane sliding over towards the side of the inflexion.

7. The smoothness of the transitions from one position to the other.

8. The tranquil lowering of the head and neck when the rider invites the horse to 'chew' the bit and lengthen the reins.

9. The readiness of the horse to go forwards on a loose rein.

10. Contented snorting.

11. The calm swinging of the tail in rhythm with the movement.

12. In the case of geldings, the absence of noise from the sheath.

Pain or just discomfort produced by the saddle is a very frequent cause of tension. The spinal muscles on either side of the vertebral column remain constantly tightened and their contraction extends to all the related muscles of the trunk and limbs. We should be able to see the rhythmical pulsations of the back muscles behind the saddle. The loosening exercises which restore the elastic activity of the back muscles are well known: they are rising to the trot, frequent periods of cantering in a light position, going over cavalletti, and jumping small obstacles. Horses with a short, and therefore relatively rigid, back should never be ridden on straight lines before they are quite calm, but cantering on a circular course has a relaxing effect.

The back of the horse may also become too tense because of pain if the interspinous ligaments – connecting the spines of contiguous vertebrae – have been strained (the outline of the back indicates the height of the spinous processes but not the position of the spinal column). If this is the case, the horse will suffer pain, even if the rider is very light.

The elasticity of the abdominal muscles needs to be improved also; to this end, the most useful exercises are the climbing of hills and work in harness, but a sledge is more suitable for the latter than a vehicle mounted on wheels. The horse can be trained to drag a contraption for levelling the surface of the manège or sand arena. We should perhaps do less mounted work with 5- and 6-year-olds, because in the horse the thin epiphyseal plates at the ends of each vertebra do not fuse before maturity. In any case, a horse with sore back

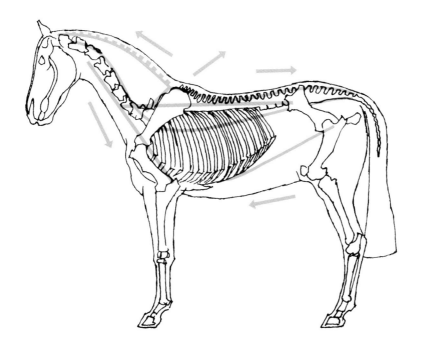

Direction of action of the most important muscles of locomotion and their effect on the joints.

muscles must be given a respite from mounted work and such treatment as is recommended by a professional equine therapist.

Human athletes know that elastic muscles, tendons and ligaments are a precondition of efficiency. Cramped muscles are the consequence of insufficient exercise if not of over-exertion; and inelastic muscles are weak muscles. Horses must be taught to allow the stretching of their back and neck muscles by moving with a low position of head and neck. I know that some distinguished riders maintain that teaching a horse to move in this attitude is illogical, since eventually the horse will have to elevate its neck, and they remind us that Otto Lörke, a famous German horseman, would get his horses to loosen by doing the piaffe. But Otto Lörke was exceptionally talented; moreover, this was not his daily practice and he did not use this method with all his horses.

There is more than one method of getting a horse to loosen tight muscles. Turning it out to graze is believed to produce this result, but this is not so beneficial as is often assumed. It is the right sort of activity that is required. There are undoubtedly horses that gallop free in long, flowing movements, but there are many that move in a hurried manner, scraping the ground in an scanty sort of canter, their rigidly erect tail betraying their tension. We must realize that physical stiffness is often a symptom of nervous stress; it is in the mind as much as in the body. Hence a perfectly trained horse should be calm when it comes out of its box and need only a few minutes of warming up before the relatively short periods of real gymnastics. The horse's mental poise is a condition of its physical equilibrium. However, the sort of placidity that we want is not the same thing as apathy and a horse's calmness is an acquired quality, the result of training and habit; it can be imparted only by a trainer who is also mentally and physically composed. No advantage can ever be gained by gymnastic work if it is started before the animal is unwound and willing to move freely forward without haste or resistance.

We must remember also that the choice of loosening exercise must depend on the experience of the horse. Exercises which are easy for an agile and well-balanced, highly proficient dressage or show-jumping horse are much too difficult for a youthful animal. Long periods of trotting, even if the rider rises to one diagonal or another, do not necessarily induce the relaxation of tautened muscles; they may on the contrary give the horse a greater capacity to sustain intense muscular tension, with the result that ever-increasing long periods of exercise will be needed to get the horse to loosen-up. Lengthy periods of galloping to tire an exceptionally highly-strung horse may produce muscular soreness and make for even more resistance. This is particularly true in the case of horses that habitually get above the bit. Apart from the back muscles, other equally important muscles involved in balance and movement may ache and also inhibit relaxation. There are therefore many instances in which it is preferable to ride 'in position' (that is with a slight degree of inflexion of the spinal column) and to loosen the outside rein to induce the horse to lower its head and neck. We must, of course, preserve impulsion and use our legs as well as the reins to obtain this position, and we must beware of not letting the horse outwit us by using the outside rein as a balancing prop. The temporary success achieved by this supposedly unorthodox method does not acquit us of the necessity of subsequently driving with the inside leg into the outside hand to get the horse to stretch the outside rein in order to offer position right or left.

Besides bodily conditions like aching muscles or a sore skin under the saddle or girth, emotional states, such as anxiety, fright, excitement, distrust or irritability can also inhibit the relaxation of taut muscles. It would then be useless to resort to the gallop; this would aggravate the nervous strain. In such circumstances, the best plan sometimes is to do nothing other than allow the horse to stand still on a loose rein.

The way a horse carries its tail gives an insight into both its physical and its mental state. The horse's disposition, the amount of energy it has, its constitution, its nervous state, and any tension, will be expressed by the carriage and behaviour of the tail. Normally the tail moves freely, in rhythm with the stride, with the tip swinging from side to side, coinciding with the change of supporting leg. If the tail does not swing rhythmically with the movement, this means that the horse is not moving freely: it is tense. The tail is therefore an infallible guide as to whether and to what extent the horse is working through its back. A horse may be tense on one side, it may not go into the hand on one side, or it may be tired. A horse which carries its tail crookedly may not necessarily have done so from birth: the crookedness may be a result of tension. If this is so, the crookedness will usually disappear at an extended canter, i.e. when the horse is really using itself. Clamping the tail down is a practice which is often found in nervous horses which are afraid of being punished. It can also be a sign that the horse is about to kick. If they do it under saddle, for whatever reason, it means that they are not *losgelassen* (free of constraint): the back muscles are not working sufficiently, and neither is the muscle which raises the tail, which works in conjunction with the back muscles.

Temperamentally rooted tension is much more difficult to dissipate than constraint based on defects of conformation. If a horse suddenly tenses after it has been working smoothly and willingly for some time, this is always caused by a character defect. There are a number of horses that become agitated within the short interval between the working-in and the test periods of a dressage competition. Nevertheless, permanent calmness is the fruit of correct work as well as of disposition. In cases of mental turmoil, punishment will seldom achieve anything other than greater loss of calm.

I should conclude this section by emphasizing that we have been talking of horses which retain the physiological capacity to achieve looseness. There are horses that may or may not be young in years but, like many human athletes, are relatively aged by sporting performance. They may not be infirm, but they are reduced in their capacity for hard work. The spirit is still willing, but the body grumbles; joints and tendons start to feel the strain. It goes without saying that true horsemen will take special care in warming up such animals, and will be mindful of the constraints placed upon their capacity for movement. It should also be the case that such riders will not misinterpret stiffness caused by wear and tear as resistance, and they will modify their demands in terms of actual performance. A genuine horseman must be able to recognize the presence of discomfort or incapacity and will treat his horse with the same care as he would treat himself. As a corollary to this, we can add that the genuine horseman will, in any case, maximize the working life of his charge by always adhering to a proper loosening and warming-up regime and by not making unreasonable demands on the horse if it is stiff after a period of prolonged immobility, over-exertion or illness.

Gait irregularities

As a general rule, the loosening exercises must start at the walk on as long a rein as practical for at least five minutes. If the horse hurries, we turn it away on a circle and, if necessary, enlarge the circle, yet still on a loose or long rein. If this is still to no avail, we can oblige the horse to overtread by making it go forwards in turns about the forehand, alternately to right and left, until it has calmed down. No other gait should be allowed before complete tranquillity is established. And we must be logically consistent; this is the key to success. Therefore when the horse walks quietly, we must not forget to praise it generously with voice and caress, for the horse must understand that we bear it no ill will. Our ultimate aim is to teach the horse that every lesson will start with perfect calm at an active but unhurried walk. It may take some time for the message to sink in but we must remember that a horse that has not learnt to stand still when we mount will be restless at the walk, and that if it hurries at the walk, it will also hurry at the trot. We must also remember that we may never drive the horse to the bit at the beginning of any lesson. On the one hand, this can mar the walk for ever; on the other hand, it will delay or hinder the attainment of calm.

Turns about the forehand at the walk ('the carousel') are a proven method of quietening horses that hurry and (in a heightened form that we shall explore further) horses that jog. Making the horse move simultaneously sideways and forwards, an effective loosening exercise called 'yielding to the leg', is not advisable before the horse is settled and walks calmly; it can damage the joints and is likely to produce tension. Leg-yielding is, however, a good balancing and loosening exercise provided calm has been established. Poles on the ground or very low cavalletti are also excellent ways of teaching a horse to walk resolutely forward, with long, regular strides, a low head position, and without a hint of superfluous energy. They should be set at intervals that suit the individual horse's natural length of stride, preferably on a circle. If they are properly positioned on the circumference of the circle, they can be used to obtain a lengthening of the strides by moving the horse a little further out on the circle.

Ambling ('walking' by lifting the two feet on one side together, alternately with the two feet on the other side) is sometimes an inherited manner of moving, and horses with this inborn gait have to be rejected for dressage, since a correct, efficient walk is a four-time movement. Often, however, the tendency is rider-produced and horses that tend to amble will usually walk properly when the rein contact is surrendered. In the Middle Ages in Europe, horse that ambled rather than walked, and paced rather than trotted, were much favoured by inexpert riders or by ladies. Selective breeding from animals that showed a preference for these gaits at birth was therefore encouraged. It is undeniable that they give the rider an agreeable sensation of being rocked in a soothing manner. It does not matter at all to the rider who just enjoys leisurely hacking whether his horse ambles or marks the four distinctly audible hoof beats of a suitably energetic walk. Nevertheless the amble is considered to be an incorrect gait. Lazy riders who lack the energy to brace their loins with sufficient firmness will induce a horse to move at an amble and will weaken the horse's back. On the other hand, incompetent attempts to produce a collected

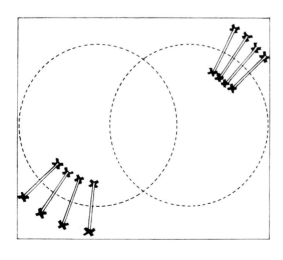

Good arrangement of cavalletti for the trot (*left*) and the walk (*right*).

appearance of the head and neck or to cadence the walk with active hands will produce the same faulty gait. It is therefore of the utmost importance for the rider to hold himself up firmly at the walk and to allow a young horse to oscillate its head freely at the walk, especially when hacking over open country. Once acquired, the habit of ambling is extremely difficult to correct.

In fact, the walk is the most difficult gait to improve, or at any rate, not to ruin. Improving the natural walk of the horse requires considerable skill on the part of a rider. It is especially in the transitions to the walk from the canter or the trot that irregularities most frequently occur when the horse is not sufficiently relaxed.

These transitions will have to be executed with great care in the case of horses that are inclined to walk badly. For example, the parades (inaccurately called *half-halts* in English) can be organized so that the first steps of the walk happen over a pair of cavalletti arranged on a circle and spaced to conform to the individual length of stride. However, cavalletti are not always available; we must then encourage the horse to chew the bit by opening our hands at the moment of the downward transition, enhancing the effect of the softness of the contact with soothing vocal encouragement. Before resorting to this particular exercise, we can practise transitions from medium trot to working trot or from medium canter to working canter. We may perhaps do a step or two of leg-yielding on a beginning of a circle at the moment of driving into walk, but – and this is the most important thing – on a lengthened rein. It is impossible for a horse to amble when moving with a deeply lowered nose, and neither can the horse do so when walking over uneven, rather ridged terrain, like a ploughed field for example, or a rutted forest drive. In any case, a horse that tends to amble must be encouraged to lower its head and neck as much as it wishes.

Ambling is an excessively leisurely way of moving. Hurrying, however, is just as inefficient. The best way of quietening a horse that hurries at the walk is to ride on long or loose reins on a winding course, guiding the horse as much as possible with pressures of the outside leg in front of the girth. A quietening use of the voice is also a helpful aid, and we can also hold the reins in one hand while stroking the mane with the other. We must continually change direction and decrease or increase the diameter of voltes and circles, and teach the horse to obey a spoken command to quieten its movements, so that we do not have to shorten the reins every time it starts to hurry. We must also teach the horse to stand still on long reins and, in doing so, we can teach it to understand the retarding signal of the legs, that is the soft, rearward pressure of both our legs behind the girth. Once a horse has learnt to react to this moderating effect of the legs, we will be able to execute all parades in a yielding fashion instead of having to maintain a hold on the reins. No other gait should be allowed before the horse has learnt that it must move calmly at the walk. An excited, over-tense horse that hurries at the walk will go at a disconnected trot, hind foot or forefoot impacting before its diagonal opposite.

When correcting these faulty forms of the walk, we will need to be especially patient and consistent. We must always be prepared to feel the slightest indication of impatience and to forestall disorderliness by the most appropriate method: either a momentary shortening of the reins, or the use of the voice, of the retarding legs, of turns and serpentines. No attempt should ever be made to collect the walk before the gait has become perfectly regular and before the horse is capable of maintaining collection more or less of its own accord at trot and canter. It is only then that the collected walk can be taught prudently, for very short periods of time, towards the end of a lesson. During this part of the lesson devoted to the collection of the walk, changes of speed *at the walk* must be avoided, for while we are teaching the horse to walk slowly in elevated, measured steps, we must not confuse it and we must not destroy the result so painstakingly obtained.

Complete freedom of head and neck must also be allowed to horses that walk skimpily; that is, those horses that do not overtrack sufficiently. In their case we must occasionally use both legs energetically, to the extent of producing occasionally a few jogging steps. I have already mentioned one of the most objectionable sins against good horsemanship – the habit of riding negligently with restraining reins while chatting with a friend during pauses in the course of work. If we need a respite, we must give it to the horse also, drop the contact and allow the horse to stretch its back and neck muscles. Remember that your horse must always remain attuned to you and attentive to your aids. Constantly going round and round the manège with even slightly restricting hands teaches the horse to become obtuse and is, besides, a guaranteed way of spoiling the walk. The tedious business of correcting a spoilt walk must be carried out on long reins, if not on completely loose ones, even when hacking across country.

Hacking is in fact salutary medicine for horses that have to do much manège work. With a few exceptions, and in nearly all circumstances, horses must be allowed to walk when we hack and to have total liberty of movement of the head and neck. The rider, however, must obviously remain alert and poised just in case the horse shies. It is also good practice to let the horse halt from time to time to nibble at a few blades of grass. There are some valid objections to this policy, but I think that on the whole it is highly commendable. Hacking ought to be a healthy easing of tension. There are many horses that hardly ever see a pasture. If this is their sad lot, it is then incumbent upon their riders to let them taste grass during leisurely outings.

Jogging is another sign of tension and is nearly always produced by bad riding. Every rule has its exceptions however, and a tendency to jog may be

Correct position of legs and trunk to allow the horse freedom of action of his back and hind legs. The trunk is very slightly inclined forwards. The contact is light.

rooted in a horse's temperament. Nevertheless, jogging shows that the horse is not 'on the aids', which means that it is disobedient to the indications of the legs and the hands. The habit can be cured in nearly all cases, but the treatment must start in the manège because it is usually the rider who must be corrected. A firm seat, by which we mean a correctly braced loin that allows a rider to preserve his balance without stiffening his hips, is an absolute condition of effectiveness. This statement is no less true for being trite and repeated ad nauseam. The walk is the gait that most clearly exposes the standard of the rider and clearly reveals whether he is properly poised and is moving in harmony with the horse's movement. It is indeed the most difficult of all the gaits in the sense that it is the one that requires the most feel and the most subtle use of the aids, the one most easily spoilt by heavy hands and a poor sense of balance. Riders generally tend to nag too much with their hands and they do not then acquire the feeling of having the horse 'in front of the legs'; that is, a horse that does not have to be constantly urged on by the legs. This signifies that we must never have more force in the hands than is necessary to control the horse. For the purpose of developing this feeling, all the exercises which favour the development of impulsion and which cultivate the sense of a tension of the reins consequent only on impulsion, must be practised with great attention. They are, to start with, the lengthening of the strides at trot and canter and the transitions from trot to canter, at first on circles, and later on straight lines. It is only when these transitions have become fluent, when the rider has learnt to relax the tension of the reins at the moment of driving forwards, only when the horse responds to the aids without stiffening its jaws, poll, back and hocks, that one can concentrate on the smoothness of the downward transitions with a feeling of still driving forwards into the slower gait (which is the meaning of parade); at first from trot to walk, and later from canter to walk. A better affinity between horse and rider will thus develop. This is actually the meaning of learning to ride; we have to admit that there are many self-styled riders who have still to discover the skill of putting the horse on the aids.

It is only when the rider has mastered the knack of using his seat, hands and legs aptly that he can think of correcting the walk of the jogging horse. As always when a bad walk has to be corrected, the beginning of the lesson must be at the walk on long or loose reins. Fixing the hands to enforce a pure four-beat walk is a grave error. A sovereign remedy is the *mill*. It is of course stressful on the joints and a very severe punishment, which must never be administered unless one is perfectly calm and has anticipated the necessity of the punishment; hence the horse's limbs must be protected by brushing boots in front and behind. The *mill* amounts to making the horse turn about a full circle several times with the aid of the sideways driving leg; it is a sort of hurried turn on the forehand with exaggerated inflexion of the poll. The effect is more potent when the horse is bent towards its hard side (usually the left). Immediately after infliction of the punishment, the horse must again be driven forwards at the walk on a long rein, and instantly be punished in the same manner if it starts to jog. When it walks quietly and regularly, it must of course be rewarded with a pat on the neck and some words of praise.

Outside the walls of the manège, the correction of jogging can be difficult. If the rider is perfectly correct, we may assume that the vice is linked to the horse's temperament. To start with, the horse should never be ridden out in the company of more than two or three others and, during retraining, hunting or other potentially exciting activities are to be proscribed. The jogging horse will have to be in the lead and must set the pace, for horses that jog are often horses that do not stride amply at the walk. If possible, we should leave the road, so that the group can spread itself on a broad front and the position of the jogging horse can be changed frequently. We must not neglect to praise the horse for good behaviour, nor to punish it instantly at the moment when it starts to jog. The other riders must constantly watch the rider of the difficult horse and note his reactions. It is for this reason that it is not possible to prevent jogging when riding in a large company. It is a good idea to dismount occasionally and lead the horse from the ground, if only to convince oneself that neither the saddle nor the bridle could be upsetting it (these being distinct possibilities, if the behaviour occurs suddenly, and is uncharacteristic). Letting the horse graze a little can do no harm – on the contrary, hustling and irritation will unsettle it even more. It goes without saying that we must have the jogging horse 'on the legs' all the time, even when hacking, because it is essentially obedience to the legs which must be instilled. We must not however grip with the calves, but just maintain a sensitive contact with the horse's sides so that our legs are always ready to act without delay. We must sit up with a straight

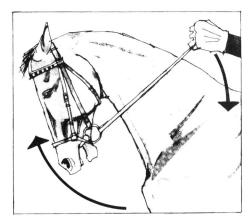

Wrong hand carriage: the hands must be lowered.

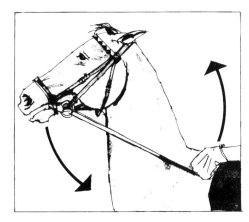

Wrong hand carriage; the hands are pressed downwards; the hands must be lifted.

Correct hand position.

The wrong way to sit on a jogging horse. It is fundamentally wrong to stick the legs out, away from the horse, so that you have no influence over it.

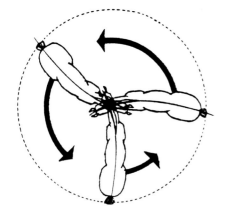

The '*mill*'. All four limbs should be protected by bandages against interference and injury.

back and drive emphatically forwards with our seat. Over open country, the remedy of the *mill* can be applied just as often and instantaneously as in the riding school; hence the horse's limbs must, again, be protected against injuries by brushing boots or bandages.

The rein-back is another form of correction, and for this purpose it is permissible to demand a greater number of steps than the six which are normally the maximum that we should request when schooling a horse. When all jogging has stopped and as soon as the horse settles into the regular walk, we must praise it and from time to time allow it to stand on a loose rein. Let me warn you that exceptional patience is needed to correct jogging, because punishment by the whip, the reins or the spurs would merely serve to increase the horse's agitation.

Another sign of excessive tension is the sheath noise which is made by geldings only. It can be a consequence of excitement, but it is often caused by a rider's wrong conception of the driving influence of the seat. Tense thighs produce tense gaits and tightened back muscles in the horse. A vicious circle is thus created. The stiffened back of the horse induces the rider to glue himself to the saddle by gripping with his calves and contracting his hamstrings, and in so doing he induces the horse to stiffen even more. A noisy sheath is a positive sign of insufficient elasticity of the muscles of the hindquarters. The noise was more frequently heard in the past when horses were prevented from moving by being tied up in their stalls for long periods at a time; it also occurs sometimes when the bladder is distended and the horse's urge to stale is repressed. But it must be admitted that the tightness of muscles is sometimes associated with a quirk of temperament, and it is then much more difficult to get the horse to relax. One can try frequent changes of gait, and alternate periods of gymnastic exercises with periods of free forward riding in a light position. Still, there are cases that cannot be cured, because the habit is too ingrained.

Stumbling and dragging the toes are gait irregularities that can have various causes. Certainly, they can be consequences of non-compliant behaviour by the horse, or of bad or inconsiderate riding, but they may also signify lameness, weakness, ill health or faulty conformation. For example, in the most general terms, there may be a basic distinction to be made between the stumbling of young horses and the stumbling of older horses. With young horses, stumbling can be caused by the horse not having yet found its balance under the rider, or not yet being able to maintain its balance in all circum- stances. In addition to ensuring that his mode of riding does not add to the horse's difficulty, the rider must undertake exercises which develop both its feeling for balance and its strength. Work over poles on the ground and caval- letti, and riding up hills and on uneven and yielding ground, especially in woods, is very good for hardening and strengthening the young horse's ten- dons and ligaments. It is important that it learns to lower its head and look where it is going, and so become sure-footed. When, as a result of these exer- cises, the horse becomes stronger and generally more developed, especially in its back muscles, it will stop stumbling. With older horses, stumbling can have a wide variety of causes. The reason may be conformation defects, such as upright pasterns or a straight shoulder. However, the horse may simply be on the forehand, having been ridden by a rider who has allowed it to lean perma- nently on the bit, so that the bit has become a 'fifth leg' for it. The cause may also lie in weakness or lack of energy, possibly made worse by overtiredness at the end of a long ride (if a horse is stumbling through tiredness, the only thing to do is get off and either lead it or take a rest). The need for attention to the feet is another possibility, in which case the farrier should be consulted. Once the various possibilities have been eliminated – and provided that no insoluble physical problems are implicated – it only remains for the rider to bring the horse off its forehand, to re-establish its balance. This entails starting basic training again from the beginning. The back muscles must be strengthened so that the hind legs are encouraged to step further under the body again. The horse must learn that it cannot simply shuffle along, but must carry itself – and its rider. Fundamentally, it is important to understand that a horse which is 'on the aids' will either not stumble at all, or will stumble much less.

Sometimes one sees horses dragging the toe of one or both hind feet on the floor of the school. This is most common in walk, but can also occur in trot. Riding school horses, which have a different rider on their back every les- son and have become stultified by riding school life, tend to shuffle away their hours in the school with stiff hind legs, and their toes dragging wearily on the ground. If there is a suspicion that a horse moving with stiff hind legs is doing so as a result of a physical disorder this should, of course, be investigated. However, even horses with essentially very active hindquarters can suddenly drag a toe across the ground. This can even happen at the beginning of the lesson, when it is certainly not caused by tiredness. It is more a question of laziness, and the only way to combat it is through active use of the driving aids. In walk, on flat ground, the horse should put its hind feet down as far forward as possible under its body, and not drag them lazily across the ground. Frequent work over grids of poles on the ground spaced at walk distances (0.8 to 1 m) will develop the activity of the hindquarters. As a progression from this, cavalletti about 15 to 20 cm high can be used, and the horse worked over these in medium trot. As we know, in medium walk the horse should tread with its hind feet beyond the prints of its forefeet. Apart from developing the ground-covering capacity, exercises over poles also activate the quarters and develop the rhythm, especially with horses which do not have a good walk rhythm. The rider should first bring his horse onto the bit, that is, establish a soft contact between his hands (which should be kept still) and the horse's mouth by pushing carefully with his back and legs. The poles on the ground should be approached straight and, just before the horse reaches them, the rider should drop his hands as low as possible, and by moving them forwards in the direction of the horse's mouth, allow it to stretch its neck downwards. The rider follows this movement, leaning his upper body forward, therefore taking his weight off the horse's back so that it can move without tension. It is very important that the rider uses his driving aids, and rides the horse straight and forwards. A horse which is being ridden forwards will pick its feet up energetically. The contact with the mouth should be maintained, but the horse should not be prevented from swinging its back by a high or rigid hand. It must be taught to move with its back, and not just with its legs. The same principles apply to the work in trot as to the walk, although the distance between the poles (or cavalletti) is increased to approximately 1.3 m (for most riders, about five of their own foot-lengths).

Sluggish horses

Having discussed a problem that may be related to laziness, we can now consider sluggish horses in general. Calmness is the first requisite of good movement, impulsion is the next – but it is just as important. 'Ride your horse forward and straight' is the oft-quoted principle of good horsemanship, but it is an axiom much sinned against by many riders whose horses are stolid chiefly because the riders themselves are too phlegmatic. If they were more concerned about the absolute necessity of impulsion, many resistances would never occur. Even a relatively small lack of impulsion (although even a small deficiency in this respect is never *insignificant*) could be put right if free forward movement were always the foremost priority of the rider, not only when training a young horse, but also when improving collection with a proficient one.

The inexperienced horse generally allows itself to be carried forwards by

its momentum and this leads to hurrying. We have to regulate the trot by rising with one diagonal or the other. However, as soon as the horse has adapted
itself to the task of carrying the additional weight of a rider, it has to learn to
move in horizontal equilibrium by flexing its hocks more pronouncedly. Most
horses instinctively discover a way of avoiding such an unnatural effort; it is
up to their rider to inspire them with sufficient impulsion. On the whole, this
is not such a difficult thing to achieve. At the beginning, before the rider's legs
are sufficiently respected, the riding crop (rather than the dressage whip) will
have to be used to preserve the freedom of movement. The spur, used with
deliberation and great discretion, can reinforce the authority of the legs in the
more advanced stages of training.

What can we do when older horses persistently dawdle? I am not alluding
here to the desensitized creatures employed by riding schools. How can those
unfortunate creatures retain their desire to go forwards? No, I am referring to
decently treated horses, often partnered by riders of considerable basic competence. Their movements may be regular, but these horses lack animation in
both the collected and extended gaits. There are no obvious faults, but there is
a lack of vital spark, and the rider is not sharp enough to inspire it. If possible,
such sluggish horses should be loose-schooled fairly regularly over obstacles of
moderate height which oblige them to exert themselves, or be made to work
on the lunge at an energetic trot. This does not mean that they must be hustled
or chased to the point of trotting disconnectedly. (It goes without saying that
insufficient nourishment, or some organic disturbance, should have been
eliminated as a possible cause of lethargy.)

The mounted lessons should be short and sharp to progressively teach the
dullard to go forward with greater vigour. Sharp spurs are not always appropriate, but if they are used they must always be long enough to enable the
wearer to use them deliberately and effectively at the precise moment when
they can produce the desired result. Neither the spur, nor the whip for that matter, can induce a horse to move more keenly either forwards or sideways if it is
used while the idle hind leg aimed at is being grounded during the phase of
recovery of balance. We can make the experiment on ourselves when we walk.
It is impossible for our left leg, for example, to extend vigorously while it is balancing our body weight; it can only do so after our right leg is ready to come
into support. It is therefore senseless to stimulate the hind limb of a horse during the first phase of retraction of that limb, when its duty is to balance the
mass. Hence it is important to learn to feel the moment when a hind leg has fin-
ished its role of shock-absorption and propulsion and is ready to be picked up.

It is, of course, for this reason that novice riders are taught the sequence of
footfalls at walk, trot and canter (see diagram on page 81). At the walk, this is
usually described succinctly in the formula: left hind, left fore, right hind, right

fore. This is a simplistic formula for a rather complex affair but it serves its purpose, because all that we need to know is that the left forefoot is picked up when the left hind foot is put down, and that this is the precise moment at which our right leg must give the stimulus. Using our left leg at that instant would be futile and would teach the horse disrespect for the legs. To a certain extent, the horse itself evinces the appropriate moment for our leg action, in that the right side of its body arches during the phase of rearward extension of its right hind, up to the moment when the foot is lifted, so the contact with our right leg occurs automatically if our legs are relaxed. All that we need do is accentuate the pressure. Inexpert riders usually apply both legs simultaneously. This pernicious bilateral swinging of the lower legs has the very reverse of a driving effect. However, this grave fault cannot be corrected before the seat is corrected. I apologize for being repetitive, but I am sure that it cannot ever be said too often that effective aids are inconceivable while the rider pulls himself into the saddle by gripping. It is the looseness of the thigh muscles that allows the legs to hang close together; it is this looseness that prevents the uncontrollable swinging of the lower legs.

It remains to be said that a horse that does not move forwards freely should never be ridden on the bit at the walk, not even for the briefest of moments. It must first learn to walk actively, without hurrying, and to go with the hip and leg action of the rider, while maintaining as straight a course as possible on a long or loose rein. During the schooling sessions at any rate, the periods of walking, between the periods of work at trot or canter, will have to be short because the horse cannot be allowed to feel that the walk provides an opportunity to idle.

From the beginning of training, the demands we can make must be proportional to the physical aptitudes and strength of the horse. Hence, our requirements will have to be heightened very progressively. Nevertheless, the horse must be made to realize that the mere presence of a rider on its back always signifies that work must be produced, energy supplied. During the schooling sessions, we can use the trot or the canter to sharpen up the horse's flagging ardour; hacking must remain a respite from hard work, but we can never allow the walk to degenerate into indolent ambling. Walking up long, moderately inclined slopes is the best kind of gymnastic exercise for promoting sufficiently vigorous activity of the hind legs.

At the trot as at walk, the horse can only obey the stimulus of the leg, spur or whip on condition that it occurs at the moment when the hind limb is about to be detached from the ground – that is, the moment when the opposite hind limb is about to come into support. We will have been taught that the trot is a two-time movement in diagonals: left fore and right hind swing forward as the other diagonal pair is about to come into support. It is, therefore, as incorrect at the trot as it is at the walk to urge the horse on by tapping with both legs (or driving with both seat bones) simultaneously. Sluggish horses must be made to trot faster than they like. At the beginning we rise to the trot and whether a rein contact is established or not is of no consequence; all that matters is impulsion and inspiring the horse with the urge to go forwards. Neither the outline, nor the correct inflexion must concern us at this stage, and we must therefore keep to as straight a course as possible.

A more potent impulsive aid will be required occasionally and, for this purpose, the riding crop should be used rather than the spurs. Since we should not be shy of losing contact with the mouth, we can take the reins in one hand, the crop in the other, and give the horse a smart smack with the whip immediately behind our lower leg as soon as we feel that the leg aid has failed to elicit a more vigorous flexion of hock and stifle. If the horse overreaches – and this cannot be avoided when it is allowed to go with its nose poked – we canter it on a large circle once or twice, return to the walk, and then drive it forwards again at an energetic trot, but without urging it on quite so much as before. It is only when the horse has understood that it will never be allowed to trail its hind legs that we can think of establishing a moderating or regulating contact, so light that it does not slow the speed or impede the unconstrained swinging of the limbs.

At the canter, the driving aids must coincide with the moment at which the inside hind is lifted and stifle and hock flex to swing it forwards. Let us again remember the sequence of footfalls at the canter. After the period of suspension, the first foot to impact is the outside hind; next, outside fore and inside hind impact practically simultaneously; finally the leading foreleg thrusts the horse forwards again into the period of free flight. This is the theoretical knowledge. What matters to the rider is the promotion of the vigorous forward swing of the inside hind, which must advance sufficiently to balance the combined weight of horse and rider. We must learn to feel the moment at which our predominantly driving inside leg can produce this effect; again, we are given the clue by the horse, because it will arch its rib cage towards the side of the swinging inside hind limb; at the same time, the horse will feel as if it were lifting up its forehand. Reinforcement of the impulsive aid of the leg by the whip can be effective only at the moment when the inside hind is detached from the ground. This is the precise instant when the inside shoulder of the horse is drawn back to the maximum limit of its oscillation.

At this stage of re-education of the sluggish horse, head position and rein contact at canter matter no more than they do at walk or trot. The only thing that concerns us is the rousing of the horse's willingness to go forwards. The corners of the riding school must therefore be well rounded, the speed as unrestricted as possible. But the horse must not run; it must leap, and so we must not chase it. It may be necessary to drive rather more on the long sides of the school. Yet, the best conditions for the development of a good cantering technique are provided by the exercise gallops for racehorses. There the horse can be made to expand itself and also develop a good breathing technique. The speed can safely be built up to the exercise 'canter' of racehorses. As the main purpose of the exercise is to teach obedience to the driving aids, the rider's legs must constantly preserve contact with the horse's sides and it is through the hips (that is, with the aid of the seat) that their repeated pressures are exerted. Riding on the knees, with the buttocks high, will simply encourage the horse to lollop.

Besides the whip, the main auxiliary aid to the leg is the spur. I have already said that constantly tapping legs are detrimental to impulsion, and so are constantly nagging spurs. Incidentally, it should be noted that it is a mistake to believe that blunt spurs are necessarily more humane than spurs with rowels. While spurs without rowels cannot produce visible wounds, they can certainly cause bruising. The length of the neck of the spurs also needs to be considered. Long spurs are obviously out of place for riding with somewhat shortened stirrup leathers, as for hunting or show-jumping. For dressage riding, the length of the neck of the spurs must depend on the length of the rider's legs, the design of the saddle and therefore the position of the lower legs, and also on the degree of arching of the horse's rib cage. Riders who cannot learn to relax their hamstrings, who pull up their legs and heels and turn their toes out will automatically, even if unintentionally, annoy the horse with their spurs; they obviously should not be allowed to wear them. Spiked rowels are certainly the most suitable for dressage. The spikes should not be so sharp as to risk wounding, yet they must be effective enough to fulfil their function, which is to quicken the horse's reaction to the legs and to prevent the loss of the horse's attention to the rider's indications. Without spurs it is impossible to motivate a sluggish horse to show a gleam of spirit.

I must stress, however, that it is incumbent upon the rider to use his spurs judiciously and to take due account of the horse's reactions, such as kicking against the spur. A sensitive horse which reacts against either the unintentional use of the spur, or its intentional but incorrect or over-harsh use, is only too right to do so. If such a reaction becomes an ingrained habit, it is always the rider's lack of skill or discernment which are to blame. The rider must check his seat, improve his knee and lower leg position, and check the design of the spurs. He must also check the way in which he applies the aids. If, for example, the horse is not obeying the sideways-pushing leg behind the girth, the rider often applies the leg (and spur) even further back, in the area behind the false ribs. In this position the leg and spur do not serve to make the hind leg step further forward: the sensitive abdominal wall further back from the position where the leg normally lies is not supported by the false ribs, and has no connection with the abdominal muscles which swing the hind leg forward. Thus the horse's only possible reaction to this signal is to kick against it. The point at which the relevant muscles can be influenced into contracting lies underneath the leg when the latter is in the normal position, that is, just behind the girth. The spur should therefore be applied just behind the girth and, if a lazy, disobedient horse then kicks against this correct aid, it should be backed up with the whip. Despite their inherent usefulness, nothing ruins a horse more, or makes it more stubborn, than too frequent and unnecessary use of the spurs.

Even if we suppose that they are always to be applied correctly there are, nevertheless, cases in which it is not advisable to use spurs, for example, with ticklish mares in heat. Such animals in particular frequently react to tickling spurs (whether applied consciously or unconsciously) by swishing and lashing with their tails. Horses which do this will have little chance of success in competition dressage. Swishing and lashing the tail as a sign of tension is a problem which will keep cropping up throughout the horse's training. A horse which is doing this is not focusing its attention fully on its rider. The whip should be used, instead of the spurs, on horses which are not very forward going, and which swish their tails.

This requirement of swift, unhesitating reaction to the legs is extremely important. It is very difficult to drive a horse forwards when it has learnt, through the apathy of its rider, that it can loiter as it wishes. The habit of disobeying the legs will, however, soon emerge again if the rider is not constantly attentive to the horse's responsiveness to the indications of the legs. This prompt obedience to the legs is a condition of effective correction of all the faults or vices that may have developed as a consequence of ignorant or incompetent training. The willingness to go forwards must be implanted into the horse's subconscious mind to the extent of becoming as irresistible as a reflex. It is not by driving the horse forwards relentlessly with constantly nagging legs that we can obtain this result, but by frequently doing transitions. No other exercises should be considered before we have obtained perfect obedience to the impulsive effect of the legs.

One of the worst consequences of disobedience to the legs is the habit of going behind the bit. A horse that overbends its neck or its poll rather than accepting the contact puts its rider in a position of total ineffectiveness. Communication with the horse's mind through its mouth is completely cut off and no control of speed or direction is then practical. Yet even a willing horse will learn to evade the control of the bit by overbending, if it is subjected to the discomfort produced by heavy or busy hands. Insensitive hands are the surest way of destroying a horse's confidence in its rider. Hands that constantly windlass, bending the neck alternately right and left (see Crookedness page 128), hands pressing down on the reins, rigidly pinched shoulder blades, socks to the mouth of various degrees of brutality, and also severe or incorrectly fitted bits…one or more of these abuses of a horse's mouth will induce the horse to evade contact with the bit. Moreover, the discomfort caused by a badly adjusted bridle that produces irksome pressure on the poll, rubbing or pinching of the cheeks or ears, too tight a throatlatch or noseband can also cause this dangerous evasion.

The horse is behind the bit and the hind legs are disengaged.

It is known, or it should be known, that severe bits are frequently the cause of some of the most dangerous forms of intractability in horses. Therefore, instead of resorting to a stronger bit when a horse pulls or gets out of control, one must always first try to discover the source of the resistance – it could be a disturbing seat or disturbing hands – and try a milder mouthpiece. A thick snaffle is kinder than a thin one; an eggbutt snaffle is less likely to cut the corners of the lips than a loose-ring wire one, but even an eggbutt can become roughened by prolonged use. A rubber jointed snaffle sometimes works wonders. Martingales also are frequently trouble-makers: when they cause a break in the continuity of the line which must run, unbroken by any angle, from the rider's elbow to the horse's mouth, they can increase the strength of the rein tension by a much greater factor than the rider imagines. A very skilful rider is the only one who has the right to resort to a martingale for schooling purposes. I will return to this subject again when talking of horses that go above the bit.

However, if a horse goes behind the bit, it is invariably because a forceful or ignorant rider has destroyed the horse's trust. Flexion of the neck behind the second vertebra, the so-called 'broken neck', is a grave delinquency, and a habit that too many riders have engendered. A horse that has discovered this evasion can run away with its nose tucked into its breast.

(*above*) Correct fitting of snaffle
and German (Hanoverian) dropped
noseband.

The 'broken neck', bent behind the second vertebra.
The rider is gripping and hanging on.

Only the experts can
be trusted with special
mouthpieces; less skilful
riders risk disaster when
they resort to them.

Hackamore.

Double snaffle.

Hackamore and
snaffle with a
coupling.

Mild curb.

Pelham with extra rein and coupling.

Breaking a habit is never easy. In the case of the horse that goes behind the bit, the first thing that must be attended to is the re-establishment of trust in the rider. Having made certain that bit and bridle are comfortable, we must first work the horse on the lunge with very long side-reins, or a loosely adjusted Chambon, until the horse lowers its neck and stretches the muscles above the vertebral column (poles on the ground or cavalletti at their lowest height are a useful aid in this respect). It may need much more than one or two sessions to obtain the desired result, which is the lowering of the neck and the lengthening of the topline at walk, trot and canter. Considerable perseverance is required, but one should not forget that all corrective work amounts to starting the education of the horse all over again from scratch, and no immediate cure exists for long-lasting dereliction of duty. The novice horse needs to develop trust in the rider; the spoilt horse must regain it.

Auxiliary reins may be indispensable, but a good seat and soft hands are the best guarantee of success. Properly adjusted, a martingale is acceptable for hunting and jumping, but a tight martingale is an instrument of torture. Running reins are as dangerous as a razor in the hands of a monkey. An expert knows how to use them to overcome resistance, but never to enforce a collected head carriage. The Chambon and the de Gogue give the horse complete freedom to lengthen and lower its neck. The running reins, often used for training young horses, prevent a

sufficient freedom to lower the neck. The standing martingale is a precaution against dangerous tossing of the head, but also restricts freedom to lower the neck and advance the nose. It is on the whole better to dispense with all contraptions.

(*Reading anti-clockwise from top left*): running martingale; running rein; Chambon; side-reins; standing martingale; pulley martingale; the commanded de Gogue; the independent de Gogue.

It is always better to start the programme of redressing faults by lungeing, because when one is mounted it is easy to wrongly establish a rein tension that would induce the horse to over-arch its neck instead of reaching for the bit. The pace must be fairly brisk, the gait regular, and the horse must be encouraged to go forwards with the aids of whip and voice; and of course it must be praised with a kind word whenever it makes the right gesture. It is only when the desired result has been achieved by work on the lunge that we can resume mounted work, on long reins, hands resting just in front of the withers, trotting on the large circle and over the low cavalletti, still resisting all desire to put the horse 'on the bit'. I repeat, we should not expect quick results. The important thing is regular forward movement; rather more speed than the horse is prepared to produce of its own accord. It may therefore be necessary to go forward into a brisk canter on the straight from time to time instead of continuing to trot endlessly at the same speed on the circle. Even at the canter, the emphasis must remain on forward movement; we can use a light seat, keeping our hands on the horse's neck in front of the withers so that they can remain passive and act like the long side-reins which, of course, have to be taken off for the mounted work.

The frequent changes of gait must prevent the horse being lulled by the monotonous rhythm of the trot or of the circle, but we must not ignore either the hypnotic effect of continuously going *large* on the track. Hence, circles must be interspersed with straight lines, shallow loops and large figures of eight, all ridden in a light, yet forward-driving seat. Before any change of position, the horse must be allowed to straighten itself for one or two strides, since any sudden change of position would disturb the smoothness of the contact achieved. Every endeavour the horse makes to reach for the bit must be praised with the voice and the caress, the *inside hand* temporarily surrendering the contact in order to stroke the mane, and then taking it up again very carefully. All downward transitions must be progressive; that is, canter to walk through one or two trotting strides, canter or trot to halt through a couple of strides at the walk.

As progress is gradually achieved, we can start to ride all the gaits in the full seat, but the pace must remain lively; this will load the hind legs more, but they must maintain their activity. The horse should have become more responsive to the driving aids, and at this stage it is very important to avoid making it work beyond the beginning of fatigue. Hence the spells of vigorous work must be kept short and interrupted by fairly frequent pauses at the halt on a loose rein. Fatigue induces dullness and we want the horse to remain bright and co-operative when it is working. Of course, it must also move straight; going forwards, but falling in on the circles or turning the hindquarters out and refusing to inflex the thoracic spine on the circles, is not sufficient submission. However, crookedness and other forms of resistance to the aids will be dealt with later on.

Hurrying

From dealing with the sluggish horse, I must return to the problem of hurrying. In this case, corrective work must also be preceded by a careful inspection of the tack, for hurrying can be a reaction to mere discomfort, short of pain, inflicted by the saddle or any other part of the tack. If no fault can be found with these, the irregularity may of course be rooted in the horse's temperament, but it is frequently developed by errors in training, or by the carelessness, insensitivity, stiffness or ignorance of the rider.

To start with, the horse must again be taught to stand still during mounting and while the rider adjusts his seat, stirrups, clothes and reins; the horse must not move before being ordered to do so. It is therefore essential to mount carefully, without displacing the saddle by hanging on to the cantle, without nudging the horse with the toe or the knee of the left leg, and to lower oneself very gently into the saddle. An assistant may be needed to keep the saddle in place. He can hold the horse by the cheekpiece of the bridle with his right hand while weighing down the right stirrup with his left hand to counter-balance the weight of the rider. He can quieten the horse with soothing words, but if the horse moves at all he must admonish it with a firm 'No' and a check with the right rein. As always when educating or re-educating a horse, a lot of patience and perseverance are essential. The horse must learn this lesson thoroughly; it will have to be repeated frequently until the habit of standing still is ingrained. We must of course reinforce the acceptance of discipline by rewarding it immediately and generously with a word of praise, a pat on the neck, or even with a lump of sugar or a morsel of bread. We will have scored a very valuable point in the process of gaining mastery of the horse once we have trained it to stand perfectly still until we give it the aid to move on; on the contrary, every advantage gained will be completely thrown away if we allow the horse, be it only once, to move in any direction before being ordered to do so. We know, of course, that when setting out on a hack, or if one rider has to close a gate, it is the height of bad manners to move on before every rider is ready to tell his horse to walk on.

Need I say it again? We must always start the work on a loose or very long rein. Restricting or active hands to enforce a head position will make the horse nervous and provoke it to hurry. Even so, some horses start to hurry as soon as they are allowed to move. In such cases, lungeing may be advisable before starting mounted work. In any case, we should never sit heavily before the horse is completely calm. A correct light seat, that just relieves the middle and weakest part of a horse's back of the full weight of the rider, must be used at the beginning; but we must not stand in the stirrups because we must not overload the forehand either. We can calm the horse by stroking its neck with

(opposite page) Trotting over poles is an excellent exercise for loosening the back muscles of the horse.

one hand and by avoiding riding on straight lines. If changing direction very frequently, circling left and then right, does not stop the hurrying, we can make a tighter volte, or turn several times on the forehand in alternate directions, riding straight on for a stride or two between each turn, to prove whether the correction has produced its intended effect. A stern, admonitory 'No' is uttered each time the horse starts to hurry, and a brief *arrest* (suppression of movement by the combined use of inside spur and rein) is sometimes permissible. We can halt, dismount, repeat the disciplinary process of mounting, or lead the horse in hand around the manège once or twice. Our pupil must be made to understand that there is no cause for excitement and that calm will always be rewarded.

But we must not forget that hurrying at the walk can be caused by a poor seat, by unsympathetic or uncontrolled hands, by tapping or gripping lower legs. If the hurrying has been caused by gripping with the calves and shoving with the seat, it may be advisable to ride for a while with rather more weight on the thighs and stirrups and closer knees. Once the horse is quietened and stops hurrying, the seat bones are loaded and the lower legs resume a gentle, relaxed contact at the girth. The voice can continue to be used soothingly.

A horse that has learnt to stand still while we mount, and to walk calmly, may well continue to go calmly at the trot. However, if it does hurry as soon as it feels that the reins are being adjusted for the trot, it must be returned to the walk, the reins must be loosened, and we will have to repeat the procedure described above. At the trot, we first rise to prescribe a pace slightly slower than the one wanted by the horse; later, we may sit lightly, with some weight on the stirrups, so that we do not yet tax the middle part of the back. This sort of half-seat allows us to delay the contact of our seat bones with the saddle for a fraction of a second after the impact of a hind foot, and to delay also the lifting of this foot. Some horses go better when this very soft seat is used than they do when one rises to the trot. We utilize all the figures of the manège: turns across the school, circles, changes of rein within the circle, shallow loops and serpentines, punctiliously softening the contact, especially with the inside rein, every time the horse lengthens its topline by lowering its head.

It is only when the horse is inured in the habit of trotting calmly in a long outline, with a completely relaxed neck carriage, that we start to canter: we will have to continue to use a light seat and to avoid going on straight lines until all tendency to hurry is quelled. Long periods of cantering should be avoided. Highly-strung horses easily get excited at the canter and will forget obedience. It is therefore better to avoid giving them the opportunity to assert their independence and allow them only short spells in this gait, interspersed with periods of walking on long or loose reins. By cantering with rather more weight on the thighs, with closed knees and less driving with the legs, we can ride slightly 'behind the movement', slowing the movements of the horse by slowing our own movements. We must manage to dictate the timing of the cantering leaps through our seat and by means of brief parades, but with otherwise very quiet hands. As at the trot, the battle can be considered won when our horse canters with a lowered neck and allows us to stroke its mane with our hands in a soothing manner. We will then no longer have to suffer the indignity of being a helpless passenger conveyed willy-nilly by a senseless machine.

There are, however, horses that hurry without going faster, and ram down against the bit to avoid engagement of the hind legs. One cause, amongst others, of this extremely unpleasant habit can be fatigue of the muscles of the hindquarters; in this case, we must keep the working sessions short, at any rate at the beginning of the redressing programme. We should never pull on both reins to try to elevate the neck; it is silly to forget that a horse is stronger than the brawniest of men, and if we try to enter into such an uneven trial of strength, we will find ourselves being taken along at the speed chosen by the horse. Provided that the horse is not increasing its speed, we must ride it onto a circle and deliver a vigorous *arrest* through the combined effect of outside rein and inside spur, thus giving the lout a sharp lesson in good manners. This energetic *arrest* must be repeated every time the horse renews its attempt to get out of control. On the other hand, if the horse increases the speed as it rams against the bit, we will have to go back to square one and teach it to go calmly by using the same method employed to quieten all hurrying horses. It may be necessary to work the horse on the lunge for some time, until it discovers the technique of calm, effective forward movement.

A good seat that allows the undeveloped back muscles of a young or novice horse to work and get stronger. The rider's hands positioned on the withers do not interfere.

The horse is bearing on the hand. The rider is gripping; her legs are ineffective and she is behind the movement.

During the whole period of re-education the horse must never be galloped in company across country. Neither should it be ridden over obstacles before it has learnt respect for its rider.

Crookedness

I am now going to look at the problem of crookedness, since a horse that does not move straight cannot be regarded as being submissive. To start with, we must understand that few, if any, horses move perfectly straight. They have, to varying degrees, an inborn tendency to go forwards with the hindquarters turned to one side, usually the right. Nevertheless, they can also be taught to move crookedly. But whether the tendency is inborn or acquired, it has to be corrected.

The cause of inborn crookedness remains to be completely understood. It more than probably exists before birth; like all mammals, including man, horses have a vertebral column that does not intersect the midline perfectly. Besides this, like humans, horses are more or less pronouncedly left- or right-footed and, consequently, will use one diagonal pair of limbs more vigorously than the other. Whatever the reason, it is a fact that horses have a soft side and a hard side; they will resist inflexion of the poll and ribs to one side and put more tension on the corresponding rein; conversely, the opposite side is only too ready to bend and it is difficult to obtain a sufficient tension of the rein; the horse does not go up to the bit on the hollow or soft side. The contact is then uneven.

It is because most horses are naturally concave to the right that all manuals of horsemanship give instructions that apply to them. A right-sided horse, observed from the rear, will be seen to place its right hind more or less outside the general direction of movement. It is symptomatic that more saliva will usually show on the left side of the horse's mouth than the right; this is because the lower jaw moves more towards the left when the horse chews and this is another reason for the greater tension of the left rein. The consequence of these facts is that the left shoulder of the horse is more loaded than the right, and the muscles of the right side of the neck will not allow themselves to relax sufficiently. The right-sided horse is said to go against the left rein and against the right leg of the rider. This is described by A. Stecken: 'The gaits cannot be regular, the contact cannot be even, the pliancy of poll and hocks cannot be obtained before the horse consents to move straight; it will not be possible either to improve the shock dampening and weight carrying capability of the hind leg joints.'

Many resistances are rooted in this inborn uneven development of the locomotor system; horses instinctively exploit this tendency to evade control by the rider's hands and to flout his orders. Obviously a crooked horse cannot move with pure gaits and will go in crooked fashion on circular as well as straight tracks.

The most striking demonstration of crookedness is afforded by the opportunity to ride on a freshly harrowed sand arena, where there are no guiding walls. We can then discover how very difficult it is to ride a perfectly straight line along the traces made previously when changing the rein or going large. We will also be able to see which is the hind leg that is not stepping in line, but it is on the circles and voltes that the crookedness will be particularly obvious. If these figures are performed with correct inflexion and with perfect regularity in both directions, the imprints of the hind hooves must cover those of the fore hooves when going either clockwise or anti-clockwise.

When we have discovered the extent of the unevenness (mirrors in the corners of the manège can help), we must proceed to straighten the horse. A horse that is concave to the right will canter with the left fore lead until the left pair of limbs starts to tire; at the rising trot, it will spontaneously put the rider on the right fore diagonal; if we let it loose in the manège, we can see that the canter on the left fore lead covers more ground with each leap than the right lead canter. A totally uneducated horse will allow itself to be lunged to the left, but will nearly always turn in to face us or attempt to run away to the left when we try to get it to circle right. A right-sided horse will nearly always run out to the left when refusing to jump an obstacle.

Premature or incompetent efforts towards collection reinforce inborn one-sidedness. The horse will evade the constraint by refusing to move the weaker hind leg in the direction of the centre of gravity; it is a tiresome ploy and a very difficult one to foil. Moreover, the frequent and thoughtless

The only correctly curved horse is the one at the top right part of the circle. The horse at top left is bent in the shape of a letter 'S'.

practice of endlessly trotting along the walls of the manège is another sure way of enhancing natural one-sidedness. The horse's shoulders are narrower than its hips; since an unstraightened horse always attempts to keep the outside of its body parallel to the wall, the narrower shoulders cannot then be placed straight in front of the broader hips. If we ride on the track, particularly to the right, we must always endeavour to bring the shoulders somewhat away from the wall. This is not done by pulling on the inside rein, but by sitting rather more to the right, that is the inside, weighting the inside stirrup more than the outside, and thus getting the right hind to engage under the mass. It is by placing the horse's shoulders in front of the hips that we learn to ride 'from the inside leg into the outside hand'.

Getting a horse to move straight does not guarantee that it will continue to move straight of its own accord, for it is normal for a horse to prefer a less arduous way of going and horses are quick to take advantage of a rider's inattention. Regardless of the rider's degree of proficiency, the horse will discover numerous ways of shirking work and the achievement of constant straightness will remain a test of a rider's patience and ability throughout the working life of the horse. Steinbrecht wrote: 'In every lesson, the natural one-sidedness will continue to cause difficulties, even when it appears to have been corrected. Crookedness is an everlasting curse. Even a very accomplished horse will evidence at times some degree of one-sidedness and this has to be corrected repeatedly by the limbering exercises on circles and two tracks.'

However competently it may be ridden, a horse will never be absolutely straight, and it would be petty to mark down a rider or a horse in a dressage test for one very small deviation from perfect straightness. However, this does not mean that we should let a horse get into the habit of moving crookedly and thus discover how easily it can avoid the engagement of the hind legs and the flexion of the hocks.

Of course, horses can be made even more crooked than normal as a result of incompetent riding, especially, as mentioned, by premature demands for collection. Restricting hands, ineffective legs, a seat that impairs impulsion, wrongly timed parades which affect only the mouth or the neck, and disregard of a horse's fitness for the stress of collected work will always induce the horse to avoid painful effort by turning its hindquarters to one side, although it may already have discovered some other way of resisting unreasonable requirements. The canter of a horse that has got into the habit of striking off into canter in a crooked position will always lack scope. It is a fault that is extremely difficult to correct.

We must now consider methods of righting crooked horses. To start with, it must be stressed that repeatedly giving and taking with the left rein when a horse leans on that hand is useless. It is the whole body that has to be straightened, and the hind legs will therefore have to be controlled. Yet the hands must obviously have an important role to play. Stiffness of the poll and the jaw and stiffness of the spinal column and the hocks are correlated. There are many horses that strongly resist the flexion of the poll and this is how they can effectively resist the flexion of the hocks. These horses can be said to be blatantly disobedient.

There are people who still believe in the wisdom of the old custom of tying a horse up in the stall in side-reins to teach it to chew the bit. This does nothing of the sort. On the contrary, it can only give the horse a first lesson in the art of frustrating the rider. More cleverly, some particularly thoughtful masters of horsemanship, realizing how much the stiffening of the hocks was related to the stiffening of the jaws, devised flexions in-hand, that is from the ground. They often went too far in this direction, but we must realize that the extreme degree of collection and lowering of the hindquarters required by our ancestors is too painful for the modern type of competition horse, which has different conformation from the old type of High School horse. Work in-hand is seldom practised any more and is even strongly censured in many quarters. Nevertheless, the stiffening of the poll and jaws to oppose the flexion of the hocks is a fact that cannot be ignored, and it cannot be corrected by driving the horse 'from behind' into a firm tension of the reins. Part of the difficulty a horse experiences when we ask it to relax its jaws resides in the presence of the parotid glands and the shape of its mandible. The parotid glands bulge more or less prominently on either side of the vertical part of the mandible. If the horse's head is turned left or right, they can be seen to bulge even more. Massage can make them retract between the branches of the mandible and this is the rationale behind the flexions from the ground. I believe that there is nothing wrong in teaching a horse to relax its jaws either from the ground or from the saddle.

The horse cannot be said to be straight if, when asked to move on a straight line, the hind feet do not step on the same tracks as the forefeet. Many factors can contribute to this lack of straightness. Some horses go wide behind and disconnect the trot when the gait is extended. The soles of the hooves show. The fault is sometimes related to the angulation and construction of the distal end of the tibial and the tibio-tarsal bones of the hock.

To this end, we stand in front of the horse that is bridled with a snaffle, and we let the reins hang under the neck. We hold the right rein in the left hand, about 5 cm from the bit ring, the left rein in the same manner with our right hand. The buckle end of the reins is laid over the left rein with about 10 cm of the rein ends hanging over the hand. We then exert a very gentle pressure with both hands on the bars of the mouth and reward the horse – by desisting instantly – as soon as it relaxes at the mouth and the poll. We may slightly vibrate on the bit with one hand, but we never actually move it from side to side. If the horse steps backwards, we get it to step forwards by stepping backwards ourselves. If we cannot get it to stand still, after two or three attempts we will have to make it stand with its tail to the corner of the manège. Then, if the horse still refuses to yield to the bilateral pressure on the bit, we can nevertheless try to get it to flex slightly laterally rather than directly vertically. It will eventually consent to submit, and we must praise it.

Once this result is achieved, we can then try to obtain the lateral inflexion of the poll by moving our right hand, fingernails facing up, a little to the side, and we gently press on the bit. The mane should slide over to this side. This slipping of the mane to one side is the maximum degree of inflexion permissible if the horse is not bent in the ribs. Our left hand, of course, must advance to the same extent as our right hand retracts. When the horse accepts the lateral inflexion, we straighten its head and repeat the same exercise on the other side. It does not usually take very long to get the horse to understand what is required and to submit.

We can then request these inflexions from the saddle. We must sit correctly upright, the loins well braced, with our legs at the girth and, if necessary,

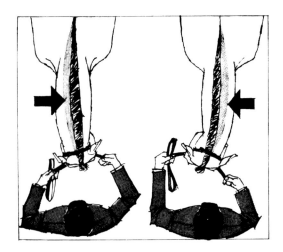

Pulling on the left rein causes the horse to tilt his poll. The ears should be on a horizontal plane.

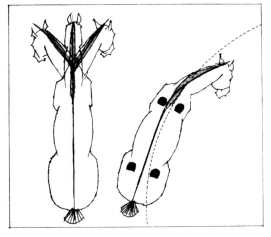

A horse that turns its neck at the withers resists the inflexion of the poll and the ribs.

slightly vibrating our legs; we get the horse to chew the bit as we did from the ground. It would be absolutely wrong to turn the neck by pulling with the arms, to *windlass*. *Windlassing* slackens the muscles which must stabilize the neck at the withers; it does cause the horse to lower its head and neck, but without flexing at the poll. The poll then ceases to be the highest point of the body and the horse's nose gets behind the vertical. Instead of acting on the bars of the mouth, the snaffle pulls on the corners of the mouth and can cut them. *Windlassing* is the expedient of the weak rider.

When a horse resists the inflexion of the poll, we must resist to exactly the same extent, by fixing our hand, bracing our loins firmly, closing the legs at the girth, and thereby making the horse advance towards our passively resisting hands. An energetic upward *arrest*, with one rein only, may sometimes be required, but we must never saw or *windlass* by moving the arms. The upper arms must be kept against the body. This is the only way in which we can feel immediately, and reward absolutely instantly, the slightest sign of understanding and submission, the slight nod that indicates the pliancy of the poll. To draw slightly more on the left rein, it is sufficient to rotate our left forearm so that the palm of our hand is turned upwards. As the tension on both reins must be equal, our right hand must of course give to the same extent as our left hand takes; otherwise we would produce a shortening of the horse's neck and a sideways tilting of its head. The ears must remain on a horizontal plane throughout the process and the inflexion must be only just sufficient to cause the mane to slip to the same side. We do not want to bend the neck. Once the horse has submitted to the lateral inflexion of the head, this is straightened and the position of the hands is reversed. Lateral inflexion of the head to the right is usually easier to obtain because horses do not normally jut the mandible out to the right. If the horse resists too stubbornly, a little vibration of the right rein is permissible, but never an actual backward or downward pull. I repeat that turning the neck at the withers does not make the poll more pliable.

In the case of particularly obstinate resistance, we can resort to leg-yielding and drive the horse on a large volte to get it to relax the tension which it puts on the inside rein by stiffening its hind legs. In all probability, it will only grudgingly yield to the pressure of the left leg, but will run away from that of the right; however it does not need much time to get it to understand what is required.

We next notice that the horse stretches the outside rein instead of pushing against the inside one; we are, in fact, riding on diagonal aids and at last we will understand the meaning of having the horse 'between the legs'. When the head is easily positioned, the inflexion of the spinal column in the thoracic region in response to the increased pressure of the inside leg becomes

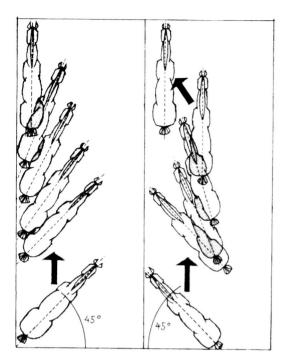

Yielding to the leg: (*left*) inside leg, right hand; (*right*) outside leg, right hand.

progressively easier to obtain as the horse's hocks also become progressively more pliant. On the side of the horse's natural incurvation, the leg may have to be drawn somewhat further back to induce the hind leg to step under the mass; on the opposite side, we must beware especially of pulling backwards because this is bound to cause the horse to tilt its poll.

When a horse has been properly straightened, a rider will be able to maintain his own poise with ease instead of having constantly to struggle to prevent himself from sliding towards the horse's hollow side and tilting his pelvis laterally. The slightest inclination of the horse to revert to its natural incurvation will be felt and corrected immediately. If we want to know whether our horse is straight and allows us to sit with easy poise, we should examine the seat of our breeches and the inner side of our boots. Since most horses tend to hollow their right side, the increased pressure of our left seat bone will leave an impression on the cloth of our breeches and the inside of our left boot will be more worn than that of the right boot. If this is the case, it implies either that we are sitting slackly or that the horse's imbalance is hindering the effortless preservation of our poise. Another sign of a crooked seat or of an unevenly balanced horse is the tendency of one stirrup to slide towards the heel. In either case, the way to correct the fault is to load one stirrup more than the other. This will not only enable us to preserve the stability of our seat; it will also compel the horse to straighten itself. Another way in which we can verify a horse's straightness is by examining the underside of the saddle, or the hair under the saddle, for signs of differential pressure on either side of the spine.

A straight horse is easily directed and positioned on circles, voltes and serpentines. A horse cannot be 'straight' on such figures if its neck is bent to a greater extent than the rest of its body, or if one or the other of its hind feet does not step in the track of its lateral opposite.

Giving the horse a *counterposition* is another ploy which we can use to make the horse straighten itself or to prove its obedience to the leg. Pressure of our outside leg behind the girth must cause a sufficiently educated horse to move its hindquarters away (turn on the forehand). A straight horse should displace its hindquarters as ungrudgingly to the right as to the left. Normally in a turn on the forehand to the right, for example, the horse's head is positioned right as the hindquarters move left. If the turn on the forehand is done in *counterposition*, the head of the horse is inflexed left, as if the horse were watching its tail out of the corner of its left eye. Remember that the inflexion must be strictly limited to the poll; it must be only sufficient to cause the mane to slide over to the left. In this turn on the forehand to the right in *counterposition*, we lean slightly to the right to load our right seat bone; it is wrong to slide over to the right side of the saddle and bend over the left hip. If the horse shows some reluctance to inflex its head left while turning right on the forehand in *counterposition*, we extend our left arm forwards from the shoulder to hold the rein directly above the horse's mouth; our right hand, in the normal position, can impact a light vibration to the rein. This induces the horse to make a swallowing movement with its tongue, which relaxes the muscles resisting the inflexion. As soon as this happens, we must drop our left arm back to its normal position. At a later stage, a mild pressure of our left leg at the girth and a bare hint of elevation of our left hand should suffice to produce the lateral inflexion of the poll. *Counterpositioning* the head on circles, or when riding through corners and on the voltes can get a horse out of the habit of bearing on the left rein. It must, of course, be well understood that riding a horse in *counterposition* is a corrective measure, which may only be resorted to for short periods.

I now come to a peculiar form of crookedness and resistance. A number of horses defend themselves against heavy-handed riders by bending their spine in the shape of the letter 'S'. They yield to the pull on the right rein by turning their head to the right, but at the same time they turn their hindquarters to the left. They are in fact disobedient to the inside and to the outside leg, and are therefore ungovernable. We correct this serious fault by making them yield to the leg; to start with on large circles, then on large voltes, increasing the radius of the circles and also turning around the forehand at the walk in forward movement. It is, however, very important to ride positively forward between each exercise. For example, if the horse goes on a circle right, with a right bend of its neck and a left incurvation of its rib cage (its hindquarters turned to the left), we correct it by placing its shoulders in front of the hindquarters; to do this, we first give the head a position left, and then we direct the horse on a fraction of a left circle. We must repeat this correction as often as necessary. From head to tail, the midline of the horse must conform exactly to the curve of the circular track. Despite the bend of the neck to the right (the usual form of this resistance), it is with our right leg at the girth that we drive the horse on (behind the girth, our leg would cause the hindquarters to turn out). When the horse consents to stretch the right rein every time we impose a position left, we can change the rein and work on the left circle, ensuring that the horse obeys the driving action of our left leg by inflexing its body correctly from head to tail, and we enlarge the circle to ride from our left leg into our right hand. We must eventually get the horse on the diagonal aids and we will then

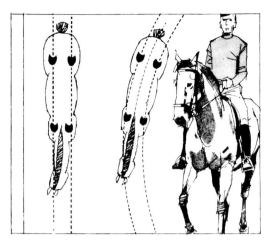

Riding in counterposition is a corrective measure that can be resorted to for short periods only.

be able to obtain smooth changes of position without any alteration of timing when we change the rein within the circle.

It is most unusual to come across a horse that bends in the shape of the letter 'S' on both the circle right and the circle left. In any case, it is always advisable to request a veterinary examination when we experience marked resistance of this form, because it might indicate a congenital and incurable abnormality of vertebrae. It is often pain that induces a horse to resist the aids and the form of resistance just described is usually associated with discomfort or pain. It would be wrong to attempt to correct the fault by coercive measures without trying to discover the source of the trouble, for this would merely intensify the horse's recalcitrance. It would be provoking opposition to try to enforce the left inflexion by pulling on the left rein. The procedure that I have explained above is a ruse that produces the desired result without exasperating the horse. In any case, the 'S'-bent horse is best corrected by unrestricted forward movement with careful changes of direction and rather more insistence on the side of the difficulty. It is only when the faulty curvature has thus been straightened that we can proceed with leg-yielding at walk and trot, although never for more than a few strides. If the horse submits as readily to the left as to the right leg, we can assume that it has been straightened.

One of our primary concerns during basic training is the stability of the base of the neck. The neck must never be turned at the withers. This does not mean, of course, that the neck has to be transformed into a rigid rod, but only that in its entire length it must never be more curved than the rest of the body, and that the latter must be almost equally flexible to right and left. I say almost, because all horses will tend to bend only too easily to one side; absolutely equal suppleness in both directions is not possible. Incorrectly inflexed horses are, of course, impossible to collect, since they resist the rider's hand actions by turning their hindquarters to one side or the other. But, worse than this, in cases of disharmony of wills, they can never be prevailed upon to submit because they will assume a position that enables them to evade the full effect of the aids.

Correction of every difficulty involves a complete return to the most basic schooling, but this process becomes more difficult and complicated when the horse has discovered that it can always frustrate the rider by overbending its neck, either vertically or laterally. Therefore, re-education is always more difficult than education. (In nearly every case, this fault has been produced by a rider who pulls or *windlasses*, thus disregarding the most important principle of horsemanship, which is that manipulations of the mouth are anathema.) Returning to basics signifies the following. Riding forward on straight lines or shallow loops, with our hands just in front of the withers and against the mane so that we do not restrict the movement or turn the neck; all circles to be large, and the corners of the school to be ridden as arcs of a large (20 m) circle, in a properly balanced position and with correct seat aids. The horse must learn to accept seat and leg aids, and in some cases we may have to emphasize the weighting down of one stirrup through a somewhat unrefined seat aid to make the horse obey and inflex itself correctly on the large circles. Riding into the corners and on small voltes to obtain more bending must be strictly avoided until the horse moves in a properly straight position.

In the case of the 'S'-shaped horse, two-track work is definitely prejudicial if the horse has not yet become perfectly obedient to the forward-sideways driving effect of either leg on circles. On no account should the horse be allowed to bend its neck towards the side of the driving leg. It is important to change direction frequently in these leg-yielding exercises and to keep the horse absolutely straight on the straight lines and properly bent throughout its whole body on the circles. When side-stepping can be done without detriment to impulsion and straightness, a very small degree of lateral inflexion at the poll is permissible. It is only when the exercises can be performed fluently at the walk, without hesitation or alteration of regular timing, that they can be practised at the trot. The aim is to obtain all changes of direction in a smooth and well-balanced manner, without ever breaking the continuity of the inflexion from head to tail at the withers. This is what is meant by stability of the neck at the withers.

A further sign of imbalance of the horse is the tilting of the poll, so that one ear is lower than the other. It is a very revealing indication of crookedness, evidenced by many horses in dressage tests of all levels of difficulty. It is indeed surprising that the fault is not pointed out as often as it should be since, in addition to indicating training defects it could, in some cases, signify physical impairment. For example, one would not compete with a horse that had impaired sight in one eye or some trouble in the ears that affected its sense of balance and would cause it to tilt its poll. Another, albeit rare, possibility is that horses with exceptionally widely spaced mandibular rami may experience pain caused by compression of one of the parotid glands. The buckle of the cavesson may also cause discomfort if it presses against the bony part of the mandible instead of resting on the soft part of the cheek.

The rider is pulling on the left rein and causes the horse to tilt its poll.

Where residual crookedness is the cause, it is especially in the right shoulder-in that horses tilt the poll; the right ear is lower than the left and the nose points left. (In the left shoulder-in, on the other hand, the same horses will tend to bend the neck the wrong way and turn the outside hind out.) Tilting the poll is a dodge to avoid stretching the right rein. We can attempt to straighten the horse's head by means of brief tugs on the right rein, with our right hand held a little higher than our left, but we need extraordinarily sensitive hands and an exceptionally good seat to do this without risking serious trouble. On the whole, it is safer to induce the horse to stretch the right rein by driving it with the right leg at the girth in *counterposition* on circles or large voltes, and by placing the forehand in front of the hindquarters as explained earlier. But when the outside ear is the lowered one in the shoulder-in right, it just shows that the rider is pulling. The horse will have to be taught obedience to the outside leg behind the girth without interference by the reins, independently of head position. To start with, we have to use the reins, but if our horse does not yet obey our right leg behind the girth, we must not hold our right hand any higher, but only a little further away from the midline (direct rein to reinforce the lateral driving effect of the leg). Our hand stays in its normal position when the horse obeys fluently the sideways driving indication of the leg behind the girth.

Inability to teach the horse to move straight shows up also in the canter transitions, in the lengthening of the canter and in the transitions from canter to halt on the centre line to salute the dressage judge; the turning out of the hindquarters is a very common fault. It sometimes happens that the rider has been negligent and does not realize how many precious points he is throwing away, but much more often the fault is caused by a bad seat and hence powerlessness. As most horses show a tendency to turn the hindquarters to the right, it is especially in the transitions to right canter on the right rein that the fault is displayed in tests of all levels of difficulty. If the irregularity is allowed to persist, it will become a habit almost impossible to eradicate. A horse will always strike off to canter with its hindquarters turned in if the rider cannot make it engage its inside hind to get it to balance and propel the mass efficiently. After a crooked strike-off, the subsequent strides of the canter will always lack expressive quality and collection will be impossible to achieve.

The irregularity would not become established if we always ensured a straight strike-off to canter either from the trot or from the walk. To start with, we must ride on a circle and enlarge it over one or two strides, thus putting the horse in a very modest degree of shoulder-in (shoulder-fore) position; this will constrain the horse to support our weight properly with its inside hind; we can then give the indication to canter with our inside leg. If we have already acquired a well-balanced and feeling seat, we will be able to sense the precise moment at which our horse can respond to the cantering aid of our inside leg; if we still lack the ability to feel the right moment, we must at least know that the inside leg must act at the moment when the outside hind comes into support, giving the inside hind freedom to swing forward powerfully; we can then be guided by observation of the horse's shoulders.

It is easy to give the horse that shoulder-fore position by enlarging the circle or the volte. On a straight course, we can think shoulder-in before giving the aid to canter. We can do this also when we have to enter the dressage arena at the collected canter. The thought of shoulder-in before the canter strike-off will prevent our horse from starting the canter with its hindquarters turned in and will ensure that it continues to canter straight and that it also halts straight. In the medium or the extended canter, we must keep the horse's shoulders in front of the hind legs by holding them away from the outside track. The forehand is narrower than the croup; therefore a horse cannot be straight if both the shoulders and the croup are parallel to the wall of the school. If the rider cannot use his legs to keep his horse straight, the horse will always lean against the wall with its shoulders, and the rider will never be able to collect the canter. We should also note that the right way to work towards collection of the canter is not the slowing of the working canter. We must educate the horse, through the frequent repetition of straight transitions into canter, to use its hindquarters to carry more weight; this is how we lighten the forehand. The canter must become an 'uphill' gait, on the lightest tension of the reins.

Habitually crooked horses, especially those that are very sensitive to a faulty tension of the reins, often appear to be lame, when in fact they are just *bridle-lame*. They do not stretch the reins evenly and they make a shorter step with one hind foot than with the other. The 'lameness' shows when they are

(*below left*) Crooked transition to canter right; right hind leg is not engaged. The rider is pulling up his right leg and bending at the waist.

(*below right*) Good position and correct aids of the rider. The canter is started out of a slight shoulder-in position and consequently the inside hind leg of the horse can support the weight effectively.

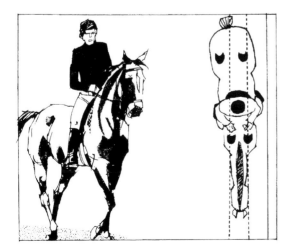

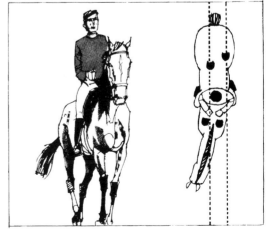

Entrance into the arena at the collected canter always reveals the straight position or otherwise of horse and rider.

trotted with a bit in the mouth and disappears if they are controlled by a halter. Bridle-lameness is an acquired, rider-produced vice, a trick discovered by a horse to evade a heavy-handed rider's attempts to obtain the flexion of the poll; the horse has learnt that it can avoid collection by stepping short with one hind leg. The first symptom of bridle-lameness is the uneven nodding of the head that can make us suspect shoulder-lameness or pain in the back. However, if the horse is lunged without side-reins and with the lunge line attached to the cavesson or halter, and then moves soundly, we can make a diagnosis of bridle-lameness. The bridle-lame horse goes against one rein and behind the other; it can be a sluggish horse or a lively one; it may step short with one foreleg or with one hind leg. The irregularity often develops when a horse is made to perform certain dressage movements before it has learnt to go forwards without being constricted by severe hands; and the lameness may be shown suddenly by a horse that has been trained to perform advanced dressage movements. In fact the bridle-lame horse is vacillating between a longing to hurry and go above the bit and reluctance to go forward. It may move evenly at an extended trot but, if asked to collect itself, it will try to get above the bit, will step short (usually with the right foreleg), and will hover at the collected trot. The only way to correct the fault is to surrender the contact and to ride forwards calmly while paying attention only to the regularity of the gait. We must not think of driving into the bit before we have obtained perfect regularity of the strides. When we take up the reins eventually, the contact will have to be very light and the tension of the reins perfectly even. We will have to regulate the movement as much as possible through our seat rather than our hands.

One other physical manifestation of crookedness is the crooked tail carriage. A crooked tail is nearly always turned the same way as the neck. It is not always a symptom of malformation; like a clamped-down tail, it is very often the mark of an obstinate horse. If the horse carries its tail in a normal manner when made to go at a free gallop, we can discount the possibility of a constitutional defect. But we will have to resign ourselves – as in so many cases – to a return to square one and re-educate the horse from scratch. Unwelcome advice, but there is no other cure.

Finally, regarding the whole problem of straightness, I must invite you to think again about the traditional figures of the manège. They are limbering exercises designed to make horses more pliant and controllable, but they are quite useless if they are not performed correctly. Properly ridden figures of the manège are proof of a horse's straightness. When turning corners and riding voltes, the inside hind must step exactly in the trace of the inside fore and the hindquarters must not be turned outward or inward. This is not an arbitrary rule; it is evidence of correct movement. The best way of checking on this, as we have seen, is to ride the figures on a freshly raked sand surface. Perfectly ridden figures of the manège are the hallmark of the good horseman.

CHAPTER SEVEN

Teaching Acceptance of the Bit

THERE ARE SO FEW TRULY submissive, easily pliable horses, and there is so much to say on the subject. The majority of riders have never experienced the pleasure of riding a pliable horse, a horse that obeys the lightest indication of hands or legs, and that uses the back and hind leg muscles to cushion the rider against the jolts of motion. We know mostly horses that stiffen their jaws and poll, their shoulders, back and hind leg and that will try, in all sorts of ways, to defy our authority. How can we enjoy having to maintain a tiring tension of the reins and a strenuous grip to avoid being tossed by the movement of an unwilling horse? However, a much more important consideration than comfort is safety. If riding is widely believed to be a dangerous sport, it is because horses, in general, are not sufficiently pliable either physically or mentally. If more horses were properly trained, accidents would be rare.

Obstinacy is revealed in various ways and is generally related to excessive tension caused by hasty training, unreasonable demands, the disturbing seat and hands of the rider and other upsetting circumstances. An obstinate horse may bear on the bit, go above the bit, toss its head, put its tongue over the bit or stick it out to one side, pull like a train or even bolt. It is usually said that such horses have a hard mouth.

A number of horses are relatively insensitive to the pressure of the bit on the bars, but a really hard mouth is the result of bad training or bad riding. Nearly all untrained horses try to balance themselves by going with too much weight on the forelegs and using the reins as a fifth leg, but their imbalance should diminish in the course of training as they learn to obey the parades more promptly. However, this is only if the rider uses his aids skilfully and is not too doggedly determined to assert his authority. Psychological insight and cunning are essential qualities for a trainer and, according to circumstances as well as to the disposition of the horse, he may have to resort to various tactics to get his own way without directly opposing the will of the animal.

Underlying principles

A good rider will never presume to correct a hard-mouthed hireling in one session. He knows the futility of the attempt and understands that if correction is at all possible, a long and systematic programme of re-education will be needed. We must remember that long-established bad habits are difficult to eradicate. A horse that has acquired a mouth of iron as a result of the use of more and more severe bits may indeed be totally incorrigible, especially if some fault of conformation predisposes it to go on the forehand. If this is the case, we should not waste time or risk accidents. The horse will never give us

Tension and excitement may cause a horse to go above the bit.

any pleasure and, if the much-abused creature could talk, it would be able to explain that it had never enjoyed the experience of being ridden. Generally speaking, however, a hard mouth is curable, but only by a cool rider with a very good seat.

Therefore, the rider's seat and the co-ordination of his aids may have to be improved before he can think of correcting the horse. Effective aids are inconceivable if the seat is incorrect. This is the first condition. The second is that the rider will have to avoid the canter for a long time, as it is the gait that is most likely to give the horse the opportunity to fight the bit; the walk mostly, then the working trot for short periods, will have to be used perseveringly. I would advise you to read again the passages relating to crookedness and to find out which are the soft and the hard sides of the mouth, that is the hollow and the convex sides of the horse's body. Failure to do this will make the task more difficult for yourself and for your pupil. Moreover – and this may well surprise you – it is on the hollow side that you will have to work first.

In the turn on the forehand at the walk, we must persuade the horse to yield in the mouth and at the poll. The forelimbs must describe a smaller circle than the hindquarters as we get the horse to walk slowly forwards, inflexed only at the poll. We extend our right, inside arm upward, to impart to the rein an almost vertical position; this will induce the horse to make a swallowing movement and to move its lower jaw to chew the bit, while the repeated pressures of our inside leg, driving the inside hind in front of the outside hind, will prevent the horse from using its left hind to push against our left hand. This procedure is especially useful in the case of horses that bore on the bit by going above it, because the inflexion of the poll induces the relaxation of the tightened neck muscles and a lowering of the neck. Nevertheless, the manoeuvre succeeds also with horses that bear down on the bit, since it enables the rider to get the horse to engage his right hand so that it supports the weight better and thus lightens the forehand. It is of course imperative to lower the right hand to a normal position at the very instant the horse yields in the mouth.

Regular repetition of this exercise to both hands, first at the walk, and then at a rather shortened working trot, will soften the tension which the horse puts on the rein and will also teach it to obey the rider's leg. Again, let me remind you that the leg can be obeyed by the horse only on condition that it presses at the appropriate moment, that is when the corresponding hind leg of the horse has ended its supportive and propelling function. Once obedience is established, we will be able to proceed with the corrective work by teaching submission first to the half-parades, next to the full parades from the trot, then to the rein-back, to yielding to the leg on circles and on the diagonal of the manège, and eventually in the two-track movements with general inflexion, shoulder-in, travers and renvers. But I must repeat that none of these exercises will achieve their purpose, the pliancy of the poll and mouth, if the rider does not sit properly; a good, relaxed position is an absolute pre-condition of feeling hands and effective legs.

We must be able to control our reflexes at all times, and it is a good plan to surrender the contact frequently to loosen our shoulders and arms; of course this does not mean that we should never resort to a severe *arrest* when the horse displays blatant disobedience or open rebelliousness. These *arrests* must be executed in an upward direction and be supported by our back and shoulders; anger must never be allowed to surge because calm must be immediately restored as soon as the horse accepts the constraint.

The last thing we should ever employ is a sharper, more severe bit. It may produce temporarily the desired result, but a hard-mouthed horse soon finds out that it can resist the effect of any bit and will become just as obdurate, if not more so, than before – unless the rider is capable of being twice as lenient as he is already. It is advisable, in any case, to examine the bars of the mouth; if they are particularly clean-cut, an eggbutt snaffle or even a jointed rubber one may have to be substituted for the one which may be causing discomfort, annoying the horse and inciting it to resist. Martingales and running reins are absolutely counter-indicated. A hard mouth is not the consequence of insufficient exercise, and it would be a grave mistake to try to cure the horse by tiring it, especially by riding at the speedier gaits. On the other hand, long, quiet hacks in a light seat and trotting over cavalletti, also in a light seat which promotes the lowering of the neck and the rhythmical activity of the back muscles, are helpful exercises.

In teaching the horse to accept the bit, the jaws are not the only part that must loosen; the whole of the muscular system must relax and be rid of unnecessary tension. We must never start driving with the seat to the hands before total calm is assured. Even so, as soon as the mild activity of the jaw ceases, or degenerates into a grinding of the teeth, we must immediately recognize that something has gone wrong and allow a pause. No horse can be expected to remain constantly attentive to the rider, or to chew the bit when fatigue sets in and causes aching of many important muscles. A true horseman enjoys peaceful riding and can see no merit in over-exerting himself or his horse; powerful driving aids should never be used in the early stages of training. Hence, the good rider will frequently lighten the tension on the reins by slightly advancing one hand or both, just to verify the leniency of the contact and the relaxation of mouth and poll. Amiable communication with the horse through the reins must persist throughout all stages of training; it is the quintessence of good riding.

Horses that move in horizontal equilibrium do not weigh on the rider's hands. Badly balanced horses, on the contrary, attempt to find a 'fifth leg' in the form of a strong tension of the reins. This is not always a consequence of bad riding for it can be the result of defective conformation or a difficult temperament. Horses with too high a croup, with weak hind legs and consequently deficient carrying power (a frequent defect of mares), tend to lean on the hands. Yet powerful hindquarters linked to a weak forehand and an upright shoulder also cause balancing difficulties. The amount of tension put on the reins by the horse varies with each individual. The better the balance, the lighter the tension will be. Conversely, however, a light tension fosters the attainment of horizontal balance. Straight hind legs with insufficient angulation of all the hind joints predispose a horse to put too much weight on its forelegs, especially when age increases the stiffness of the joints. The extent to which balance can be improved must obviously depend on the degree of the fault of conformation. But even a horse with an unfavourable conformation must not be allowed either to roll along at the trot with most of its weight on the forehand, or to seek a prop on the hands. Provided the beat is regular – and at the beginning one may have to trot on circles only, the working trot being the most appropriate gait – it is fairly easy to get the horse to relax its neck muscles and to lower its neck if one frequently loosens the tension of the inside rein by advancing the hand, while continuing to drive with an active inside leg and a light pressure of the outside guarding leg. We must change direction frequently, indicating the change of position clearly; we will turn about the forehand in movement, make the horse enlarge the circle by yielding to the pressure of our inside leg, and also practise all the exercises in *counterposition*.

The tension of the reins cannot be equal when a horse is unevenly balanced, but it is on the hollow side that we start the corrective work, because this is the side of the lazy hind leg, which neither propels nor supports adequately. It may even be necessary sometimes to exaggerate the lateral position of the head – but only temporarily to overcome a particular difficulty – the action of the hand being always supported of course by the *activity* of the inside leg. Our main concern is the development of the strength of the horse's weak hind leg, but if we do not change the rein frequently, we will provoke resistance caused by fatigue and stiffness. Work along these lines should produce relaxation of the cramped neck muscles, and we can then proceed carefully with the gymnastic exercises designed to increase the flexibility of the hocks; due regard must of course be given to the limits imposed by conformation.

I have been describing a programme of correction for the horse that resists the hand by going above the bit. Yet again, wrong training, bad riding or the horse's temperament may induce it to bear down on the bit and thus defeat the rider with a weak seat who tries to limit the speed by hanging onto the reins. Nonetheless, the corrective work is essentially the same as described above. However, it should be obvious that when a horse bears down on the hand it must be taught to engage its hind legs without being encouraged to lower its head and neck. It is effective use of legs and seat that is required to cure the fault, but this does not mean that one constantly assaults the horse with legs and spurs or pelvic convolutions, while restricting the forward movement with set hands. Determined application of the spurs once or twice and a sharp *arrest* must occasionally be used to convince the horse of the error of its ways; otherwise, broadly speaking, the strategy is the same as the one outlined above. It is always by riding 'forwards' that we put the horse on the bit and on the legs.

The rider is gripping and hanging on. The horse is propping itself on the reins.

The impact of gait irregularities

Imbalance and uneven tension of the reins, which effectively prevent complete acceptance of the bit, can be caused by other irregularities of the trot or the canter. These have to be understood and corrected before the horse can be said to go properly 'on the bit'. We have already examined the irregularities of the walk: ambling, jogging and hurrying. The trot, however, is also impure if a hind foot or a forefoot impact later than its diagonal opposite. Usually this happens when a rider has attempted to enforce collection before sufficiently developing the carrying capability of the hind legs, or has tried to lighten the forehand by actively elevating the neck, thus preventing the relaxed activity of the back muscles and breaking the connection between hindquarters and mouth.

It is when the speed of the trot has to be increased to a medium trot that the gait will be seen to become disconnected if the horse has not been properly trained to use its back muscles. It hurries instead of lengthening its strides; it can be observed from the rear to go wide behind, with stiffened hocks, and to show the soles of its hooves. Alternatively, it may clack (forge) when urged on, because its hind foot is coming down before its forefoot is out of the way. The horse is then said to 'hurry behind'. This clacking is often heard at competitions when rain-soaked ground has become poached or pitted with the hooves of the many participants, and the bad going emphasizes any flaws in equine movement.

Horses that disconnect their trot must never be driven into a speedy trot before their topline has been lengthened; their back and shoulders loosened so that their forelimbs can make more ample gestures. And the first thing to attend to is the perfect regularity of the beat. Relative elevation, that is, a lowering of the hindquarters rather than an active elevation of the neck, results from flexion of all the joints of the hindquarters; this is what lightens the forehand, frees the shoulders, cadences the trot and expands the gestures of the forelimbs. Although the cure depends on the competence of the rider, injuries caused by overreaching, and the unpleasant clacking noise can, in the meantime, be minimized by a good farrier.

When the general attitude of the horse at the working trot has been improved and the beat has become perfectly regular, one of the best exercises for developing the elasticity of the hind joints and a correct lengthening of the strides is the transition from shoulder-in to medium trot on the diagonal; but riding on circles at a quickened working trot, and occasionally increasing the speed by lengthening the strides is equally beneficial. This is how we proceed:

Disconnected trot, hurried in front. The hind leg will have to alight too soon because the foreleg of the same side is picked up too early.

(*below*) Disconnected trot, hurried behind. The left hock is snatched up too soon, causing the left foreleg to support all the weight.

after a half-parade, with a firmly guarding outside leg, we drive the horse forwards on a tangent of the large circle towards the next point of the circle,
where we engage the hocks by means of another half-parade, to turn the horse
about the hindquarters, and proceed to the next point on the circle. It is of the
utmost importance to prevent the turning out of the hindquarters in the
change of direction; hence the importance of obedience to the outside leg
behind the girth. The turning out of the hindquarters would defeat our object,
which is the lightening of the shoulders through the increased flexion of the
hocks. These repeated changes of speed and direction will increase the horse's
responsiveness to the aids and deprive it of the possibility of hurrying and
trotting disconnectedly. At this point of training, it would be a grave mistake
to increase the speed on the long sides of the school, but we may occasionally
verify the horse's obedience to the driving aids by lengthening one or two of
the strides along the short sides. It is only when the horse has become sufficiently compliant to legs, seat and hands that we can think of increasing the
speed on the long sides, although we must be prudent and avoid doing so
immediately after turning out of the corner; until the improved balance is
confirmed, it is preferable to ask for medium trot in the second half of the long
side, as we approach a corner.

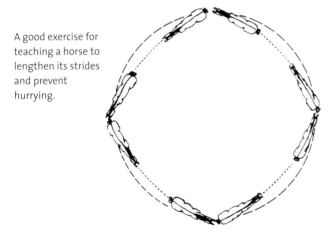

A good exercise for teaching a horse to lengthen its strides and prevent hurrying.

Still another form of a faulty trot with insufficient scope is shown by
horses that throw the forelegs stiffly from the elbow at the extended trot and
hover in the collected trot. Just like the irregularity described above, it is a sign
of excessive tension of the spinal and related muscles of the trunk. The
muscles of the trunk, or mass muscles, which must function equally as shock-
absorbers and locomotive agents, do not work with sufficient elasticity; that is,
they do not allow themselves to be sufficiently lengthened and, consequently,
do not shorten efficiently either. These horses move the shanks from the stifle
or the elbow, and in Germany we call them *shankmovers*.

Shankmovers are produced by insufficient attention to relaxation and calm, and excessive demands in the early stages of their training. (Excitable Thoroughbreds that have been held in by jockeys during their racing training are prone to display this action.) Thus, while it is the weakness of those mass muscles that causes the horse to stiffen the joints of the hindquarters, this form of movement often results from the horse being psychologically as well as physically constrained. The rigidly tensed back makes it impossible for the rider to sit easily to the movement, and so he pulls himself down into the saddle by tightening his hamstrings. Conversely, the cramped, forced seat of the rider aggravates the horse's discomfort and causes it to tense its back even more; thus a vicious circle is established.

The way of curing the fault, and there is no other one, is to attend to free forward movement in perfect rhythm, stepping over cavalletti, quiet hacking and riding over undulating ground in a light, back-relieving seat and sitting to the trot as little as possible. All attempts at collection must be relinquished. The rider must discipline himself. When this return to basics has produced an entirely satisfactory result, the demands on the hindquarters can be increased, but always with lenient hands and a soft, easy seat.

We can now study the irregularity of the canter and learn to understand why a four-beat canter is a disconnected canter. It may be a natural ungainliness which is impossible to correct, but the four-time canter is often rider-produced, that is by restricting hands, ineffective legs and stiff hips and loins. It is always wrong to attempt to teach the horse to collect the canter by slowing the working canter. We must start the work of collecting the canter by frequently repeating transitions from the walk or the collected trot into canter, while paying great attention to the straightness of the horse's position prior to driving it forwards. Transitions from medium canter to working canter are also preferable to a slowing down of the working canter, but even then, we must avoid destroying impulsion by shortening the period of suspension, that is executing the half-parades during this phase of the movement. Driving forwards on the circle is another effective procedure. In fact, the horse must learn to collect itself.

Nodding of the head at the collected canter is another fault that reveals the stiffening of the back muscles. Thick-necked horses with a badly coupled head cannot produce a graceful canter, and this defect can be aggravated by a neck that is too low at its base of attachment to the thoracic spinal column. Horses with this sort of unfavourable conformation tend to go above the bit. It can be an acquired fault, or a natural one that should have been corrected as far as possible during the early stages of training; it is also frequently related to weakness of the back, which makes weight bearing uncomfortable, if not actually painful.

Nothing, of course, can be done to alter the shape of the lower jaw, but the poll can be made more supple and the mouth softer by resorting to all

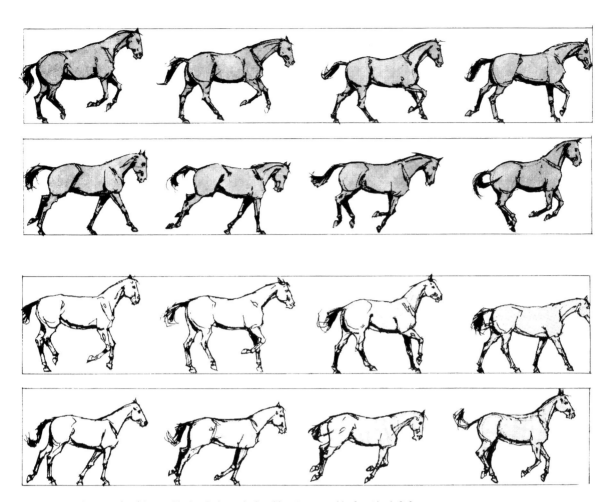

Disconnected canter: (*top*) hurried behind; the right hind has impacted before the left fore;
(*bottom*) hurried in front; the left fore has impacted before the right hind.

Flexions from the
ground to teach the
horse to chew the bit.

the exercises explained above. Hand massage of the parotid glands and work in-hand may help, but there is, obviously, no remedy for very bad conformation.

Horses that go above the bit

Apart from faulty conformation, stiffening of the back muscles for any reason will make a horse go above the bit. Work on the lunge before riding may be beneficial. The essential thing is to get the horse to lower its head and neck so that the tightened back muscles can lengthen. In this case, a position of the head very slightly behind the vertical is acceptable in the early stages of the corrective work, but still the most important thing is easy forward movement, and for this, soft and steady hands are essential. The lowering of the head and neck relieves the back muscles of the effort of supporting the weight of the rider; they can then fulfil their proper function, participate in the general movement, and hence become stronger.

When I am asked to ride a horse with a conformation that makes me suspect that it is an inveterate 'star-gazer', I first sit still and observe its reaction. Then I make the horse walk and I go quietly with its movement without urging it on with pressing legs and seat. If possible, I will not even establish a rein contact. If the horse raises its head when I adjust the reins to a light contact, I preserve the lightness of the contact and let it go at the trot, but sit lightly. I will ride on a circle, usually to the right, since the right side is nearly always the soft side. Maintaining the very light contact with my inside hand and inflexion of the poll to the inside, I will enlarge the circle with my inside leg at the girth.

I may have to wait a very long time for the first sign of submission, the lowering of the neck, but as soon as it shows I allow the horse to move on a straight line, and press on a little to lengthen the stride. If the horse again comes above the bit, I return to the circle and use firm pressures of my inside leg to make the horse lengthen its stride and start to stretch the inside rein. This is the time to change the rein and to ride in the same way in the opposite direction, alternately rising to the trot and sitting very lightly. I will not ride on straight lines for a long time. Eventually, the circle can be decreased somewhat. This is the right way to induce the lowering of the neck; we should never enforce it by pressing our inside hand down. On the contrary, our inside hand may have to be held rather high while our inside leg increases its pressures until the horse gives up its resistance and drops its nose; our hand must then also drop immediately to a normal position.

It would be senseless to ride straight lines, especially along the walls. It is only on circles and fairly large voltes that we can use our inside leg effectively.

We can also get the horse to relax at the halt, but we must not make it rein-back, nor lower its head by sawing or *windlassing* with our arms. We merely give a slight inflexion to the head with a more or less elevated hand position, and vibrate mainly the inside leg; the other leg need not, however, remain completely inactive. The slightest sign of submission must be generously rewarded. Consistent work in this manner should obtain some progress in the right direction and get the horse to grasp the notion of what is correct and what is incorrect.

Once the tightened neck and back muscles are properly relaxed, we can proceed with the usual gymnastic development of the elasticity of the hindquarters. Our hands will always have to be extremely soft and sensitive, and we must eventually succeed in obtaining the relaxation of poll and jaws merely through a careful bracing of the loins and a gentle pressure of the legs. Horses that go above the bit are in fact very tender-mouthed, and they will occasionally get behind the bit. However, when this happens, we will have gained so much experience and confidence that we will instinctively utilize the event to drive the horse forwards into a lengthened trot or even into a canter on a large circle.

Riders of horses that get above the bit nearly always resort to one or another of the auxiliary reins: side-reins, running or standing martingales, running reins or the Chambon, although, as Seunig says, 'the best auxiliaries are soft, steady, unconstricting hands and a soft but effective seat'. The running martin-gale, in the wrong hands and adjusted too tightly, increases the pressure on the bars of the mouth; the slightest hand fault is therefore greatly aggravated and the horse's dislike of the bit will be increased. The rider may have sufficient feel and intelligence to detect a loss of rhythm, a tightening of the back muscles, a slackening of the contact, and will detect the source of the disturbance; why

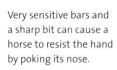

Very sensitive bars and a sharp bit can cause a horse to resist the hand by poking its nose.

then does he use the martingale? He will succeed just as well without it. As regards the running rein, its purpose is not to impose a correct head position in the hope of obtaining collection; expertly used, it can be of some corrective use, but in the wrong hands it is as dangerous as a razor in the hands of a monkey. I think that the Chambon, loosely adjusted, is the most useful of all these gadgets. It automatically induces the horse to lower its nose if it lifts it up too high, and a less than very skilful rider is not therefore tempted to act in the wrong manner. Side-reins are most objectionable because they do not allow the horse to stretch its top muscles as much as necessary.

Other evasions of the hand

Further to the need for sensitive hands, we should consider the bad habit of the horse which opens its mouth. Although this can, occasionally be a defiant attempt by the horse to wrest control, it is far more commonly a rider-induced problem. One way for a horse to evade the action of a hard hand is to open its mouth wide, and it will do so especially if it has not learnt to flex at the poll. A non-elastic hand is usually the starting point of the trouble. The liaison between the driving and the restraining aids is broken, and often the horse is also stiff in its quarters and rigid in its back. The best way to combat this is by reviewing and developing the horse's *durchlässigkeit* (suppleness), and by performing lots of transitions from one gait to another. Particularly recommended are flowing transitions from canter to trot and transitions from trot to walk and straight back to trot. The reins are held elastically, with the joints of the hands absorbing the movement. If the horse sets itself against one rein, the rein is immediately vibrated. Transitions from working trot to medium trot and vice versa are also good, as are the same exercises in canter – particularly on a circle, and with frequent changes of rein. If opening the mouth is not accompanied by other symptoms, tightening the drop noseband will help. A Flash noseband is particularly recommended because it does not make it so easy for the horse to open its mouth.

As with opening the mouth, head-shaking or tossing is occasionally a sign of temperamental insubordination, and it may also indicate pain from ill-fitting tack (such as a pinching saddle or over-tight browband) or dental problems (which require veterinary investigation). More commonly, however, it is rider-produced, although the present owner may have acquired the difficulty at the same time as acquiring the horse. However, even if our own seat and hands were not the original cause of the resistance, if we are not to resort to a martingale for ever, we will have to return to basics and to all the exercises that loosen the back and neck. In any case, the first condition of successful correction is a good seat, and of course light hands. The second condition is patience; the horse's trust in the hands has to be restored, and it cannot be restored if punishment is inflicted in the form of a sock in the mouth. Very soft hands, a very soft seat and a great amount of tact are going to be needed. Since severe parades have to be avoided, the voice should be used as much as possible either to calm or to stimulate, especially if the horse is rather hot-tempered. A brief prod with the spurs at the moment the horse tosses its head is better than any form of punishment by the hands, but we must remember that, like all punishment, punishment by the spurs has to be instantaneous, unexpected and consistent. Eventually, the threat of the spur must suffice to convince the horse that its bad behaviour cannot be tolerated. This is not to say that the lesson will be remembered in the excitement of hunting or competition. In those circumstances, it is of course prudent to use a *properly adjusted* martingale.

A tight running martingale with a short-cheeked curb bit is an instrument of torture. Notice the wide-open mouth of the horse and the anguished expression of its eyes.

Nose-diving, to wrench the reins out of the hands, is just another form of instinctive defence against heavy hands. It is a vice usually associated with general constraint, a stiff or slack back, or a feeling of imbalance. Need I say again that the first thing that may require attention is our seat or our hands? Restricting hands, employed to enforce a painful or uncomfortable head position, prevent a horse from finding out how it must balance the weight of the rider. Many dressage tests therefore require a surrendering of the contact, not only at the halt and the walk, but also at trot and canter. This is to discern the quality of the training and show up any irregularities of gait or general constraint.

It must be said, however, that some horses are truly perverse. When allowed to 'chew the reins out of the hand', they start by lowering their head and neck deceitfully, then suddenly wrench the reins from the hands. In this particular case, a strict *arrest* with the spurs and one rein (in an upward direction) is justifiable punishment. We must always be consistent, and so the punishment has to be administered with utmost promptitude every time the horse repeats this show of independence, until it is properly subdued. The rein-back is an exercise that can be used to improve the pliancy of poll and hocks and also to punish obstinate resistance.

The most dangerous form of obstinate resistance to the aids is grudging obedience to the parades, or total disobedience to control by the hands. Riding a horse that stubbornly fights the bit is as frightening as being at the wheel of a juggernaut rolling downhill when its brakes have failed. Before we dare to risk our life and limbs by riding these wayward creatures, we must make them pliable. To start with, we can practise the work from the ground as previously described (see pages 131–2). Much will have been gained if we obtain some degree of relaxation of poll and mouth. In the mounted work, we must ride as much as possible on circles and do all downward transitions progressively, using a light seat. However, since the horse that fights the bit is not an inexperienced remount, easily confused by the simultaneous use of legs and hands as an order to stop, we can use our legs calmly with a backward pressure to make the horse understand that we want it to slow down. The transitions must be practised first from the walk to the halt, then from the trot to the walk, but we will have to refrain from cantering until the half-parades are equably obeyed. Of course, the horse must never be allowed to hurry, and we may well have to correct our seat. We should learn to brace the small of our back if we have not yet discovered the power of this aid, because we must not hesitate to use all our aids energetically if the horse is frankly mulish, but we must never pull backwards and never press the hands down. In those very special circumstances, we may use a severe and completely unrefined punishment with one rein, giving the horse a shock by jerking up on the bit, fingernails of the acting hand facing up, back and shoulders well braced. This rough *arrest* must be preceded by a brief, punishing prod with both spurs.

We can also punish the horse by making it step backwards once or twice. If it refuses to comply, it cannot be considered to be ignorant; the rein-back is a lesson that the horse must surely have had at some time. Refusing to step backwards is a sign of blatant defiance; a really rebellious horse may rear rather than consent to make one backward step. We must of course eliminate the possibility of physical disorder, such as, for example, the condition known as

The rider is pressing his hands down; the horse is resisting the hard pressure on the bars of the mouth and goes above the bit.

shivering; however a sound horse does not find the rein-back a painful movement. Nevertheless, trying to force the horse to rein-back by pulling on the mouth certainly does cause pain, provokes resentment and can damage the joints. Therefore, if the horse refuses to move, we must make it turn on the forehand, towards its hollow side first. We may at this stage unload the hind leg by leaning very slightly forwards, and also somewhat shorten the rein on the side of the forefoot around which the turn must be made. This should induce the horse to make a short backward step with the hind foot that has been lifted. We will thus have scored the first point to our advantage, and we must be generous and reward the horse immediately. We must not forget that we must use our inside leg to detach the hind leg from the ground; the horse cannot displace its hindquarters before it has lifted a hind foot. The exercise will have to be repeated frequently, but the horse must be allowed to step forwards as soon as it has made this single step. A correct rein-back may not be painful; it is nevertheless a fairly strenuous exercise.

An assistant on the ground can be very useful. We know that the rein-back is a movement in more or less perfect diagonals; a horse cannot rein-back from the halt unless it is standing square; it cannot lift up a hind leg if the opposite one is either turned out or left behind and is not supporting weight. Neither can the horse step backwards if it is standing like a saw-bench, with all four legs straddling. These are things that our assistant can see. Then, as we incline our trunk slightly forward (a permissible position at this stage), the assistant can tap each knee of the horse alternately with the whip, and we support his action with one hand, then the other. Our lower leg presses backwards, about 10 cm behind the girth. No more than two or three steps should be demanded before allowing the horse to move forwards to the place where the exercise was commenced. We then halt, reward, go forwards another step or two and repeat the procedure. We can also utter clearly the command 'Back'. Exceptionally stubborn horses do exist and they may show their wayward behaviour by beginning to rear or by rearing frankly, in which case we must not hesitate to send them forwards by means of a very sharp punishment with the spur precisely at the moment when their forelegs come down. Holding one hand up, we force the horse to do the *mill* (recommended for the correction of jogging) and at the same time we use our legs to try to make the horse step backwards. The extreme inflexion induced by the *mill* completely thwarts any attempt to rear. The rein-back will not be correct, because the correct movement must be straight, but at this time, we need not bother about straightness. All that matters is understanding and obedience. When this is obtained, little difficulty will be experienced in obtaining a straight rein-back. Our assistant can also help by using the reins or pressing on the horse's nasal bone. Should the horse run backwards, or step backwards with disconnected diagonals, we must be content with one, or at the most two steps, and advance calmly one or two steps, then repeat the exercise, not neglecting the calming aid of our voice. But if the horse persists in running backwards, we must punish it by forcing it to step backwards even faster, leaning slightly forward and using the right and left reins alternately on the side of the foreleg that is picked up. After going backwards for one or two horse-lengths, we firmly brace the small of the back, lean backwards and use both our legs or even the spurs to send the horse forwards on a loose rein; in this manner, we cannot confuse it.

The scheme which I have just explained is a corrective measure. When we have succeeded in destroying the opposition, we must proceed to teach the correct rein-back. There are many riders who do not know that the rein-back must remain a forward movement, in the sense that it is obedience to the command of the legs telling the horse to go forwards; however, as soon as the horse has detached a diagonal pair of limbs from the ground, instead of yielding with our hands, we resist, and at this stage, we remain perfectly upright; the lower legs, acting slightly behind their normal position at the girth, determine the number of steps required. The degree of compliance which we have obtained must never be allowed to lapse. We may not be able to improve on it, in fact we may not need to if we are not contemplating a dressage test in which up to six steps may be required, but if the horse shows the slightest sign of disobedience to the parade, our reaction must be immediate; if submission is not absolutely unconditional, riding is indeed a very dangerous sport. However, slavish subjugation should not be expected; even highly trained dressage horses have an occasional whim and will need to be reminded that the rider is always the boss. Every rider must feel that he is the one in control.

Pulling backwards is not the correct way of getting a horse to step backwards.

To follow on from this theme, obstinate disobedience to the hands is shown by horses that pull. Pulling is an unnerving vice that can completely destroy the pleasure of hacking, hunting or competing in horse trials. The pulling horse eventually exhausts the rider, who can then do nothing else than allow himself to be carried away like a dead body; he can hardly be called a rider. Pulling horses are not totally unmanageable; they remain steerable but take such a strong hold on the bit that the most energetic parades make little if any impression on them. The vice is often temperamentally conditioned and it is then extremely difficult to eradicate, especially when – as is often the case – it is associated with a ewe-neck, weak or hollow back or weak hind legs.

Pulling horses bear downwards on the bit, seeking a 'fifth leg' from the reins. The tendency is not invariably innate, as a horse may pull when ridden by a heavy-handed rider and behave himself for a softer-handed one. In fact one can quickly transform a horse that tends to lean on the hand into a confirmed puller. Provided that an exceptionally difficult temperament or a gross fault of conformation, that makes it impossible for a horse to control itself at the gallop, is not at the root of the fault, the habit can be corrected. However, it must be clearly understood that a pulling horse cannot be controlled by a rider who hangs on to the reins or by a more severe mouthpiece. Both aggravate the resistance. If we tried, for example, to use a curb with long branches, a high port and a tight curb chain to control a hard-mouthed horse, far from curing the vice we would run the risk of converting the pulling horse into a senseless, panic-driven bolter. We will, therefore, have to go back to basics. The horse will have to be taught obedience to the legs and hands and will have to learn to move in horizontal balance, these corrections being implemented according to the procedures described earlier in this chapter, which I need not repeat here.

The periods of schooling must never be protracted; they will have to be carried out first in the manège, then in a larger but still enclosed place and finally, if possible, in a field. When we have obtained perfect submission to the aids at the slow gaits, we can canter on a circle (not too large a one to start with), using a light but effective driving seat which will enable the horse to use its back muscles efficiently for balance and propulsion. We rest our hands on either side of the mane, just in front of the withers; our wrists must remain pliable and we must always be disposed to soften the tension of the reins by advancing our hands in the direction of the mouth. When we are sure that the horse is cantering calmly, we enlarge the circle prudently and increase the speed for a while to that of a training 'canter', riding in a light 'jumping seat'. Our legs, resting against the horse's sides, play an important role in regulating the tempo. If the horse starts to get excited and to hurry, we decrease the circle and reduce the speed progressively. Eventually, we must be able to sit to the calm, free-moving canter and the horse must learn to move in self-carriage without weighing down on our hands. Periods of rest at the walk must not be disregarded; we do not want the horse to get tired and get out of balance because of fatigue and stiffness of the back and hindquarters, and during these intervals at the walk the reins must be as long as practical. To either hand, the horse must remain calm and must not attempt to go faster than we wish; better that he should go a little more slowly and have to be driven onwards. We can make a 'bridge' with the reins; this will help us to keep our hands quietly on the mane. (In 'bridging' the reins the left rein is crossed over the withers to the right side, and the right rein to the left side, so that the reins are held in the normal position, but each hand holds both reins. This ensures that the hands – – which are both held at the same height – have a steady, firm grip, and that the action of the reins is 'quiet', and not backward.) All downward transitions must be performed most carefully, with hands as prompt to yield as to resist. The milder the mouthpiece the better, and a jointed rubber snaffle, with a Flash or Grakle noseband, should be tried. If we have to tighten the noseband somewhat, it must never be to the extent of impeding the breathing, for this can make a horse panic. While a Flash or Grakle are less likely to pinch the nostrils than a Hanoverian noseband, even these can upset the animal if they are fitted too low.

Cantering in a 'jumping seat' with the small of the back 'tightened' slightly relieves the horse's back of weight and allows it to swing. The hands lie on the crest and have a 'yielding tendency'. The lower legs should lie lightly but positively against the horse's sides. The canter strides should cover plenty of ground. A horse which is pulled together from the front and not ridden from behind will not be capable of covering the ground.

Some strong pullers are, in fact, much less headstrong when the control of the head is achieved by a hackamore rather than a bit, and there is absolutely no objection to its use for hunting or show-jumping. During the period of re-education we ought in any case to avoid the exciting influence of a crowded field or riding-in area at competitions. (Young and inexperienced horses should be accustomed systematically to activities such as hunting, in order that they do not develop bad habits such as 'taking off' through becoming

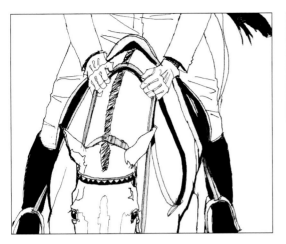

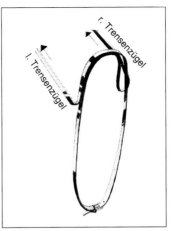

Making a 'bridge' is a good way of keeping the rider's hands steady and at the same time giving him some security. Moreover, the feeling of the hands against the sides of the withers has a calming effect on the horse.

over-excited.) When we go hacking, we should never be accompanied by more than two or three riders. They must be willing to keep the speed within safe limits and to be considerate, and also to let us find out if our horse behaves better at the head or the rear of the group. If we come to a field where we can gallop, we ought to trot for a while and order the canter rather later than the horses expect; since they will sense the impatience of their riders, we must be wary of tensing ourselves. If a wood has to be traversed, it is when approaching it that one gallops and not on the way out; this is contrary to the instinct of the horse, which is to enter wooded terrain with caution and leave it as quickly as possible.

The habit of hanging on to the reins can easily turn a pulling horse into a manic bolter. In contrast with the puller, however, the bolting horse breaks away by throwing its head up and is then absolutely impossible to control. If

A passenger transported by a pulling horse.

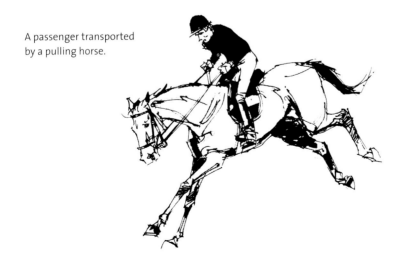

this happens on a straight road, the rider is in a dreadful predicament. We can thank our lucky stars if the horse bolts in a wide-open space, as we may be able to turn its head to one side so that we can guide it on to a circle that we gradually decrease in size until we bring the horse back under control. We are more likely to succeed if we pull the horse's head to its concave side, this being the side on which it is less likely to resist. On a narrow path, this is obviously quite impractical. We can then try to take a very short hold on the reins and lift up our hands to the level of the horse's ears, so that we can give it a truly violent wrench against the corners of its mouth: all niceties have to be forgotten in these circumstances. If location permits us to do so safely, driving the horse even more forwards, on a light contact, may both serve to tire it and get it back onto the aids. Regarding the rider's posture, this will depend to some extent on the manner in which the horse 'takes off', but in all circumstances the very worst thing would be to lean backwards with legs outstretched and hang on to the reins, since this position reduces the rider to the role of helpless passenger. Simply sawing at the bit will make a bolting horse panic even more, and

Sawing at the mouth makes a bolting horse panic even more.

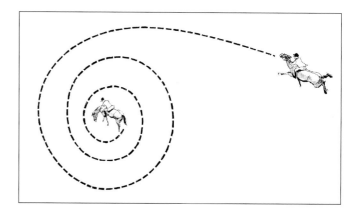

Where circumstances permit, a horse which goes out of control should be ridden on a spiral-shaped track to bring it to a halt.

merely pressing the hands down, in the absence of any postural adaptation, is absolutely useless.

In the case of the horse which threatens to 'take off' through excitement, raising the horse's head very high, combined with energetic use of the seat and legs ('sitting into the horse'), can serve both as a preventative measure and, provided that the horse does not get 'first run' on the rider, to bring it back onto the aids. However, a horse which 'takes off' in a panic usually does so with its head in the air and its back hollow. In this case, the rider should try to lower the head by adopting a correct, light 'jumping seat', with legs in support against the horse, and by keeping his hands relatively low and as light as is practical. As a general rule, in maintaining control of horses thought likely to 'take off', it can be helpful to hold the hands at the same level as the horse's mouth, in keeping with the well-known rule: the higher the horse's head, the higher the rider's hand, and the lower the horse's head, the lower the hand.

This is the appropriate moment to stress the importance of submission to the hands. We are taught that it is with the legs and the seat that we must get the horse to go 'on the bit', and that the reins must be used purely for guidance. This prescription to ride the horse *from behind* can be misleading however: we cannot dominate a horse with our legs alone; it is the rein that imposes

A pulling horse cannot be brought back under control if the rider's legs are nowhere near the horse's sides (*above*). The rider in the bottom picture has adopted a 'jumping seat' and lowered his hands, and so has more chance of getting his horse back 'on the aids'.

An excited horse attempting to 'take off'.

An upright posture and raised hands can assist in maintaining control.

obedience to the leg of the same side and the hands that give the rider mastery of the horse. We cannot hope to obtain the pliancy of the hocks if we have not first obtained the pliancy of the poll and the relaxation of the jaws. In saying this, I am certainly not implying that we get the hocks to flex by pulling backwards, and riding from front to back so to say: I mean that a horse cannot be properly collected, straightened, positioned or bent if it stiffens its poll.

Bad habits involving the tongue

Having taken stock of horses that push against the bit, lean on the hands and go above or behind the bit, we can now consider how they can frustrate all our efforts to control them by using their tongue. It has to be said that, again, this form of wayward behaviour is nearly always caused by human mismanagement. Horses will find all sorts of ways to counteract the incorrect and at the same time often very painful actions of an unskilful or hard hand. Some horses will try to counteract the constant 'strap-hanging', hammering, and rough action of uncontrolled hands by twisting and turning their tongues: they may put the tongue over the bit, or stick it out of the side of the mouth. Since they also know how to conceal the fact that they have done so, their unskilled riders often fail to realize (or at least do not do so straight away) that their horse is not correctly on the bit.

These forms of mismanagement are, of course, related to work under saddle, but problems can begin at a much earlier stage. First, let me say that there are rare cases of foals that play with their tongue in the first months of life before they have ever had a bit in their mouth, but this behaviour seems linked to a nervous disposition and probably to loneliness in early life. Such rarities aside, it is axiomatic that young horses should never be left alone in their box with a bit in their mouth, since this induces them to use it as a toy. Once they have formed this habit, it is always very difficult to correct them.

Bad habits involving the tongue can also be caused by ill-fitting bits. Particularly in the early stages of riding young horses, care must be taken to ensure that the bit is neither too narrow nor too wide. There should be one centimetre protruding from the mouth on either side. The joint of the bit should not be worn, have sharp edges, or pinch. It is a well-known fact that the thinner the bit, the more severe it is. Especially with young horses, a somewhat thicker, milder bit should be favoured and a jointed rubber snaffle is also worth trying. The height of the snaffle in the mouth should be such that the lips are not drawn upwards. However, a snaffle fitted too low will encourage a young horse to play with the unfamiliar object in its mouth. It will try to spit it out or to push it forward with the tongue. If the bit is too low in the mouth and the young horse has a very mobile tongue (very fleshy tongues are less mobile), it may get its tongue over the top of the bit. This is one way that tongue problems start. The horse will try again and again to get rid of the annoying object in its mouth. So, from the outset, you should be careful not to fit the bit too low. Once the horse has come to terms with the bit, and has confidence in the rider's hand, it is unlikely to adopt this habit. In avoiding fitting the bit too low it is, however, equally important that it is not fitted too high, and therefore too tight in the mouth, since the consequent discomfort can engender other forms of fussiness and a reluctance to go forwards freely. If the horse has a naturally 'busy' tongue, rather than attempting to restrict its mobility by adjusting the bit markedly too high, a better solution is to fit a Flash noseband. This restricts the breathing less than a drop noseband and yet makes it more difficult for the horse to open its mouth and get its tongue over the bit.

Although problems with the tongue may not be rooted wholly (or even partly) in the type of snaffle used, there are circumstances in which specific patterns may help to alleviate the difficulty. One example is a snaffle with a double, spoon-shaped tongue grid, the idea being that the 'spoons' lying on the tongue should prevent the horse from getting its tongue over the top of the bit. Provided it is resorted to at an early stage in the development of the habit, a tongue grid sometimes produces good results, but is useless in long-standing cases, highlighting the point that this vice is more readily avoided than cured. Some people recommend a straight bar snaffle with a large tongue grid, but this can cause considerable pain if the tongue is very thick and its channel narrow, and we must remember that the reaction of horses to pain is always to fight against it, and this is especially so when the pain is inflicted to the mouth. Further to this, I can say only of the old remedy of tying the tongue down with a bootlace, that it is a monstrous usage which frightens a horse out of its wits.

Sometimes problems with the tongue are signs of nervousness and tension. In such cases, rather than trying to prevent movement, it may pay to encourage mobility in the horse's mouth. Bits can be acquired which have several small links built into the joint for the purpose of making the horse's mouth more mobile. Double-jointed snaffles (French snaffles) and snaffles with a double mouthpiece have a similar action. With all such bits, great care should be taken in choice and fitting, to increase the possibility of their alleviating, rather than exacerbating, the problem. Riders wishing to address this issue whilst competing at dressage should ascertain which patterns of bits are permitted under the relevant rules.

Even if a horse has exhibited no tongue problems whilst ridden in a snaffle, that is no guarantee that such problems will not arise during the transition from snaffle to double bridle. The extra bit in its mouth can cause the horse to open its mouth or play with the bits with its tongue. Problems can also be caused by inexperienced riders handling the reins, especially when the horse is ridden more on the curb than the bridoon. It is important for the hand to be light and not to have a pulling action. Holding the reins in the 3:1 position (i.e. right snaffle rein in the right hand, the other reins in the left) is beneficial, because the right hand can make adjustments more easily. It must not be forgotten that with the reins in the 3:1 position the left hand must be held in front of the middle of the rider's stomach, otherwise the right curb rein is over-tightened!

However, as with the snaffle bridle, the most fundamental point about the double bridle is that it should fit correctly. First of all the choice of curb is important, since being ridden with a curb is a big change from what the horse is used to. A thin mouthpiece is more severe than a thick one, especially if the horse does not have very fleshy bars. The higher the port, the more severe the bit's action. The port also serves to accommodate the tongue and give it freedom to move. Horses with thick, fat tongues should therefore be fitted with a bit which leaves plenty of space for the tongue. The width of the bit must also be correct. If the mouthpiece is too narrow, the cheeks of the bit press against the lips and cause discomfort. If it is too wide it will not remain still in the horse's mouth, but will be pulled backwards and forwards through the mouth. Moreover, the curb chain will also move about. The proportions of the upper and lower cheeks, and the length of the upper cheek in relation to the lower should also be considered, because the shorter the upper cheek and the longer the lower cheek, the stronger is the lever action. Likewise, the less the difference in length between the upper and lower cheeks, the milder the curb's action. The lower cheek is normally twice the length of the upper cheek. The position of the curb chain must also be checked carefully. It is hooked first onto the right-hand hook, and then turned to the right (i.e. twisted round) until it lies flat and evenly in the curb groove. With horses that have curb grooves only thinly covered with flesh, a rubber or leather curb guard may help. If possible the chain should be made up of broad, flat links. The ring in the middle is for the so-called 'lip strap' to pass through, and should always be on the outside of the chain. The lip strap is for use on curbs with straight cheeks, when the horse is in the habit of 'snatching' at the cheeks with its teeth. Another way of preventing this habit is to use a curb with 'S'-shaped cheeks (show-hack bit). However, these bits are no longer very popular.

The curb chain makes the lever action possible. It also limits it (to forty-five degrees from the line of the mouth). Too much play in the cheek (where it makes an angle of more than forty-five degrees) is less of a fault than not enough play (less than forty-five degrees), and can even be recommended for early training in the double bridle. Particular care should be taken that the curb bit (and indeed, the whole double bridle) fits in all respects because otherwise faults can develop which, if they become habits, are very difficult to cure.

Once factors relating to the introduction and fitting of bits have been excluded as causes of tongue faults, we must consider other possibilities. For example, drawing the tongue out to one side is a sign of resistance to the painful pressure on the bars of one side of the mouth; it is significant that the tongue is always protruded towards the so-called hard side and there must be some connection between this habit and the natural one-sidedness previously discussed. Also, we should note that contraction of the muscles of the tongue is always associated with stiffening of the back and neck muscles; hence we cannot correct this fault without obtaining the loosening of the muscles of the neck and back. To this end, we must realize that factors such as discomfort caused by a faulty seat or physical injury, or some defect of conformation, may hinder the flexion of the poll and the relaxation of the spinal muscles, and we must do what we can to address such points if we are to have any hope of curing the problem with the tongue. We should also note that trying to enforce collection before the muscles of the back and hindquarters have become sufficiently strong provokes anxiety or resentment, and may thus provide the horse with both physical and psychological reasons for developing faults with the tongue.

Furthermore, we should note that, whatever the root cause, these problems are a sign that the horse is not happy about something, or even that it is in pain. Therefore, look out for this problem when buying a horse. A horse, even a young one, which puts its tongue over the bit or lets it hang out of the side of the mouth will be a constant source of problems, even for a good rider.

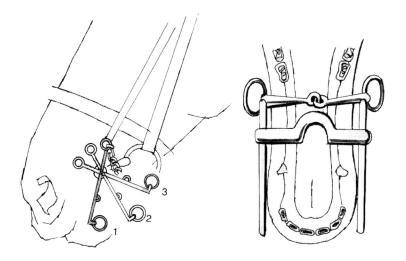

(*Left*): Positions of the cheek of the curb. 1. The bit 'cannot move': adjustment is too severe. 2. Correct position – cheek at forty-five degrees. 3. Too much play in the cheek – the bit is almost completely ineffective. (*Right*): The correct position of curb and bridoon on the lower jaw.

If, despite our best efforts to avoid them, we are confronted with bad habits involving the tongue, we must never simply ignore them, because the more difficult the schooling exercises become, the more the horse will seek to evade the action of the bit by twisting its tongue about. The important thing is, then, to prevent the development of the vice into a stubborn habit that cannot be eradicated. Hence, as a first response, as soon as we feel that a young horse has got its tongue over the bit, we must dismount and put the bit back into its right place.

In the case of the tongue hanging out, it usually does so, as mentioned, on the side the horse leans on the bit. Often it does not actually hang out in full view, but is inserted like a cushion between the bit and the bar of the mouth to soften the action of the bit. In this position it is less noticeable. One possible cure lies in temporarily taking a stronger contact on this rein, and at the same time applying the leg on the same side more strongly. The hand then yields immediately if the horse retracts its tongue. The horse must be praised straight away if this method succeeds. This fault will take time and patience to cure. The rider should keep reminding himself that it is wrong handling (whether his or another rider's) which is to blame, and consequently he is the only one who can put matters right. With patience and more patience, and through a quiet, sensitive hand, supported by a supple seat, he must reschool his horse from this bad and unpleasant habit. However, horses may sometimes also squeeze their tongue out between their incisor teeth (a habit which may not be immediately noticed by the rider) and this can be dealt with by judiciously tightening the (Flash or drop) noseband.

At this point, I should perhaps make some distinction between those habits of the mouth and tongue that signify serious problems and resistances, and those milder variations that can perhaps be considered more as idiosyncrasies. For example, getting the tongue over the bit or protruding it to the side are signs of resistance; not so the habit of pushing the tongue forwards between the front teeth. Only a few millimetres may show, and the tip of the tongue may be invisible when the horse chews the bit. Very attentive and obedient horses sometimes have this idiosyncrasy and it is quite unimportant.

Gnashing and grinding the teeth

An unpleasant habit adopted by some horses is gnashing or grinding the teeth. However, a distinction must be made between violent, angry gnashing, usually with laid-back ears and accompanied from time to time by opening of the mouth, and a quieter version performed with a closed, wet mouth. The first kind is always a serious fault, and shows that the contact is not steady and the horse is not in harmony with its rider. Horses which do this are not free from constraint: they are physically and mentally tense and are unlikely to accept the bit – or the other aids – fully until the underlying tension has been addressed. If this is the case, the remedy is to give the animal a break from work and to content oneself for a considerable period with long, quiet hacks in open country. The easing of stress provided by riding on a long rein will also strengthen the horse's back muscles and improve its balance. Moderately undulating terrain is particularly beneficial for this purpose. When work is eventually resumed, priority will have to be given to the loosening exercises to promote the lengthening of the muscles of the topside. The second kind of grinding, however, signifies something distinctly different. This discreet, barely audible, rhythmical grinding may be considered an aesthetic blemish, but it is pretty harmless; it is, in fact, an indication of contentment rather than of obstinacy or annoyance and the horses concerned have a good contact and are in harmony with their riders.

(Marked grinding of the teeth can also indicate some malaise: the teeth may need rasping, the permanent cheek teeth may be erupting, a wolf tooth may have to be extracted, or a wrongly directed molar may be irritating the gums. When young horses grind their teeth, a veterinarian should be asked to examine their mouth. Moreover other areas – the feet or the back for example – may hurt sufficiently for the horse to display irritation in this manner.)

Horses which mouth and rattle their bits are not completely free from constraint. They do not have an even contact, and are avoiding paying attention to the rider. This fault is thus a sign of incorrect training. However, as with grinding the teeth, there are two kinds of mouthing the bit: a noisy rattling with open mouth and a soft 'clink' with closed mouth. In writing of the double bridle, Seunig states: 'In contrast to the noisy gnashing and clattering which coincide with the rhythm of the gait, the soft "clink" of the bit is not a fault but quite the reverse: it is welcome music to the rider's ear. It takes the form of an almost inaudible, non-rhythmic "clink", produced by the tongue falling back into its channel, after the swallowing action resulting from correct mouthing, and allowing the two bits it has lifted to drop back into place, with the mouthpiece of the bridoon clinking against that of the curb as they do so.' Thus, with a double bridle, the occasional gentle clinking of curb and bridoon is evidence of the correct movement of the lower jaw with closed lips (which we call chewing the bit), a welcome sign of easy overall motion. On the other hand, a loud clapping of the bits indicates uneven tension of the reins and inattention to the rider. In this case, we will have to accept that the horse is not ready to be ridden in a double bridle and that we must return to the use of a snaffle and to corrective basic training. The curb should, in any case, never be used before a horse has learnt to use its back muscles properly, to move straight and to stop resisting the hand either by leaning on it, by going above or behind the bit or by putting uneven tension on the reins. Bitted with a snaffle, the horse must allow itself to be inflexed equally easily to right or left, and to accept collection without passive or active resistance. No trace of opposition to the action of the bit in the poll and mouth, or in the hocks, should remain. This means that the gaits must remain perfectly regular and unconstrained and that the horse must be properly 'on the bit' – in other words, absolutely obedient to the slightest indication of hands or legs. The more immediate and precise effect of the curb will then allow us to avert momentary inattention or laxity, but the pliancy of hocks and poll must previously have been obtained by thorough education in a snaffle.

CHAPTER EIGHT

Lawless Horses

I T IS GENERALLY ACKNOWLEDGED that very few horses are born vicious and perverse; hence we have to presume that lawless horses are usually the product of human mismanagement at some stage. I am not implying, of course, that these horses are constitutionally virtuous and compliant. A horseman should, however, be able to appreciate very quickly the temperamental and physical attributes of the animal that he undertakes to ride or train, and to adapt his conduct accordingly. If trainers and riders in general were more understanding, there would be fewer lawless horses, by which I mean horses that gambol irrepressibly, or buck, cat-leap, repeatedly shy, balk, rear or jib. The horse's instinct will suggest many ploys to obstruct his rider's design; even horses that have been trained to accept a high degree of pliancy will occasionally show a streak of wilfulness. I am not thinking only of the skirmishes that occur when horses begrudge the pressures of strenuous work, but also of some examples of blatant insubordination, like refusal to stand still during the awarding of prizes at competitions, rearing when one attempts to put on a headcollar, and various other aberrations. I have seen, on more than one occasion, horses leap out of the arena or rear in a Grand Prix test.

Equine lawlessness is too dangerous to be tolerated. Horses must be trained to the highest degree of submission, and it is from the very first day of training that we must consistently strive to attain this end. We cannot afford to believe that the process of educating our horses – or ourselves, for that matter – is ever completed. They will continually have to learn to understand new demands or situations, and to be confirmed in their submission to previous requirements. Still, we must realize that every horse is an individual, subject to the influences of past or present environment, of different sensations and inherited tendencies. The basic principles of training are invariable; they are the result of centuries of observation and experiment made by intelligent horsemen. Methods, however, must be adapted to each individual case; to conform unquestioningly to any system or conventional practice is not good horsemanship.

Nevertheless, a basic logical consistency is the best guarantee of quick, correct results. There is no denying that stubborn horses exist; provided we can perceive their pig-headedness in good time, there are ways of making them suitable for a restricted usage. But the first condition of obedience is understanding, and apparently stubborn horses are often just rather obtuse. Many resistances are based on perplexity. If a bewildered animal is maltreated for its assumed obstinacy, the seeds of recalcitrance immediately take root. Also, a horse may feel that it can trust its rider never to torment it and it will eventually comply with modest requirements; yet its instinct may drive it to forget its instilled obedience when it is required to perform a more difficult task. The better we can develop in a horse a feeling of trust and dependency upon the

Serious resistances are sometimes seen even in the highest levels of competition.

rider, the less the possibility of disobedience will occur to it. It is well worth developing these qualities to the highest degree. Total subservience in all circumstances is too much to hope for but, from the point of view of safety, the subordination of the horse's will to that of its rider must be obtained.

I have said that the first condition of obedience is understanding – on the horse's part. However, if we are to confront what we term lawless behaviour by the horse, it is also important that we understand those aspects of the horse's make-up and psyche that may contribute to this behaviour. This brings us back, in general terms, to the subject matter of the first chapter, and we will explore some of the specifics in the passages that follow. For the time being, however, we should consider that our own underlying attitudes to riding may contribute to how our horses behave.

In the context of shying, for example, horses that are regularly ridden out-of-doors soon become less easily alarmed and may be reassured by the presence of their unflustered rider. By contrast, horses that are always ridden in a manège, and that may have become fairly responsive to the aids in this secluded environment, are usually infuriatingly jittery outside. In any case, horses that are frequently ridden on the road or about the countryside are quieter and more agreeable to ride than those miserable creatures which, for most of the hours of day and night, have nothing to contemplate other than the walls of their box. There are some dressage riders who never go out hacking, maintaining that trappy ground can make horses stumble; or that peaceful hacking encourages their horse to move in a slovenly way and is therefore detrimental when a horse has to learn to move in collection. These are absurd pretexts; in the first place, all horses must learn to look after themselves over uneven terrain and the rider can choose the best line – if he is not constantly watching the animal's head position. The second excuse reveals astonishing ignorance of the principles of dressage and balance. The conception of dressage as something that is only rehearsed in the manège in preparation for a short test in a dressage arena is the reason why quite a number of dressage horses behave very badly as soon as they are away from the marked arenas. Their riders seem to forget that a horse that is not quite submissive to legs and hands is not a well-trained horse, and that pliancy of the poll and the hocks should be obtainable anywhere. This matters much more than the spectacular movement that is nature's gift to a few horses. Disobedience in the show-jumping ring or the dressage arena entertains some spectators who witness it from a safe distance. Anywhere else, a disobedient horse is a danger to itself, to its rider and to third parties.

Let us now consider the various manifestations of lawlessness, see how we can counteract the horse's recalcitrance, and examine methods of correction.

Shying

Persistent shying is a form of lawlessness, and shying is a vice that can become a dangerous habit if the rider does not understand its cause or resorts to irrational methods of prevention or correction. Before we consider ways of preventing the growth of this tendency into a habit, there are two things that we must understand. The first is the flight reflex and the second is the horse's sense of vision.

The compulsive flight reflex of horses is a frequent cause of disorder. The nature of the frightening object is immaterial for, so far as the rider is concerned, what matters is his own predicament. Some horses merely balk or jump aside to ensure a sufficient escape distance from an alarming object, while others immediately bolt. There are horses that shy away suddenly from things that have never startled them before; others may shy only once when they perceive something strange, but having found out that it is really harmless, they will ignore it on subsequent occasions. We will never be able to fathom quite why one individual may suddenly behave 'uncharacteristically', or behave so differently from another, just as we may wonder vainly why the stirring of a bird in a hedge will upset one horse but not perturb another, or why a speck of white paper on the ground can seem so threatening to some horses, despite the opportunity to appraise its problematical nature by sight, sound or smell from a safe distance. The answer probably lies in some combination of temperament, self-confidence, learnt response and the acuteness of the various senses. However, it is a fact that the flight reflex is deeply rooted in the constitution of horses. If frightened horses will disregard the strongest impulses of thirst, hunger or sex, it is understandable that they should forget their habit of obedience to their riders when they find themselves prey to such a strong emotion.

So far as the visual sense of horses is concerned, we must understand first, that their eyes are not placed absolutely frontally as in man and monkeys, but are positioned somewhat obliquely or laterally. Consequently, they are able to view two separate pictures at the same time, one on either side of the body. What their mind perceives is not a three dimensional view, but a wide panorama with ill-defined features. Their field of vision is much larger than ours, but the images are rather blurred. The more or less all-round vision of the horse (the range may be close to 360 degrees) enables it to keep its entire surroundings almost completely in view when its head is close to the ground to graze. Second, the cornea of the horse's eye has a greater vertical than horizontal curvature, and this produces further distortion of the image; for example, spots to a horse look like rods. Moreover, the pupil of the eye is oval, and this gives good protection against bright light, but behind the retina, a

Shying at unfamiliar objects and sudden movements is an instinctive reaction.

fluorescent film increases light reflection and this enables horses to see much more than we can in the dark.

Professor W. Blendinger, who has made a thorough study of the psychology of horses, states that:

1. The vision of the horse cannot be said to be better or worse than ours. It was designed by nature to suit the needs of the animal in its wild state, and we can have only a limited conception of the way in which horses see the world.

2. The horse can watch its environment almost equally well from all angles but cannot bring things into clear focus like we can.

3. The rather lateral position of the eyes makes it difficult for the horse to see distinctly objects situated straight in front of its head and deprives it of a sense of perspective.

4. Its ability to focus simultaneously on so many things around it restricts its ability to concentrate on a particular object. From the point of view of training jumpers, this is an interesting observation; it means that horses have to be educated to look attentively at an obstacle.

5. Adaptation to see things in very bright light or in almost total darkness is a characteristic of the horse's eye, but it is not designed to adapt to rapid changes of brightness.

6. The ability to detect very slight movement is much more acute in the horse than in humans.

7. Finally, it is not true that horses are completely colour-blind. They can certainly distinguish reds, yellows, greens and blues, though less precisely than humans, and they appear to see yellows and greens better than blues and reds.

(I should add here that some horses habitually start specifically at objects lying on the ground. This may be because they have exceptional difficulty in focusing; it might be wise to have their eyes examined by a veterinarian. Although these horses, also, must get used to a great variety of sights and sounds, it is safer to present these to them as much as possible on safe home ground.)

Need I say that human facial expressions are absolutely meaningless to horses and that our smiles or scowls are wasted on them. On the other hand, if we suddenly changed our appearance by turning up in a large sombrero, by exchanging the whip for an umbrella, or approached them creeping on all fours, we could scare them out of their wits. Horses are very timid creatures and any unfamiliar sight can release their flight reflex. Man usually thinks before he acts; safety for horses depends on flight before thought. In fact,

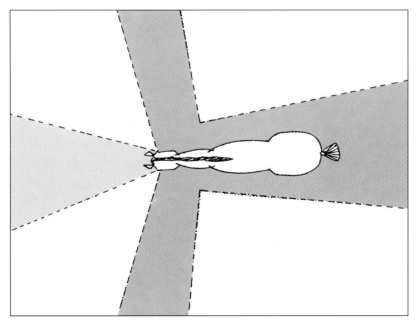

When the head is straight, the horse's field of vision comprises either the area bordered by lines in front or the sectors on either side and to the rear. It does not comprise the front area and the two side areas at the same time (according to Smythe).

horses do not think, in the sense of analysing; they have no capacity to analyse the possibility of danger when confronted with a new experience.

Yet, even although we must acknowledge the horse's visual sense and instincts, it would be a serious mistake to tolerate every manifestation of apprehension, since doing so would subjugate our own demands of the horse entirely to its own instincts. Young horses, for instance, often shy just because they are fresh, the jumpiness being simply a release of high spirits. Some riders, out of a laudable tolerance of youthful ebullience but misguided permissiveness, allow a young horse to make a fuss over any unfamiliar sight and to prepare itself to start, jump or recoil by snorting and looking at the object with a great show of apprehension, just like a spoilt child showing off. We must not confuse such play-acting with genuine fear and allow it to persist in displaying this silliness: the right course of action is to put the horse in *counterposition*, make it look away from the excuse for excitement and ride past it with total unconcern. In doing so, we may prevent what began almost as a game from developing into something more serious: highly-strung horses in particular are quick to seize slight pretexts of agitation, but we cannot allow them to become flustered every time a bird is roused.

Therefore, the horse cannot be allowed to feel that shying is a commendable reaction and it is senseless to pat it as a sign of approval every time it jumps, especially since we must always be prepared for a sudden unseating movement by maintaining at all times a firm and ready seat. In re-educating the horse we must, however, be judicious in our actions. For example, while, as we shall see, progressively desensitizing the horse plays a key role in combating shying, it is a great mistake to compel a horse to have a good look at something that worries it by driving the horse at the object head-on; this just increases its apprehension. A worse mistake still is to punish with whip, spur or voice every expression of the flight reflex, since the horse will associate the punishment with the object it fears. Hence, we must never lose our patience despite the unsettling effect on ourselves of the sudden movement of the horse. Even when shying is just a symptom of bumptious behaviour on the part of a horse, punishment serves merely to exacerbate its impatience.

Fortunately, fearfulness diminishes with increasing experience and maturity, especially when a horse is frequently ridden out over countryside by a calm and competent rider. Nevertheless, although strolling on a loose rein is very pleasant, it is not a prudent thing to do when a horse is liable to start for no accountable reason, or when we are likely to encounter a farm tractor or a large coach on a narrow, winding road. Moreover, while the horse's vision is a major factor in many cases of shying, it is not the only contributory sense. The horse's sense of hearing is also much more acute than ours, and the animal is liable to panic long before its rider can distinguish the noise of an approaching vehicle. Besides which, horses have a very acute sense of smell and can be upset by certain odours that we may not notice or that do not perturb us. (Certain smells, such as blood and smoke, cause intense fear in horses, as they do in many living creatures.) It is therefore foolhardy to ride with loose reins on the roads; we can find ourselves dangerously out of control during the short time it takes to adjust the reins to a suitable length. Of course, I do not mean that we should be so timid ourselves as to ride on an unnecessarily short rein, for keeping the horse curbed would merely increase its jitteriness. However, we do have to retain a prudent amount of control and it is certain that the horse must not learn that it will be allowed to run away at its own discretion!

(*Left*): Incorrect position for passing an object which the horse has shied at. (*Right*): The correct way is to turn the horse away and push it past in a shoulder-in position. In this way it does not step backwards and so evade even more.

The company of a calm horse may have a tranquillizing influence on a jittery one, but even a placid horse can never be totally reliable in all situations, because fear is extremely contagious. Therefore, if you are the owner of an animal that is easily upset by certain things, to the point of becoming almost uncontrollable, it would be imprudent to confront such things head-on, simply because you are in company. Instead, you should give such objects a sensibly wide berth and, if their relative presence alarms your horse less than before, consider this a step in the right direction. Whenever you can, anticipate trouble, and ride past suspicious objects in *counterposition*. In saying that you should anticipate trouble, I am speaking simply of watching out for objects that might provoke shying and ensuring that your seat is correct: if trotting, revert to sitting trot and, if cantering in a light seat, assume a full seat. However, you should be careful not to tense up, or to ride more energetically than is necessary, since these actions will simply increase tension in the horse. In some circumstances, it may be advisable to dismount and lead the horse, but always walk between the horse and the object of its fear, even if you then have to lead from the off side. I need not tell you what the consequences could be if you were on the wrong side. Always pass the reins over the horse's neck when leading and, when you ride, maintain a firm seat even when calm has been restored. A proper seat does much to inform a horse that it cannot get away with disobedience.

All horses have to be educated to realize that many of the things that may alarm them are innocuous and they must therefore be exposed *progressively* to as large a variety of sights and sounds as possible. That horses can be educated to ignore a wide variety of startling events is shown by the composure of well-trained animals at competitions: sudden thunder, flapping programmes and newspapers, flags waving and swishing, or a parade of noisy hounds leave

The correct way to lead a horse. Note the lack of stiffness in the arm, which is bent slightly; the reins are separated by the index and middle fingers, and the end of the reins is held under the thumb. If this method is used, a shying horse can be brought back under control promptly.

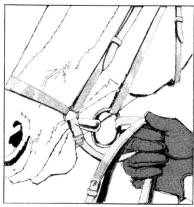

them unperturbed. It is just a matter of desensitizing them gradually and teaching them to ignore unusual occurrences. Further to this, it seems that horses will often not fully accept fixed objects they are afraid of until they have sniffed them and touched them with their nose repeatedly. They will turn away and then come back and examine the object again, just as carefully. Fear is accompanied by curiosity. Usually, in the inner struggle, it is curiosity which wins – although the battle may flare up again later! This natural form of

Shying can be redressed by a gradual process of desensitization in a safe environment.

gradual acclimatization gives us a further clue as to why it is inadvisable to compel a horse to confront the object of its fear head-on, at first meeting.

However, we must not forget that every horse is an individual and that not all horses will behave with the same degree of equanimity or otherwise in all circumstances. The fundamental rule is to deal with the concerns and reactions of the individual horse, not to make judgements about its behaviour based on one's experiences with a different horse. To demonstrate this point, in the days of cavalry, military remounts (that had to be trained en masse as quickly as practicable) would be deliberately startled by the sudden appearance of large sheets of paper on the floor of the manège or exercise ground. The paper would flutter in the breeze, and crackle when clods of soil thrown up by horses' hooves fell on it, and the new horses either jumped – or took no notice. If we have a horse that is inclined to be spooky, we can use a modified form of this practice at home, to acclimatize the horse to a whole range of unfamiliar objects: we can partly bury a large sheet of paper in the arena surface, place a variety of objects in the manège and have someone walk about the vicinity with an open umbrella. Although some of the objects used – such as sheets of paper and umbrellas –are specific items that the horse may encounter outside, there is additional value in teaching the horse that unfamiliar objects (of any sort) are not necessarily to be feared. Of course some horses, such as those used by police services, have to be trained to develop an exceptional level of impassivity to all sorts of objects. Our horses, kept for pleasure, do not have to display such a remarkable degree of stoicism, but a somewhat impassive horse is certainly more fun to ride than a jittery one.

Prams, umbrellas, handbarrows or any other common, every-day object can cause a horse to shy. Training at home can help to desensitize the horse.

Balking at water

Water is one of the things that some horses distrust much more than others. Although fear of water is an atavistic instinct, any tame horse that refuses to step into water in perfectly safe circumstances must be considered unruly, and it would be ridiculous to have to contend with obstinate resistance every time we met a puddle or needed to cross a little stream. It is therefore on safe home ground that a horse must be taught to step over or into water. This education should start in the stable yard and here the horse can first be accustomed to water by having its feet washed and hosed. Start with the hind legs, because horses are usually more willing to allow these to be washed than their forelegs. Put the water in a bucket, use a sponge, not a hard brush, and do not use very cold water. If you encounter difficulties, have someone hold up the forefoot on the same side as the hind leg you are washing. Initially, do not let the puddle formed on the ground get too large. Once the horse is accustomed to having its feet washed in this way, proceed to using a hose (initially with a moderate flow) and hose the legs from knee and hock downwards. Gradually increase the level of flow.

Following this, you can start to lead the horse through puddles forming in the yard, and to ride it through puddles of rain whilst out hacking. Obviously, we must be sure that the ground on the other side of the water is not a bog in which the horse can get stuck and thereby feel that its wariness was well founded and that we cannot be trusted. Much patience may be needed during the period of familiarization with water and all means of persuading the horse should be employed, except a beating. This is a case in which a horseman's discernment can play its part because, while one purposeful stroke of the whip at the right moment can be persuasive, flogging the horse is an infallible way of increasing its obstinacy and reinforcing its fear. We must never engage in a fight with a horse that resists out of fear, since the horse can always pitch a vastly superior strength against ours. We must therefore resort to wiliness rather than violence and ponder upon the easiest way of getting out of a tricky situation. It may be wise, at first, to use an experienced lead horse, but the emphasis here is on 'experienced'. If all the horses in the company are equally chary, one of them may be allowed to take some form of detour and thus tempt the fainthearted to join it. Sometimes, the best policy is to dismount and lead on foot, choosing to start with the narrowest and least frightening crossing place.

One thing we should certainly not attempt, in seeking to persuade a horse to jump into or over water, is to approach it by building up speed from a considerable distance; this will never prevent a recalcitrant horse from putting its brakes on at the brink. If we cannot persuade the horse to clear the obstacle from a distance of 2 or 3 m, driving it vigorously from a distance of 50 m will simply give it greater latitude to run out. Another point for consideration it that it is imperative to give ample freedom of the reins when crossing water, because the horse must be able to lower its head and neck to aid its balance. Therefore, we will have to steer it with seat and legs and, as the nervous horse will probably decide to leap suddenly into or over the water while we are

Persuading a horse to enter water. (*above*) In the early stages, an assistant can be useful, to encourage the horse and perhaps splash its forelegs or lead it in if necessary.

(*left*) A willingness to immerse the forefeet is usually an encouraging sign.

183

unprepared, we should take the precaution of holding on to the mane, a neck strap or even the pommel of the saddle. An unintentional rap in the mouth at this stage would be a disaster.

A little forethought is always profitable, and we may be able to plan our hack so that we approach the water on our way home. In this case, although we may have to wait patiently for up to fifteen minutes for the horse to consent to negotiate the water, we are increasing the likelihood of its doing so. In the case of defeat, we may have to return to the scene of our discomfiture or to some other part of the stream – if the horse appears to have a marked distaste for water, we should at first choose a narrow, shallow stretch of water with a very firm bottom. We should take with us two or preferably three assistants armed with a lunge line and lunge whip. The line must be passed around the horse's croup, above the hocks. Rather like persuading a reluctant horse into a horsebox, two of the assistants then pull the horse forwards with the lunge; the third pushes from the rear, or encourages the horse with the long whip, but without chastising it. Patience and quiet are essential; the horse must not be distracted by shouts and frenzied gestures. If it puts a forefoot on the verge, sprinkling the leg with a little water, in mimicry of washing it, may encourage it to step forwards. The rider now stays in a ready position and keeps the horse straight mainly with his legs; although the hands may play some part here they must, nevertheless, give the horse complete freedom to use its neck and they must therefore not press downwards nor hold back. As described above, the horse may well jump extravagantly and the one thing that is guaranteed to harden its obduracy is a jab in the mouth at that moment.

(Some horses, once they have consented to put a foot into the water, start pawing the water. Various explanations have been given for this, but in the context of a horse being introduced to water, it is usually an encouraging sign.

One way of getting a horse to cross a stream. Patience and quiet are imperative. Punishment is out of place.

However, with horses that have no fear of water, this action may be a prelude to the horse lying down! It is by no means unknown for horses and riders to completely submerge, so if you ever feel your horse's knees start to buckle when it is in water, you should take instant action with a powerful upward action of the rein, combined with driving leg aids and a loud 'No!')

Initial success in introducing the horse to water can be followed by two or, at the most, three repetitions of the lesson. If things are proceeding well, it may be appropriate to try a different – although not yet more difficult – point of entry. If at any time the horse's opposition develops to the point of rearing, we will have to conclude that we are faced with complete lawlessness, and here is not the place to provoke rebellion or to try to destroy it. Rearing will be considered later, and the horse's propensity for using it as a form of defiance will have to be conquered before other situations which may induce it can be addressed.

There is no pleasure to be found in riding out of doors if a horse cannot be relied on to jump small ditches and other water-filled obstacles without hesitation or flurry. After we have got the horse to surmount its instinctive apprehension in the manner just explained, further progress will be much easier to achieve and the horse's confidence will increase with experience. After all, jumping over a ditch that is no more than 2 m wide requires nothing more than some lengthening of a normal canter stride that is well within the scope of any horse. Therefore, it is just the horse's confidence and obedience that need to be improved. If natural obstacles are not available close to the stable, an artificial water jump can be constructed, using light blue sheeting or a shallow, painted wooden tray. It may even be possible to add a film of water from a bucket or hose to add authenticity. Initially, a small brush fence on the take-off side, or a low pole over the middle, will make the obstacle easier for the horse. In similar fashion, it may be possible to dig a shallow ditch and fill this with water, if required. With all obstacles of this type, the actual size should, initially, be subsidiary to the principle of gaining the horse's confidence. Once a horse has become truly confident, albeit at a very small water jump or ditch, it is likely to jump any such obstacle within its scope with little fuss. If, however, it is overfaced before it has become confident, this may lay the foundation for a lifelong suspicion of, or aversion to, such obstacles. As with so many aspects of equitation, the key is to make progress slowly.

As is the case with horses that shy habitually at objects on the ground because of their abnormal vision, some horses will always show a strong aversion to jumping over water, probably for the same reason. It would be silly to expect such horses to do well in competitions that include a water jump and it may be advisable to find routes through the countryside which do not make this demand of them. In most cases, however, teaching horses to overcome their natural aversion to water is a matter of developing their obedience and their confidence in their rider.

Balking at obstacles

Of course it is not only water that horses have to learn to clear by jumping. Learning to jump is an essential part of the education of all young horses, even if they are not suitable material for specialized show-jumping. In the early stages of this education, it is extremely important to avoid setbacks which could instil permanent aversion to jumping. Every sound horse is capable of jumping obstacles of moderate height, although some horses will have a better style than others. But the subject of this book is not the development of jumping style. I will just deal with disobedience: that is, stopping or running out in front of the sort of obstacles which are well within the scope of any young horse.

(*right and opposite above*)
Run-outs and refusals can mar the enjoyment of competition.

(*left*) Any tendency to refuse can bring the added problem of indecision. Here we see the predicament of a horse that has hesitated between stopping and going. It is going to have to lift itself up like a helicopter.

Obviously, we must always ensure that neither pain in the back nor the legs could punish a horse for its obedience and give it justifiable grounds for refusing (to this end, we should avoid jumping -— especially on firm ground – the day after a horse has been shod). Otherwise, when a horse starts to balk at jumps, we can be sure that its rider is at fault. He may have overfaced the young horse at the beginning of training. It is absurd to make a young, igno-rant horse jump big obstacles, even without a rider on its back, just to discover the extent of its talent. This dealer's custom is stupid and is one of the princi-pal causes of reluctance to jump. The ambitious owner of a talented young horse, who indulges in this custom, will then enter it in every competition going – perhaps as often as once a week, and probably train it over obstacles every day. Then the owner will wonder why the horse is turning sour and will proceed to chastise it. The horse may, for a time, jump out of fear of punish-ment, but eventually will dig in its toes. This is how inveterate refusers are produced and they are always extremely difficult to redress.

Since it is really distrust of the rider that is at the root of most difficulties, trust in the rider is the first thing that has to be restored. It is difficult enough to create faith in the rider when a horse is inexperienced; it is infinitely more difficult to revive trust that has been abused. Generally, it is fairly easy to gain a horse's confidence in the first year of training; nevertheless, such confidence is as fragile as an exotic plant and just as easy to destroy. In the early stages of training, it is always a mistake to make a fuss over an occasional stop and to punish the horse with a beating or by chasing it over obstacles with a whip, thereby forcing it to jump out of fear. A presumed assistant, standing by the

fence to allegedly encourage the horse with shouts and gesticulations, will serve further to unnerve the horse completely. It is folly to make a horse jump because of dread of punishment. Horses that have been ridden into the ground by riders that push behind and hold in front with a running rein may refuse to jump because they have been deprived of the use of their hind legs for balance. Demanding training for show-jumping should never be undertaken before basic training on the flat has taught the horse to move in horizontal equilibrium.

When a horse is on the way to becoming a confirmed refuser, it has to be trained all over again from scratch, which will include trotting over poles or low cavalletti, and bounce-jumping over low obstacles, mainly to develop the cantering technique. No attempt should be made to make the horse round itself by the use of the reins; this would upset it and increase its agitation. At a later stage, broader, sloping and inviting obstacles can be carefully introduced.

During the training sessions, the jumping work must be interspersed with loosening work on the flat. It is good policy to alternate lungeing over an obstacle with mounted jumping and, throughout the period of re-education, all temptation to teach the horse to speed up or to jump more cleanly by rapping it in one way or another must be strongly resisted. The emphasis must be purely on style and regularity. The rider must also avoid using strong driving

Riders sometimes have to share responsibility for refusals. Here, the rider has sensed the impending refusal but his seat is so weak that he cannot prevent it.

At the second approach to the same obstacle, the horse hesitates but jumps despite the fact that the rider has impeded it by getting in front of the movement.

189

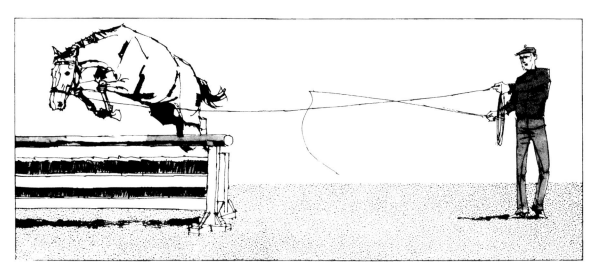

When lungeing a horse over obstacles, avoid catching the lunge line on the jump stands by making sure that they are low.

Gymnastic bounce-jumping.

aids, which easily impair the horse's equilibrium. Of course, most of the time, it is not only the horse's own style that has to be improved. The rider must discipline himself and develop a correct jumping seat, not just over the obstacles but also between them. The speed and the contact must remain steady. With horses that have developed a tendency to run out, it is preferable to start the canter as frequently as possible with the leading leg on the horse's concave side (usually the right), to carry the whip in the opposite (left) hand and to approach the obstacles as close as is practical to their right side. All transitions to canter must be done quietly, without ever urging the horse on to go faster.

It is, of course, understandable that a horse should refuse to jump, or will jump badly, if sunlight is shining straight into its eyes and it cannot judge the height of the approaching obstacle. Sharply contrasting lighting conditions, such as floodlit arenas in which the jumps are glaringly lit but the areas between are pools of darkness – or lighting that casts heavy shadows around the jumps – may cause confusion and diffidence in the most genuine horse. If competing under such conditions, it is advisable to avoid standing around in the dark before entering the brightly or glaringly lit arena. This is because, although the horse's vision can adapt to greater extremes of light and darkness than man's, it takes quite a while to do so.

Regarding vision, we must not underestimate the horse's need to assess each obstacle according to its own sight which, as we saw earlier, is somewhat different from ours. You may have noticed well-trained horses going round a course of jumps moving their heads somewhat up or down or to one side before they jump. These horses are not evading the aids, but are simply trying to get their eyes in the best position to size up the obstacles, and it is noticeable that their astute riders permit them to do so. As a corollary to this, we should also understand why horses that throw up their heads as a form of resistance – especially in the last few strides of the approach – are so ready to stop. When their head is carried high, the sight of the obstacle hits the blind spot on the retina. The horse will see the ground at the foot of the obstacle too late to estimate the height it has to jump; its hind feet will be over-engaged and it will then slide helplessly into the fence. Again, it is to basic dressage training that one must return to get the horse to stretch its back muscles and lower its head and neck. The obstacles used during this training should be inviting spreads rather than uprights.

Another possible cause of refusals and other jumping problems lies in the colours of the jumps. Horses see colours differently from us. According to Grzimek, the horse sees a smaller range of colours than we do and, although it can apparently distinguish the colours yellow, green, red and blue, it sees yellow and green more clearly than red and blue. It also sees colours in a different intensity from man, hence dark colours (dark red, dark blue) make it more

Horse's field of vision before a jump, when the head is raised. The horse cannot see the ground in front of the jump, except the last 1.2 m (according to Smythe).

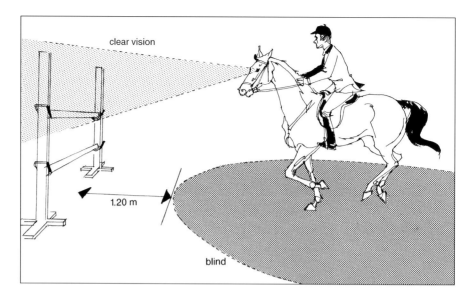

Horse's field of vision before a jump, when the head is lowered (according to Smythe). Note the difference in the field of vision depending on the position of the head.

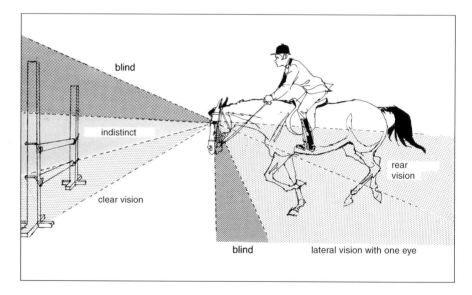

difficult for the horse to discern the jump, while light colours (yellow, green, white) make jumping easier. Interestingly, it has been shown that more mistakes are made at jumps built of blue poles than poles of other colours. We can learn from this that what is, for us, a brightly coloured course with poles, planks, gates, walls and pots of plants of many different colours, looks much less colourful to a horse. Furthermore, in some cases, the obstacles that we may interpret as looking easy for the horse may be quite hard for it to sum up, whilst others, that we might think could prove difficult or spooky, may appear to the horse to be quite straightforward. Thus learning to reassess jumps from a 'horse's eye view' may help us to avoid errors in presenting the horse at the obstacles.

Regarding competitive show-jumping, we should realize that even well-trained horses cannot always produce top performance; they may be tired or feeling below par. In competition, some horses lose their nerve if they hit the first fence, which is why good course-builders make the first obstacle as inviting as possible. Sometimes it is the nervousness of the rider that is sensed by the horse; a horse may stop or run out in front of a particular obstacle because the rider himself dreads it; with another more confident rider, it is probable that the refusal would not have occurred.

There is evidence that horses can, in some sense and to some extent, count. An example of this is that horses which have been trained always to rein-back a set number of steps may hesitate distinctly if asked for an extra step. In the context of show-jumping, while most repeated refusals have obvious causes, it seems that some horses learn that, after three refusals, they can leave the ring. Elimination for this, or other, reasons may engender frustration and other strong emotions in the rider and, since beating the horse in full view of the judges can invite fines and suspension, some riders will administer severe punishment behind the scenes. Of course, in many cases, it is the rider and not the horse that deserves the punishment; anyhow, if punishment is justified, it must be inflicted without the slightest delay at the moment of the transgression. No judge will censure a rider for dealing a smart stroke of the whip to the culprit that shows out-and-out disobedience. However, punishment delivered even a short while after the wrongdoing is meaningless to the horse and is thus resented. Horses are constitutionally unable to repent. It is not sensible, either, to chase a horse over jumps in the practice area after a disappointing performance; in fact, there is no surer way of souring the animal. A decent and intelligent rider will reflect calmly over the circumstances of the refusal and will work out a rational programme of correction to be carried out at home.

Before competing it is good practice, so far as is possible, to familiarize the horse with all types of obstacle likely to be encountered in the ring. If, in competition, a horse balks at an obstacle that is totally strange to it, it could be said to be disobedient to the rider's aids, but the main fault may lie in the rider's lack of preparatory schooling. In some such cases, the organizers of the competition may permit the competitor to acquaint his horse with this obstacle after the end of the event. However, after a series of refusals (or in order to avoid them), it is advisable to proceed cautiously and to devise a wise plan of re-education. The obstacle that causes the problem will have to be lowered and the horse's confidence built up by careful progression of demands. The horse's confidence can be destroyed irremediably by hastiness.

Jibbing and napping

Opposition to the authority of the legs can take the form of jibbing, in which the horse declines to move forwards – although a horse that refuses to come out of its box (see Stable Vices pages 49–50) is as much a jibber as one that digs in its toes when commanded by the legs to enter the show-jumping ring. The vice usually reveals apprehension or dislike of the expected work, but the herd extinct may be involved also. It is natural for horses to feel reluctance at being separated from their fellows; in their wild state, the herd represents safety. It is also understandable that some horses should be more reluctant than others to be separated from the herd, because of their individual character and their position in the herd hierarchy. In the context of the herd instinct, a horse that refuses to move forwards away from the 'herd' could be said to be jibbing, while a horse that attempts to move in the direction of the 'herd', especially in oblique fashion, against the rider's wishes, could be said to be napping. As suggested above, the physical influence of other horses may sometimes be replaced in the horse's mind by what it perceives to be 'safety': it will be reluctant to leave, or anxious to return to, an environment it considers safe, and equally reluctant to confront one it considers dangerous or unpleasant. If this is the case, the same basic principles can be applied for resolving the problem as those I am about to describe for horses that are reluctant to leave their fellows.

Horses that refuse to move out of the rank of their fellows must first become accustomed to occupying different places in the row, then be made to walk sometimes towards it, past it and ahead of it. For educating a horse to behave itself in company, the old cavalry methods are excellent. Two of the young remounts would be made to walk ahead of the troop, while the others had to remain standing until a sufficient distance was established (which still preserved eye contact). When the whole troop resumed the march, the same distance would have to be maintained. The large exercise grounds at the disposal of the cavalry for the training of remounts are not always at the disposal of clubs and commercial establishments, but a suitable location, such as a fairly large field, should normally be available. The underlying principle remains valid; a horse that will not allow itself to be separated from the rank is a badly trained, hence disobedient, horse that must be re-dressed. The rider of the unruly horse must of course be especially competent. Firm loins rather than strong legs are required, as is determination. But an understanding of the horse's psyche is also important. When faced with danger, horses bunch together. When a horse is afraid, it runs *to* the other horses, not *away* from them. Horses should not, then, be hit to make them leave the others, since fear engendered by the punishment will reinforce their instinct to cling to their fellows. Instead, they should be praised and rewarded for leaving them: the horse must make the association in its mind 'When I leave the others I get something nice'. In this respect, if the horse is confirmed in its habit, it may be expedient, at first, to have an assistant on the ground to lead it away from the others; in this way, the rider can simply apply reasonably firm seat and leg aids, and will not be tempted to use undue levels of coercion.

When dealing with jibbing and napping, it is advisable to do a lot of riding alone, outside in a safe environment as well as in the school, to build up the horse's self-confidence, and its confidence in, and obedience to, you. On the occasions when you do join a ride, employ variations on the old cavalry practice described earlier. Keep changing your position in the ride, ride past it and to the front, turn off from the back of the ride and ride in the opposite direction. Another good exercise is to ride out forwards from the ride when it is lined up at the halt. Sometimes the ride should go on ahead while the nappy horse remains behind, and sometimes the ride should hang back while it goes on ahead. There are all sorts of possibilities and variations. The rider should select the exercises which will best help the horse to overcome its fear of leaving the 'herd'. With frequent practice, combined with praise, the horse will gradually give up the habit.

Crushing the rider

One particularly unpleasant vice of horses – and this is a really depraved one – is the deliberate attempt to dislodge the rider by crushing him against the walls of the manège. Fortunately, it is not a very common form of rejection of the rider's authority and the victims are weak riders. The habit is generally formed when a horse can no longer tolerate the discomfort suffered at the hands of an overbearing, ignorant rider. The horse may be physically incapable of complying with the demands made upon it, but intelligent enough to recognize the weakness of the rider and to find out one way of getting rid of the encumbrance. Moderately stubborn horses are not rare, but their true obstinacy manifests itself only when they are asked to perform a task in a way that makes the task more difficult or unpleasant, or when the incipient obstinacy is not recognized early enough. A wrong approach to training will destroy every trace of goodwill that may have existed, and they become thoroughly pig-headed. It is also the case that dim-witted, indolent horses strongly resent orders that they do not understand, and their mulishness steadily increases. The ignorance and obdurate behaviour of certain riders, as much as their physical gaucherie, will provoke equine insubordination. For example, we often see riders who punish disobedience by forcing the horse to move backwards when its head is elevated and its back is hollow. In this attitude, stepping backwards is very painful and damaging to a horse's back and joints, let alone its mouth. The rough and ready parades that some riders indulge in to discipline a resistant horse are also cruel and irrational, but the cost to the rider is often high in terms of veterinary bills. Riders must be able to control their own body and limbs, to feel and put right their own faults, before they have the right to accuse the horse of stupidity or cussedness.

Of course, as with many vices, it may be that the rider who is required to address the problem is not the one who has engendered it. A horse that tries to dislodge the rider by crushing him against the wall has managed to escape from the aids, especially the aids of one leg: it evades the action of the leg on the side it rubs against the wall in an attempt to scrape the rider off. We must therefore make the horse obey this leg again. It would be quite wrong to try to pull the horse away from the wall with the opposite rein: this would only serve to make the side which is not obeying the leg even more convex, and enable the horse to press itself and its rider even harder against the wall. Instead, we must do the opposite: in order to make the side against the wall hollow, we bend the horse slightly so that its head is towards the wall, placing more

A horse trying to crush its rider against the wall (*left*). The rider should not (attempt to) pull the horse away with the inside rein, since this will only result in his outside leg being squashed even more against the wall (*centre*). Rather, the rider should try to make the horse hollow on the outside (place it in a counterflexion as it were) and obtain obedience with the outside leg (*right*).

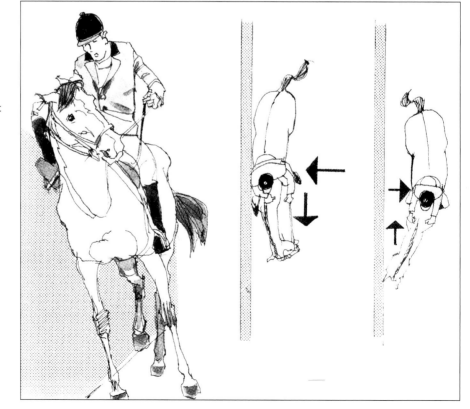

weight on the seat bone of this side (without collapsing the hip!) and moving the horse around its forehand away from the wall. The horse must then be taught respect for the legs by means of the usual exercises: turns around the forehand in forward movement, yielding to the leg, enlarging and decreasing the circle.

Kicking under saddle

A few points here about kicking under saddle to supplement the earlier reference in Redressing Spoilt Horses to kicking against the spur (page 116). Owners of kickers are to be pitied: they may be charming people in themselves, but the dislike directed against their horse will also be aimed at them. This is certainly unfair, because there is no completely effective cure for horses which kick out when ridden. Although he will do everything in his power to discourage it, the best of riders cannot absolutely prevent his horse from lashing out when in a group or equestrian gathering. The best course of action to avoid any sort of kicking accident is for all concerned to keep their distance at all times. This advice includes such precautions as not shaking hands with other riders if congratulating them on some competitive success, or if meeting as friends whilst hacking. Even if you think you know the other horse well, it is better not to do so, as all sorts of things have been known to happen when horses get this close. Instead, make an appropriate salutation from a safe distance.

In the hunting field, any horse known to be a kicker must have a red ribbon firmly secured to its tail by way of warning. However, this does not absolve its rider from a duty to take all practical measures to avoid causing an accident. For example, it would be highly irresponsible for the rider of such a horse to press regardless into a crowded gateway. On the other hand, no one riding in close company should assume that another horse will not kick, simply because it is not attired with a ribbon. Any horse, feeling crowded or threatened, may lash out as an instinctive reaction, even though it is not a habitual kicker.

Further to this, we should note that even horses that are 'habitual' kickers in the sense that they have a history of kicking out may not necessarily do so all the time. When they kick depends on their nature and on the underlying reasons – whether there is a sexual reason, whether they feel generally disagreeable, or whether there is some undiscovered cause. If the kicking is purely a reflex action (that is, something the horse does subconsciously), there is unlikely to be any warning. However, many horses give some indication that they are about to kick, by making obvious threatening gestures such as laying back the ears, baring the teeth or pushing their quarters towards the object of their dislike. Provided the rider recognizes the symptoms in time, these can be corrected accordingly by sharply raising the head and neck, transferring as much weight as possible onto the quarters, or leaning right back. Any punishment for kicking or attempted kicking must be given immediately.

Rearing

I will now talk about rearing, the extreme example of lawlessness. It is, of course, total defiance. By refusing to go forwards and refusing to make contact with the bit, the rearing horse discovers a highly effectual way of annihilating the rider's assumed dominance. A horse evidently cannot rear when it is moving forwards. And so the first signs of rearing are jibbing, running backwards or half-rearing and, if the rider is at all timid or spiritless, the horse learns quickly that it can easily evade every intention of its human passenger. Therefore, as soon as the horse shows the slightest preparation to rear, it must either be sent forwards ruthlessly or, if it is completely off the bit, it must be bent completely in the direction of its soft, hollow side. It cannot rear when it is balanced on one hind leg.

Sometimes, however, the horse can catch its rider off guard and achieve a full rear. If this happens we must of course lean forwards – since leaning backwards can make the horse overbalance – and we should not be too proud to hang on to the mane or to clasp the horse's neck. Hanging on to the reins spells disaster. In this particularly critical situation, it is prudent to take the feet out of the stirrups.

Rearing horse. The rider on the *left* is sitting correctly, with the upper body leaning forward. He is yielding the reins completely, and so avoiding the risk of the horse falling over backwards. The rider on the *right*, on the other hand, is hanging onto the reins and simply asking for the horse to go over backwards. He is not sitting in the saddle, and his legs are no longer against the horse and so not in a position to react by punishing or driving the horse on with the spur when the moment comes.

(*opposite page*) Rearing is an extreme example of lawlessness.

The best way of getting out of the predicament is to take a very short hold on the rein corresponding to the horse's soft side and pull its neck *sideways* but of course not *backwards*. The shorter the hold we can obtain the better because when its neck is sharply bent the rearing horse is compelled to lower its forelegs. As soon as they touch the ground, we must drive forwards with utmost determination. If the horse does not obey our legs and rears again or threatens to do so, we must once more bend its neck forcibly and *mill* energetically with the aid of hand and leg on the same side until the horse is exhausted. We may have to fix the hand behind our thigh.

The punishment has to be very severe indeed and repeated every time the horse shows the slightest intention of repeating the resistance. Absolute promptness and determination of reaction are imperative. But remember that a horse cannot understand punishment that is not completely coincident with the fault. Punishing too late or when calm is restored is always worse than useless for it exacerbates opposition. It is evidently senseless to punish a horse that has overbalanced and risen to its feet again; it cannot be expected to understand whether it is being beaten for falling or for standing up on all four feet. Sitting on a horse's head and flogging the animal while it is lying on its

A horse canot rear when its head is turned sharply to one side.

side has sometimes been said to be a potent correction, but I cannot say that it is practical since two strong men must be available at the time, one to sit on the horse's head and the other to wield the whip. It is in any case difficult to imagine that a horse enjoys throwing itself over. If the horse falls and gets up, the wisest plan is to remount without more ado and to be prepared to react instantaneously in the manner described above if the horse threatens to re-enact its disobedience.

Once a horse has been convinced that rearing is a useless resistance that invariably receives the same dire retribution, it must be taught again to obey the leg. Correction is always a lengthy affair; still, it has to be deeply impressed upon the horse's mind that the leg aid always means totally ungrudging forward movement; obedience to the legs is the indispensable keystone of submission. The notion that the rider's authority can ever be flouted must be erased without a trace. However, it is not strength that counts and it would be pointless to try to develop particularly strong legs. Obedience must become ingrained in the horse's mind and readiness to obey instantly the various indications of our legs has to become eventually an unconscious reaction. It is the rewarding of obedience that is the convincing agent of persuasion and, like punishment, reward can only be understood if it is immediately granted upon the slightest sign of submission. The feeling of pleasantness induced by the reward develops a constantly increasing desire to please. It is known that horses are sensitive to praise and that all *unspoilt* horses are prepared to volunteer co-operation when they understand what is required, provided that obedience automatically brings about an easing of pressure. A rider who uses strong leg pressure will always be slow to react appropriately.

Obedience is not, of course, inborn and certainly some horses are more willing to comply than others. Moreover we must realize that horses are not automatons; however well trained they may be, it is inevitable that they will occasionally feel that obedience can cause them some inconvenience. A rider who does not understand the mentality of animals always risks losing face. Sometimes, it is wiser to let matters rest for a while rather than to chance the outcome of a conflict in the horse's favour by virtue of its greatly superior physical power. Nevertheless, what J. Fillis said is true: 'Sooner or later, in the course of training, disagreement between rider and horse is going to occur; we cannot be certain of a horse's submissiveness if we never give orders that it would rather not obey.' Another percipient horseman, G. Le Bon, expressed the same notion: 'A horse can never be convinced of the ascendancy of its rider before it has lost the issue of a conflict of minds.'

This certainly does not mean that riding must be constant contention between horse and rider; only that if we do engage in a contest, we must be absolutely certain that the situation is heavily weighed on our side and that the issue cannot be in doubt. But if there were never any friction, it would be because the horse had never been asked to work beyond its natural inclination. Generally speaking therefore, it is a principle that a horse cannot be allowed to argue. Still, there are many instances of equine misbehaviour that ought to make the rider search his own conscience. For example, horses quite often display a show of resistance when they must go into the show-jumping ring but, after the salute to the judges, most of them will enter into the spirit of the game and perform as best they can. On the other hand, if the resistance culminates in running away from the rider's legs either sideways or backwards, or even rearing, we may justifiably suspect that too much has been demanded of the horse, or that it fears pain and punishment at the hands of its rider. If the rider had a little intelligence, he would have realized that the only cure for the horse's rebelliousness in such circumstances is a completely new start: peaceful hacking, elementary dressage and much time allowed to forget abuse of trust.

Bucking

Finally we can consider bucking, which in some forms is just another case of crass insubordination, but we must make a distinction between proper bucking and capering. Capering is a display of exuberance and joyfulness which horses frequently indulge in when they are let loose in the paddock and are allowed to let off steam. Movement is a necessity of life for young horses, an irresistible compulsion. To deprive them of it by keeping them confined is to do violence to their nature. The first capers of a horse turned out to grass cannot be called bucking. When a spirited horse under saddle puts in a couple of gambols when allowed the first canter of the day, it should not be severely repressed; we should be able to keep our seat and refrain from chastising it. With closed knees, well-depressed heels, our buttocks eased off the saddle but not lifted up high, and with a slight forward inclination of the trunk, we can easily dampen the impact of the capers through the elasticity of all the joints of our legs. We must keep our hands at the level of the mane and, if the circumstances require it, we can hold on to the mane – which in this instance may be a practical expedient rather than a sign of timidity. However, if the leaps become too unrestrained, a check with one rein (in an upward and never a downward direction) together with a curt reprimand must tell the horse quite clearly that we have had enough of its antics. In any case, horses cannot be allowed to indulge in high jinks every time they feel the grass under their hooves; they must learn to behave and to understand that it is the rider's convenience that matters. We should also be aware that this playfulness is infectious and when one horse starts to kick up its heels, others will often start to imitate it. Furthermore, such excitable behaviour may trigger actual kicking out in a horse predisposed to doing so. Therefore, while capering to let off steam may be tolerated up to a point, it must not be permitted in circumstances where it might inconvenience other riders, neither must it be allowed to become a habit, nor to degenerate into bucking which is a manifestation of pig-headedness.

Bucking as a sign of disorderliness is a different matter. It is like the tantrums of a spoilt child. Instead of going forwards as the capering horse does, the lawless horse bucks on the spot and sometimes leaps sideways or whips round. Some horses even throw themselves over. As with rearing, the important thing in such cases is to compel the horse to go forwards. Bucking is usually a warning of impending trouble, whereupon one must administer a hefty stroke of the whip and an energetic upward tug on one rein to bring the horse to its senses, to lift up its head and to send it forwards. The whip in this case is a more telling remedy than the spurs. When the rider has to contend with actual bucking rather than capering, he must sit deeply, brace his loins very firmly and lean backwards somewhat. Inclining the trunk forwards in this instance exposes one to the risk of being rudely catapulted should the horse produce two or more powerful buck-jumps one after the other. Holding on to the pommel of the saddle or to a neck strap with one hand is not being chicken-hearted, but we must keep one hand free to hold the reins because it is important to hold up the horse's head. A horses cannot buck if it cannot lower its head.

It is of course crucially important to stay on, for once a horse has discovered that some riders are easy to eject out of the saddle, it finds bucking an entertaining game which it can indulge in whenever it feels that its rider has a weak seat. Some crafty horses are not so brazen as to project the rider through the front door but are adept at unseating him by jumping sideways, veering suddenly or cat-leaping and, having effectively unsettled their passenger, lose

Correct seat during vicious bucking.

It is certainly no disgrace to hold on to the front of the saddle on a bucking horse. In this way you can pull yourself down into the saddle (*left*). The rider on the *right* will most probably be catapulted over the horse's head at the next buck.

203

The horse will be prevented from bucking if the rider can only raise its head.

no time in completing his downfall. If confronted with such antics, one must try to lift up the horse's head by means of vigorous upward jerks with one rein and contrive, if possible, to pull the head sideways, thus depriving the horse of the support of both forelegs. If this tactical move succeeds, the horse must be sent forwards energetically. When defending one's position during an attack of bucking, one must push the stirrups forwards to assist the bracing of the loins and the backward inclination of the trunk.

However, the cause of bucking will have to be investigated. It can be a symptom of pure block-headedness, but it can also be a revolt against tactless and unreasonable demands. In the latter case, the remedy is easy: the pressure must be reduced. On the other hand, if the horse has taken advantage of a weak rider, a competent one will have to convince the horse of the superiority of man over beast. It is highly probable, however, that the horse will play up again when it next carries a lighter and weaker rider. Unfortunately, the weaker rider is often the owner of the problem horse and it is a fact that unruly horses are usually begotten by weak owners.

Yet there are other causes still. The tiresome, so-called 'cold-back' is one. As mentioned earlier (Problems in saddling and bridling) 'cold-backed' horses have to be saddled and mounted with extreme solicitude. Other sensitive animals may blow themselves out when first saddled and girthed, and using undue force to tighten the girth quickly aggravates their resistance. Such a horse may find the pressure of girth and saddle initially quite uncomfortable and, by ignoring this fact, a thoughtless rider can quickly produce a bucking horse that will be very difficult to reform. (The sudden manifestation of uncharacteristic bucking fits should always trigger an investigation into the suitability of saddlery and the physical condition of the horse's back.)

It is believed that crib-biting and wind-sucking may predispose a horse to bucking because of the effect upon respiration. There are some wind-suckers that appear to digest their food well and they are less likely to object to being girthed-up; nevertheless, it is always advisable to ride a wind-sucker on straight lines at the beginning of work and to refrain from bending or gathering the horse before it is completely loosened.

Certain sexual abnormalities are associated with vicious or crafty behaviour. Rigs (cryptorchids) can be very aggressive and need firm handling. Their belligerence is often exhibited in the form of irrepressible bucking. Their counterparts, nymphomaniac mares, tend to be equally unruly. Normal mares in season are often ticklish, excitable and tense, and this might predispose them to bucking on occasion, but this behaviour is cyclic. Nymphomaniacs, by contrast, are constantly awkward because their hormones never give them periods of ease. Surgery will usually subdue problems caused by sexual abnormality in either gender.

Some horses buck simply because they are inordinately ticklish; they will kick up their heels if anything touches them lightly behind the saddle. A renowned dressage horse was so sensitive to the light touch of a rider's coat-tails that these always had to be pinned up securely. Ticklishness is not a vice but an uncontrollable reflex. Nothing can be done to remedy it, but one can and must avoid provoking it by letting items of clothing come into contact with exaggeratedly sensitive skin over the horse's loins. The skin covering the belly can be just as ticklish and a bucking attack may occur when the horse is galloped over loose soil or a light covering of snow and flecks thrown up by the horse's hooves hit the belly. The resulting high jinks may be unpleasant for the rider, but it would be very wrong to punish the horse. Punished unfairly, any horse will become resentful and resistant.

Conclusion

I N THIS BOOK AN ATTEMPT has been made to bring together information which may be useful for the handling and riding of the horse. I mentioned at the start of the book that, once the horse ceased to be used intensively as a working animal, much of the knowledge and 'horse sense' which was previously taken for granted was dissipated. However, in recent years, research into equine behaviour has begun to increase in importance. Mention of this subject is no longer greeted with a sympathetic smile, and at least the seeds have been sown for a greater concern with the psychological welfare of our animals. It is my contention that everyone who is intensively involved with horses should make their own small contribution to this field of behavioural research, simply because this broad subject has yet to be explored fully.

In saying this, I would stress the point made in the opening chapter that we should not try to understand the horse by 'humanizing' the behavioural characteristics of our charges, but should try, instead, to discover how a *horse* would feel in different circumstances. We should be conscious of the fact that the horse was certainly not created by nature to be ridden, to be jumped over very demanding fences, or to perform dozens of changes of leg at canter. If it is to be asked to perform exercises which go beyond the basic requirements of nature, the rider must not only prepare it to do so physically, but must learn to deal with it correctly from a psychological point of view – from the point of view of equine psychology, that is. Furthermore, we should remember that *equine* psychology is pertinent to the whole equine species, and we should not narrow our thinking by assuming that certain equine characteristics are peculiar to some particular breed or type.

Given our imperfect understanding of equine psychology, our own limitations as riders and the horse's own mental capacity and instincts, I do not claim that the foregoing review of problems in the control of horses is exhaustive. In

Total relaxation of rider and horse after successful completion of a test.

the first place, there are far too many possible causes (and permutations) of problems and resistance to permit an all-embracing, in-depth study. Besides which, the variety of ploys that horses light upon to exploit the ignorance or inadequacy of their riders and preserve their independence is remarkable. Furthermore, we cannot always know *with certainty* whether horses disobey our orders because they do not understand what is required or because compliance would cause them inconvenience, discomfort or pain. I believe, like Waldemar Seunig, that horsemanship is a science in which nothing can be said to be absolutely right or wrong. Hence it is not possible to prescribe an infallible recipe for the cure of every possible form of resistance. My intention, rather, has been to point out that all forms of intractability are based on some root cause, and that there are several direct or roundabout ways of gaining an indispensable mastery of the horse. To this end, it is imperative that in all our dealings with horses, we remain in complete control of our actions and emotions and that we always remember that our demands upon the horse may require an effort that could potentially be painful or stressful. All civilized countries have enacted laws for the protection of animals, to the effect that no pain, mental distress or injury may be caused to a creature without justifiable grounds. Nevertheless, if we are to consider ourselves horsemen, it should not be the law of the land that constrains our actions, but our own self-governance. While are entitled to believe in the right of our dominion over horses, we are not entitled to conduct ourselves as despots.

It now only remains for me to wish you every success in your dealings with horses!